William J. Gedney's Comparative Tai Source Book

OCEANIC LINGUISTICS SPECIAL PUBLICATIONS

Numbers 1 through 25 are no longer available.

1. English in Hawaii: An Annotated Bibliography. Stanley M. Tsuzaki and John E. Reinecke. 1966.
2. An Ivatan Syntax. Lawrence Andrew Reid. 1966.
3. Manobo-English Dictionary. Richard E. Elkins. 1968.
4. Nguna Texts. Albert J. Schütz. 1969.
5. Nguna Grammar. Albert J. Schütz. 1969.
6. A Grammar of Kaliai-Kove. David R. Counts. 1969.
7. Chrau Grammar. David D. Thomas. 1971.
8. Philippine Minor Languages: Word Lists and Phonologies. Edited by Lawrence A. Reid. 1971.
9. Japanese Pidgin English in Hawaii: A Bilingual Description. Susumu Nagara. 1972.
10. Kapampangan Syntax. Leatrice T. Mirikitani. 1972.
11. Isneg-English Vocabulary. Morice Vanoverbergh. 1972.
12. Outline of Sre Structure. Timothy M. Manley. 1972.
13. Austroasiatic Studies, Parts I and II. Edited by Philip N. Jenner, Laurence C. Thompson, and Stanley Starosta. 1976.
14. A Bibliography of Pidgin and Creole Languages. Compiled by John E. Reinecke, Stanley M. Tsuzaki, David DeCamp, Ian F. Hancock, and Richard E. Wood. 1975.
15. A Handbook of Comparative Tai. Fang Kuei Li. 1977.
16. Syntactic Derivation of Tagalog Verbs. Videa P. De Guzman. 1978.
17. The Genetic Relationship of the Ainu Language. James Patrie. 1982.
18. A Grammar of Manam. Frantisek Lichtenberk. 1983.
19. The History of the Fijian Languages. Paul A. Geraghty. 1983.
20. For Gordon H. Fairbanks. Edited by Veneeta Z. Acson and Richard L. Leed. 1985.
21. The Causatives of Malagasy. Charles Randriamasimanana. 1986.
22. Echo of a Culture: A Grammar of Rennell and Bellona. Samuel H. Elbert. 1988.
23. A Guide to Austroasiatic Speakers and Their Languages. Robert Parkin. 1991.
24. Tonality in Austronesian Languages. Edited by Jerold A. Edmondson and Kenneth J. Gregerson. 1993.
25. Tinrin Grammar. Midori Osumi. 1995.
26. Toward a Reference Grammar of Tok Pisin: An Experiment in Corpus Linguistics. John W. M. Verhaar. 1995.
27. An Erromangan (Sye) Grammar. Terry Crowley. 1998.
28. From Ancient Cham to Modern Dialects: Two Thousand Years of Language Contact and Change. Graham Thurgood. 1999.
29. Grammatical Analysis: Morphology, Syntax, and Semantics: Studies in Honor of Stanley Starosta. Edited by Videa P. De Guzman and Byron W. Bender. 2000.
30. Nhanda: An Aboriginal Language of Western Australia. Juliette Blevins. 2001.
31. Bislama Reference Grammar. Terry Crowley. 2004.
32. Otto Dempwolff's *Grammar of the Jabêm Language in New Guinea*. Translated and edited by Joel Bradshaw and Francisc Czobor. 2005.
33. A Grammar of South Efate: An Oceanic Language of Vanuatu. Nicholas Thieberger. 2006.
34. William J. Gedney's Comparative Tai Source Book. Thomas John Hudak. 2007.

Publications may be ordered electronically from www.uhpress.hawaii.edu or by mail from University of Hawai'i Press, 2840 Kolowalu Street, Honolulu, Hawai'i 96822, USA.

Oceanic Linguistics Special Publication No. 34

William J. Gedney's Comparative Tai Source Book

Thomas John Hudak

University of Hawai'i Press

Honolulu

Printed in the United States of America

13 12 11 10 09 08 6 5 4 3 2 1

Library of Congress Cataloging-in-Publication Data

Hudak, Thomas J.
William J. Gedney's comparative Tai source book / Thomas John Hudak.
p. cm. — (Oceanic linguistics special publication ; no. 34)
ISBN 978-0-8248-3190-5 (pbk. : alk. paper)
1. Tai languages—Phonology, Comparative. 2. Proto-Tai language—Phonology.
I. Gedney, William J. II. Title.
PL4113.H83 2008
495.9'1—dc22

2007041673

Camera-ready copy for this book was prepared under
the supervision of the series editor.

University of Hawai'i Press books are printed on acid-free paper and meet
the guidelines for permanence and durability of the Council on Library Resources

Printed by IBT Global

CONTENTS

ACKNOWLEDGMENTS

This volume could not have been produced without the generous assistance and good humor of numerous individuals. Much of the early work, creating formats and proofreading, for example, benefitted from the expertise of Chelle Brookes, Aloysius Canete, Alberto Perez-Pereiro, Joseph Maranville, and Michael Zier. References and encouragement were kindly provided by Karen L. Adams, Dawn Bates, Anthony Diller, Jerold A. Edmondson, Thomas Gething, Yongxian Luo, and Christopher Miller. At Arizona State University, two individuals contributed large amounts of their time and energy: Barbara Stark took time from her own research and created the map for this volume, and Marsha Schweitzer was always there to explain the mysteries of the software and to rescue me from never-ending computer errors. And at the University of Hawai'i Press, one could not ask for a more efficient and knowledgeable editor than Keith Leber. To all of these people, I extend my heartfelt gratitude and thanks.

ABBREVIATIONS

The Proto-Tai category of each cognate follows its gloss or the lexical item in question. Languages and dialects represented by the same set of symbols are separated by commas: S, W, B, Sh ʔaw^1; otherwise, semi-colons are used: LP ʔaw^2; LM ʔaw^4. In the Saek section (p.53), OG refers to the older generation and YG to the younger. For the Tai dialect of Lungchow (LC), 'current in the countryside' refers to the 1930s and 1940s when Li did his research.

SW Southwestern Tai Dialects

S	Siamese (Standard Thai)
W	White Tai (Tai Khaw)
B	Black Tai (Tai Dam)
Sh	Shan
LNK	the Tai dialect of Nong Khai
LCH	Lue of Chieng Hung
LMY	Lue of Muong Yong
CM	the Tai dialect of Chiengmai

CN Central Tai Dialects

LP	the Tai dialect of Lei Ping
LM	the Tai dialect of Lungming
WN	the Tai dialect of Western Nung
BV	the Tai dialect of Bac Va
LC	the Tai dialect of Lungchow
PS	the Tai dialect of Ping Siang
NM	the Tai dialect of Ning Ming

N Northern Tai Dialects

Y	Yay
Sk	Saek
WM	the Tai dialect of Wuming
P	the Tai dialect of Po-ai

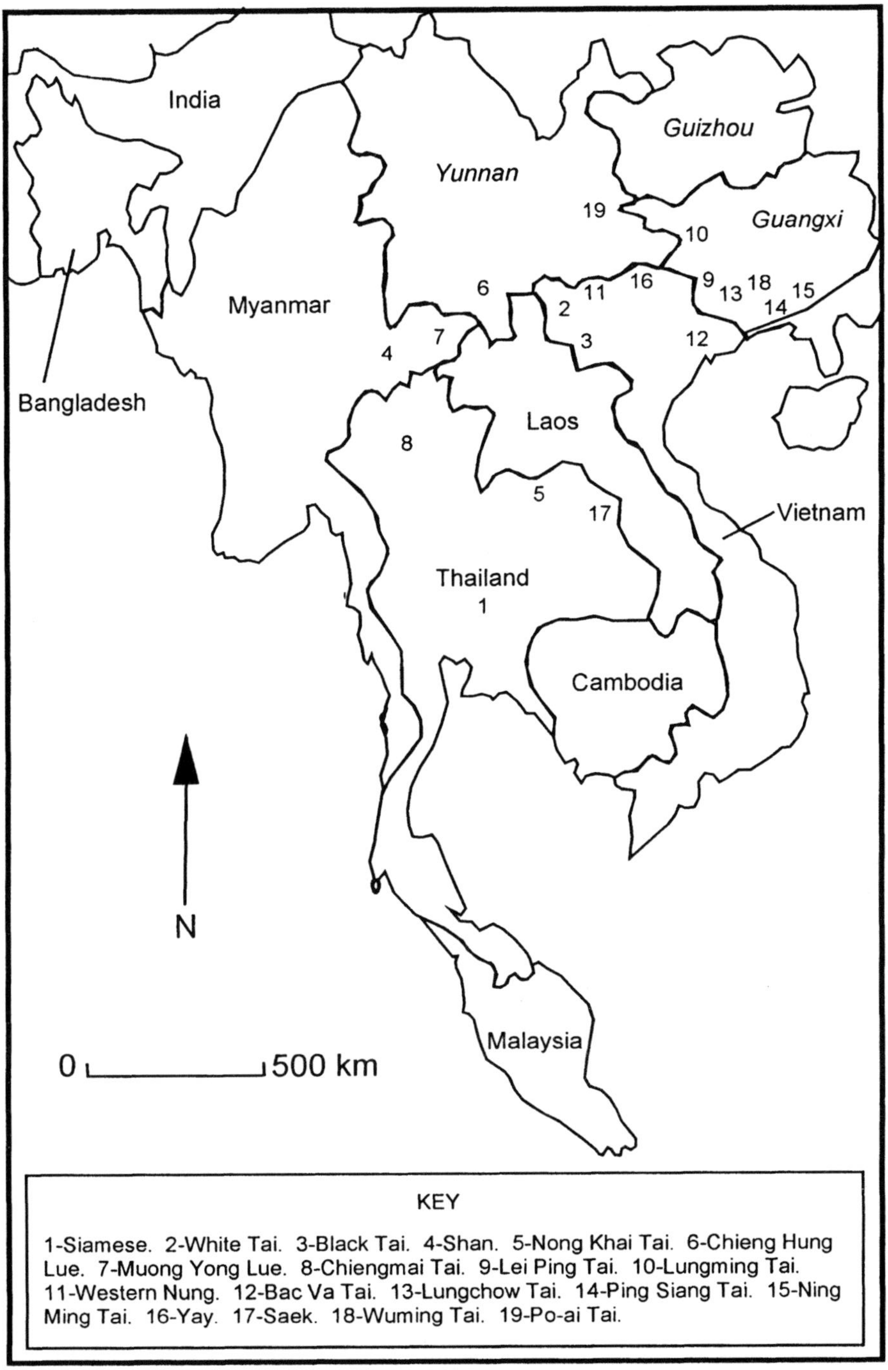

Map 1. Tai-speaking areas in Southeast Asia and Southern China.

CHAPTER 1: INTRODUCTION

The Tai language family extends from Assam in the west to northern Vietnam in the east, from southern China in the north to the Malay peninsula in the south. At the far western end of this area, in Assam, the related, but extinct, literary language Ahom can be found. In adjacent Myanmar (Burma), the main representatives of the Tai family include Shan and a variety of dialects on the border of Assam and Yunnan. The Lue inhabit the Sipsongpanna region of southern Yunnan, northern Thailand, and Laos. Further south, the whole of Thailand is covered by Siamese and Tai local and regional dialects. A similar situation occurs in Laos where Lao dialects extend throughout the country as well as into northeastern Thailand. Unlike the other Tai languages which are spoken by minority groups, those in Thailand and Laos are socially and politically dominant. Moving into northern Vietnam, White, Black, and Red Tai appear in the northwest and varieties of Tay (formerly identified as Thô) and Nung in the northeast. Yay is spoken in the extreme northern part of Vietnam in the area of the Hong (Red) River and the Lo River (Rivière Claire). Tai dialects in southern China, related to the Nung of northern Vietnam, have been grouped together by the Chinese under the name Zhuang, although individual linguistic studies identify dialects by localities such as the Tai dialect of Lungming or the Tai dialect of Lungchow. Finally, at the farthest point east on the island of Hainan there also exist a number of dialects closely related to the Tai family. Edmondson and Solnit (1997b:1) estimate the total Tai population to be greater than 80 million.

In two major publications Fang-kuei Li (1959, 1960), using phonological and lexical criteria, divided the Tai family into three main branches: the Southwestern with Siamese, Lao, Shan, White, Black, and Red Tai, etc.; the Central with Tay, the dialects spoken at Lungchow, Lei Ping, Ping Siang, Ning Ming, etc.; and the Northern with Yay, Saek, the dialects spoken at Wuming and Po-ai, etc. For the most part linguists follow this tripartite division, although Gedney (1989:62–66) has proposed that the Central and Southwestern probably represent a single group with gradual transition between the languages within it. Haudricourt (1956), on the other hand, suggests that the Northern and Central branches may very well form a single group. For both Gedney and Haudricourt, then, the Tai family may ultimately consist of two major groups rather than three. Both Luo (1996:17–18) and Edmondson and Solnit (1997b:10–12) discuss this tripartite division and the related issues raised by Gedney and Haudricourt.

With the exception of loanwords, all of the different varieties of Tai are monosyllabic. Each syllable has a tone, an initial consonant or consonant cluster, a vocalic nucleus (vowel or diphthong), and an optional final consonant. The tones of each of the Tai dialects had their origin in an earlier system of three tones on open syllables (those ending in a vowel, semivowel, or nasal) and no tonal contrast on checked syllables (those ending in p - t - k). Those tones on open syllables have been conventionally designated as A - B - C and the fourth category, the checked syllables, as D. The tones in each of these categories underwent phonemic splits, conditioned by the phonetic nature of the initial consonant of each syllable. The phonetic nature of these initials can be divided into four different tiers: 1) voiceless fricatives such as [s], [f], [x], [h] and voiceless aspirated stops [ph], [th], [kh]; 2) voiceless unaspirated (plain) stops [p], [t], [k]; 3) glottal sounds, glottal stop [ʔ] and preglottalized consonants [ʔb], [ʔd], [ʔy]; and 4) voiced sounds. With the D category, the splits were further conditioned by whether the vowel was short or long. As the following chart demonstrates, this four-way split between initials and tones allows for a possible total of twenty proto-tones for any one Tai dialect, although no dialect has shown all these possibilities. Most Tai dialects range between five and seven tones.

Initial\Tone	A	B	C	D-short	D-long
voiceless friction sounds	1	5	9	13	17
voiceless unaspirated stops	2	6	10	14	18
glottal sounds	3	7	11	15	19
voiced sounds	4	8	12	16	20

Research on this family of languages and dialects began in the nineteenth and early twentieth centuries; however, most of this research was done by individuals with little or no training in linguistics. The results of this lack of training were publications filled with errors and inaccuracies. Of course, there were exceptions such as the Siamese and Shan dictionaries, but by and large these early studies must be approached and used with caution. Even so, these early lists are valuable for they give a general idea of the phonological structure of the word and at the same time provide evidence of the word in a particular language or dialect. It was only in the mid-twentieth century that the rigorous scientific investigation of these languages was begun by Fang-kuei Li who worked primarily on the Tai languages in southern China and their relationship to Siamese; André-Georges Haudricourt who worked on the Tai languages in northern Vietnam and southern China; and William J. Gedney.

William J. Gedney's work with the Tai family began in the 1950s with his investigations into Siamese and then in 1964 with other Tai languages. Emphasizing tonal and phonological systems, Gedney worked with native informants first to determine the tonal system of the dialect (Gedney 1972). With the tones described, he then moved on to a more general list arranged according to cultural and semantic spheres (Hudak 2004). In cases where the informant was particularly adept, Gedney was able to elicit every phonologically possible syllable as in his Yay, Saek, and Lue dictionaries (Hudak 1991a, 1993, 1996). Generally, Gedney would use Siamese, Lao, or Black Tai to elicit the data, and only rarely did he resort to English and an interpreter as in his work with the Tai dialects at Lei Ping, Lungming, Ping Siang, and Ning Ming. Because of the close similarity, culturally and linguistically, between Siamese and the languages being investigated, Gedney was able to arrive at clear and exact one-word translations.

Elicitation sessions were taped, replayed, reviewed, and then transcribed with the aid of the informant checking for accuracy. These word lists and texts were recorded in notebooks, indexed word-by-word and syllable-by-syllable on 3x5 slips, and organized into comparative lists. These slips and lists came to play an important part in Gedney's scholarly work: 1) they provided the data for his Tai linguistic research (Bickner et al. 1989); 2) they were the source for his courses on comparative Tai; and 3) they were to form the basis of a book on comparative Tai. They were also often borrowed by students and other linguists for their own research. The book, never completed, was to provide accurate and reliable data of a variety of dialects so that additional phonological studies could be made of individual dialects as well as on the entire language family. Gedney was particularly interested in the role these data would play in the reconstruction of the Proto-Tai language family and in determining its wider genetic relationships. A meticulous and cautious investigator, Gedney frequently took a 'wait until we have more data' attitude on the wider genetic affiliations of the Tai languages as set forth in the Tai-Kadai and Kadai hypotheses (Luo 1996:14–18, Edmondson and Solnit 1997b:2–4).

For the proposed book on comparative Tai, Gedney compiled a list of 1159 words, in their cognate forms, that were common to the Tai languages in the three branches of the Tai family. For the Southwestern (SW) branch, he used Siamese (S), White Tai (W), Black Tai (B), Shan (Sh), the Tai or Lao dialect at Nong Khai (LNK) in northeastern Thailand, the Lue dialects at Chieng Hung (LCH) in Yunnan and Muong Yong (LMY) in Myanmar, and the Tai dialect spoken in Chiengmai (CM). For the Central (CN) branch, he included the Tai dialects found in China at Lei Ping (LP), Lungming (LM), Lungchow (LC), Ping Siang (PS), and Ning Ming (NM). He also incorporated the dialect designated as Western Nung (WN) spoken in extreme northern Vietnam and the Tai dialect at Bac Va (BV) in northeastern Vietnam. For the Northern (N) branch, he chose Yay (Y), found in northern Vietnam, Saek (Sk), a linguistic island in northeastern Thailand and across the Mekong in Laos among Southwestern Tai languages, and the Tai dialects in China at Wuming (WM) and Po-ai (P). Data for the dialects at Lungchow, Wuming, and Po-ai came from Li's remarkable individual studies of these dialects (1940, 1944, 1957a, 1957b, 1977). For each of these cognates, he also indicated the Proto-Tai tone category to which it potentially belonged.

The data reproduced for this source book of comparative Tai were taken from the slips and lists compiled by Gedney over his career. As part of the original plan, an individual phonological description for each dialect or language, which includes the location where it is spoken, has been added. The second part, the comparative section proper, allows the comparison of the sound system (the consonants, vowels, and tones) of the cognate forms in the above languages and dialects. Following this section are the complete references and an index of the 1159 cognates.

For ease of comparison to the original sources from which the data have been taken, the original notation system has been retained and explained in each phonological description. Thus, in some dialect descriptions final vowels, which are phonetically long, are written with a single vowel, [a], while in others double vowels are used, [aa]. Throughout the data, however, Gedney consistently treated the syllable-final semivowels as consonants and wrote them with the consonant symbols [w], [y], and [ɰ]. In addition, the unrounded mid back vowel [ɤ], characteristic of the Tai languages, has been used throughout this volume rather than the less accurate [ə]. Traditional names of the languages used in the literature have also been kept, although variations are noted. A map has been included to show the general location where these languages and dialects are spoken.

It is hoped that this volume will make a contribution to Tai language and dialect studies and that it will help to clarify, and perhaps put to rest, a variety of controversies that continue to surround the current historical studies related to the Tai language family.

CHAPTER 2: SOUTHWESTERN TAI DIALECTS

The Southwestern branch of the Tai family covers the largest territory and has the largest number of speakers. Probably the most well known languages in this branch are Siamese or Standard Thai in Thailand and Lao in Laos, where both are politically and socially dominant in their respective countries. Other languages and dialects can be found in northern and northeastern Myanmar as well as in Yunnan in southern China. While many of these languages are considered to be mutually intelligible, Luo (1996:81) notes that some are so different, for example, Chinese Shan and Lue, that they must be considered only distantly related even though they are geographically quite close.

Following Li, Luo (1996:81–82) lists the following characteristics as the most salient features for distinguishing the Southwestern branch from the other two: 1) the original proto-voiced stops *b, *d, and *g have developed into voiceless aspirated stops /ph/, /th/, and /kh/; 2) proto-labial clusters *br and *bl have become an aspirated labial stop /ph/ and proto-velar clusters *gr and *gl have become an aspirated velar stop /kh/; 3) the proto-voiceless velar fricative *x has been retained in some dialects such as White Tai; 4) proto *hr and *r have been laryngealized; 5) the proto-initial clusters *thr and *xr have merged into the laryngeal fricative /h/ in most dialects; 5) the proto-voiced velar fricative *ɣ has become a voiceless aspirated velar stop /kh/; 6) there has been a three-way tone split in all three tone categories A, B, and C along with a variety of tone mergers; and 7) there is a set of lexical items different from the other two branches.

Cognates used to represent this branch include the following: Siamese or Standard Thai (S), White Tai or Tai Khaw (W), Black Tai or Tai Dam (B), Shan (Sh), the Tai or Lao dialect found at Nong Khai (LNK) on the border of Thailand and Laos in northeast Thailand, the Lue dialects at Chieng Hung (LCH) in Yunnan and at Muong Yong (LMY) in northeastern Myanmar, and the Tai dialect in Chiengmai (CM) in northern Thailand.

Siamese (StandardThai) — S

Belonging to the Southwestern branch of the Tai language family, Siamese (Thai), the national language of Thailand, is probably the most recognized of the Tai languages. Significant studies have been made by Haas (1942a, 1942b, 1946, 1956), Gedney (1947, 1961, 1989), Henderson (1949), Abramson (1962), and Noss (1964), to name a few. Two notable dictionaries include McFarland (1944) and Haas (1964).

Phonology

As in other dialects and languages of the Tai family, the phonological pattern of Siamese is based on the syllable. Each syllable has distinctions in tone, initial (consonant or consonant cluster), nucleus (vowel or diphthong), and optional final consonant.

Tones

On open syllables (those ending with vowel, semivowel, or nasal), Siamese has five tones. Here pitch levels are based on the Chao 5-pitch scale.

> 1 - mid level, 33: khaa^{1} - stuck
> 2 - low level, 22: khaa^{2} - galangal
> 3 - falling, from mid-high to low, 41: khaa^{3} - price
> 4 - high level, glottalized, 55: khaa^{4} - to trade
> 5 - rising, mid-low to mid-high, glottalized, 24: khaa^{5} - leg

Checked syllables (those ending in p - t - k) with short vowels exhibit tones phonetically similar to tones 2 and 4 of open syllables: mat^{2} 'flea', mot^{4} 'ant'. Checked syllables with long vowels have tones phonetically similar to tones 2 and 3 of open syllables: ʔaap^{2} 'to bathe', luuk^{3} 'child'.

The five tones of Siamese had their origin in an earlier system of three tones on open syllables and no tonal contrast on checked syllables. Those tones on open syllables have been conventionally designated as A - B - C and the fourth category, the checked syllables, as D. The tones in each of these categories underwent phonemic splits, conditioned by the phonetic nature of the initial consonant of each syllable. With the D category, the splits were further conditioned by vowel length. Table 1 shows the patterns of these splits in Siamese.

Table 1
Pattern of Tonal Splits in Siamese

Initial\Tone	A	B	C	D-short	D-long
Voiceless friction sounds	5	2	3	2	2
Voiceless unaspirated stops	1	2	3	2	2
Glottal sounds	1	2	3	2	2
Voiced sounds	1	3	4	4	3

Consonants

Siamese has the following initial consonants:

> Voiceless unaspirated stops. p - t - c - k - ʔ: pii^{1} - year, tat^{2} - to cut, cay^{1} - heart, kaw^{2} - old, ʔim^{2} - full.

Voiceless aspirated stops. ph - th - ch - kh: phom^5 - hair, tham^1 - to do, chaaη^4 - elephant, khii^2 - to ride.

Voiced stops. b - d: baaη^1 - thin, daam^3 - handle.

Nasals. m - n - η: muu^5 - pig, nay^1 - in, ηuu^1 - snake.

Voiceless spirants. f - s - h: faa^4 - sky, sat^2 - animal, huu^5 - ear.

Sonorants. l - r - w - y: lek^2 - iron, raw^1 - we, wan^1 - day, yaak^3 - difficult.

Initial clusters consist of a consonant plus [l], [r], or [w]. There are no final clusters.

Clusters with [l]. pl - phl - kl - khl: plaa^1 - fish, phluu^1 - betel, klɯa^1 - salt, khlam^3 - abundant.

Clusters with [r]. pr - phr - tr - thr (rare) - kr - khr: praay^1 - to scatter, phraan^1 - hunter, tram^1 - to endure, thri^{4}sadii^1 - theory, kraan^3 - coarse, rough, khraam^1 - indigo.

Clusters with [w]. kw - khw: kwaaη^1 - deer, khwaay^1 - water buffalo.

Final consonants include nasals m - n - η and voiceless stops p - t - k -ʔ. For final w - y, see ***Diphthongs***.

Nasals. m - n - η: num^3 - soft, spongy, baan^3 - house, thuη^5 - bag.

Voiceless stops. p - t - k - ʔ: sip^2 - ten, phuut^3 - to speak, paak^2 - mouth, kɛʔ^2 - sheep.

Vowels

Siamese has nine vowels, three high: i - ɯ - u; three mid: e - ɤ - o; and three low: ɛ - a - ɔ, all of which may be either short or long. All vowels are phonetically long in final position and written with a double vowel.

High. i, ii - ɯ, ɯɯ - u, uu: thin^2 - place, thiip^2 - to kick, nɯη^2 - one, thɯɯ^5 - to hold, carry, buk^2 - to invade, thuup^3 - incense.

Mid. e, ee - ɤ, ɤɤ - o, oo: ten^3 - to jump, thee^1 - to pour out, ηɤn^1 - money, chɤɤn^1 - to invite, khon^1 - person, look^3 - world.

Low. ɛ, ɛɛ - a, aa - ɔ, ɔɔ: tɛm^1 - full, tɛɛη^1 - melon, cat^2 - to arrange, caan^1 - dish, phrɔʔ^4 - because, dɔɔk^2 - flower.

Diphthongs

There are three centering diphthongs, ia - ɯa - ua: thian^{1} - candle, sɯa^{5} - tiger, hua^{5} - head.

Other diphthongs may be analyzed as a vocalic nucleus plus a final w - y.

> Diphthongs with final [w]. iw - iaw - ew - eew - ɤw - ɤɤw - ɛɛw - aw - aaw: hiw^{5} - hungry, khiaw^{5} - green, rew^{1} - fast, leew^{1} - bad, pay^{1} rew^{1} pay^{1} rɤw^{1} - go fast!, pay^{1} thiaw^{3} pay^{1} thɤɤw^{3} - to go around, lɛɛw^{4} - finished, ʔaw^{1} - to take, ʔaaw^{2} - bay, gulf.
>
> Diphthongs with final [y]. ɯy (rare) - ɯɯy (rare) - ɯay - uy - uay - ɤy - ɤɤy - ooy - ay - aay - ɔɔy: hɯy^{4} - not so!, hɯɯy^{4} - not so!, nɯay^{1} - indifferent, puy^{1} - fluff, suay^{5} - beautiful, ʔɤy^{4} - an exclamation, khɤɤy^{5} - son-in-law, ʔooy^{1} - ouch, may^{3} - not, baay^{2} - afternoon, rɔɔy^{4} - hundred.

White Tai (Tai Khaw) — W

A member of the Southwestern branch of the Tai language family, White Tai is found in the extreme northwestern part of Vietnam, and possibly over the border in parts of Yunnan. The chief center is the town of Lai Chao (mɤŋ^{4} lay^{5}), with another center further to the north in Muong Te (mɤŋ^{4} tɛ^{4}). The White Tai refer to themselves and their language as tay^{4} dɔn^{2}, probably because of the white blouses worn by the women. The usual word for 'white' in White Tai is dɔn^{2}, while the cognate for Siamese khaaw^{5} 'white' is xaaw^{1}.

Excellent studies can be found in Minot (1940, edited and republished in Hudak 2001, 1949a, 1949b), Donaldson (1963), and Donaldson and Edmondson (1997). Gedney (1964) and Fippinger and Fippinger (1970) offer comparative studies. A comprehensive dictionary can be found in Diêu and Donaldson (1972). Hartmann (1985) offers a discussion of the White Tai alphabet.

Gedney obtained his data at Tung Nghia, near Dalat, Vietnam, in 1964 and can be found in Hudak (1994). Most of the data come from an informant from Muong Te by the name of Dao van Thuong (thɤŋ^{6}).

Phonology

As in other dialects and languages of the Tai family, the phonological pattern of White Tai is based on the syllable. Each syllable has distinctions in tone, initial (consonant or consonant cluster), nucleus (vowel or diphthong), and optional final consonant.

Tones

On open syllables (those ending with vowel, semivowel, or nasal), White Tai has six tones. Here pitch levels are based on the Chao 5-pitch scale.

1 - level, slightly lower than mid, 22: kaa^{1} - crow
2 - high-rising, 45: kaa^{2} - all the way to
3 - low-rising, glottalized, 24: kaa^{3} - young rice plant
4 - level, somewhat higher than mid, 44: kaa^{4} - stuck
5 - level, somewhat higher than mid with a rise and fall, 454: kaa^{5} - price
6 - falling, glottalized, 31: kaa^{6} - to trade

Checked syllables (those ending in p - t - k) with short vowels exhibit tones phonetically similar to tones 2 and 4 of open syllables: sat^{2} 'animal', mot^{4} 'ant'. Checked syllables with long vowels have tones phonetically similar to tones 2 and 4 of open syllables: ʔaap^{2} 'to bathe', laat^{4} 'to cover'.

The six tones of White Tai had their origin in an earlier system of three tones on open syllables and no tonal contrast on checked syllables. Those tones on open syllables have been conventionally designated as A - B - C and the fourth category, the checked syllables, as D. The tones in each of these categories underwent phonemic splits, conditioned by the phonetic nature of the initial consonant of each syllable. With the D category, the splits were further conditioned by vowel length. Table 1 shows the patterns of these splits in White Tai.

Table 1
Pattern of Tonal Splits in White Tai

Initial\Tone	A	B	C	D-short	D-long
Voiceless friction sounds	1	2	3	2	2
Voiceless unaspirated stops	1	2	3	2	2
Glottal sounds	1	2	3	2	2
Voiced sounds	4	5	6	4	4

Consonants

White Tai has the following initial consonants:

Voiceless unaspirated stops. p - t - c - k - ʔ: pɔ^{5} - father, tu^{1} - door, cɔn^{6} - spoon, kaaŋ^{1} - middle, ʔaaŋ^{2} - basin.

Voiceless aspirated stops. ph - th - ch - kh: phaa^{3} - cloth, thiw^{1} - to whistle, chay^{2} - egg, kho^{3} - to cook.

Voiced stops. b - d: bɤn^{1} - moon, dɔn^{2} - white.

Nasals. m - n - ɲ - ŋ: mɯŋ^{4} - you, naa^{3} - face, ɲuŋ^{4} - mosquito, ŋaay^{5} - easy.

Voiceless spirants. f - s - x - h: faa^{1} - lid, sɔŋ^{1} - two, xay^{1} - tallow, hɤ^{2} - sweat.

Sonorants. v - l - y: vaan^{1} - sweet, loŋ^{4} - dragon, yɔy^{6} - to drool. In slow, careful speech, initial [y] is often pronounced as [z] through Vietnamese influence. Gedney groups the spirant (fricative) [v] with the sonorants because of its sonority and low level of friction. In addition, [v] and [w] are in complementary distribution, with [v] appearing initially and [w] after a consonant.

Initial clusters consist of a consonant plus [w]. There are no final clusters.

Clusters with [w]. kw - khw - ŋw - xw: kwaa^{5} - to visit, khwe^{2} - to dig, ŋwaa^{5} - fig, xwan^{4} - smoke.

Final consonants include nasals m - n - ŋ and voiceless stops p - t - k -ʔ. For final w - y - ɰ, see ***Diphthongs***.

Nasals. m - n - ŋ: tɛm^{3} - to write, tɯn^{2} - to wake up, kwaaŋ^{1} - deer.

Voiceless stops. p - t - k - ʔ: hup^{2} - to smoke, sut^{4} - to sip, mak^{4} - to like, ʔɯʔ^{2} - squash. In close transition, final glottal stop may be deleted and the vowel reduced: maaʔ^{2} 'fruit' may be realized as maa^{2}, maʔ^{2}, or ma^{2}.

Vowels

White Tai has nine vowels, with a length distinction only in [a]. All vowels are phonetically long in final position, although written with a single vowel with the exception of [a] which is written with a double vowel.

High. i - ɯ - u: thi^{2} - closely spaced, tɯ^{4} - to hold, pu^{4} - betel.

Mid. e - ɤ - o: le^{4} - to lick, mɤŋ^{1} - ditch, ʔot^{2} - to plug.

Low. ɛ - a, aa - ɔ: tɛ^{6} - truly, kam^{1} - handful, ʔaan^{1} - saddle, kɔ^{1} - clump.

Diphthongs

In White Tai, the diphthongs ia - ɯa - ua have been lowered to the monophthongs e - ɤ - o, respectively: me^{4} - wife (Siamese mia^{1}), hɤ^{4} - boat (Siamese rɯa^{1}), ho^{1} - head (Siamese hua^{5}).

Other diphthongs may be analyzed as a vocalic nucleus plus a final w - y - ɰ.

> Diphthongs with final [w]. iw - ew - ɛw - aw - aaw: siw^1 - pimple, new^1 - tough, sticky, kɛw^6 - to chew, kaw^3 - nine, daaw^1 - star.
>
> Diphthongs with final [y]. uy - ɤy - oy - ay - aay - ɔy: ʔuy^3 - guava, mɤy^5 - stiff and tired, koy^3 - banana, lay^1 - to flow, laay^1 - many, hɔy^1 - mollusk.
>
> Diphthongs with final [ɰ]. aɰ: baɰ^1 - leaf.

Black Tai (Tai Dam) — B

Black Tai is a member of the Southwestern branch of the Tai language family with its chief center located at Son La (mɤŋ^4 laa^5) in northwestern Vietnam. Other locations appear south of the White Tai-speaking area and in and around Dien Bien Phu. In Thailand, known as Lao Song (laaw^1 sooŋ^3) by the Siamese, Black Tai speakers can be found in the areas of Ratburi and Phetburi. In the United States, a large group of speakers resides in Iowa. The Black Tai refer to themselves and their language as tay^4 dam^1 or tay^4 lam^1, a name generally attributed to the black blouses the women wear or to the fact that they originally lived in the area of the Black River (Rivière Noire) in northern Vietnam.

An early dictionary of apparently the Son La dialect was done by Diguet (1895) in a largely impressionistic transcription. More recent dictionaries have been done by Hartmann (1981) and Baccam et al. (1989). Gedney (1964) and Fippinger and Fippinger (1970) have provided comparative studies while Fippinger (1975) has investigated Black Tai syntax. More recently, Hartmann has written on Black Tai scripts (1985, 1986) and literary texts (1981, 1992, 1994).

Gedney obtained his Black Tai data in 1964 from two sources: 1) a family from mɯaŋ^4 piaŋ^4, a town about forty-four kilometers northwest of Son La; and 2) a teacher, bak^5 kam^4 s ɔ^1, from baan^3 ciaŋ^4 di^1, a village about thirty-five kilometers northwest of Son La. These data can be found in Hudak (1994).

Phonology

As in other dialects and languages of the Tai family, the phonological pattern of Black Tai is based on the syllable. Each syllable has distinctions in tone, initial (consonant or consonant cluster), nucleus (vowel or diphthong), and optional final consonant.

Tones

On open syllables (those ending with vowel, semivowel, or nasal), Black Tai has six tones. Here pitch levels are based on the Chao 5-pitch scale.

1 - level, slightly lower than mid, 22: kaa^{1} - crow
2 - high-rising, 45: paa^{2} - forest
3 - low-falling, glottalized, 21: ʔaa^{3} - to open
4 - high level, 55: naa^{4} - rice field
5 - level, somewhat higher than mid, 44: kaa^{5} - price
6 - falling, glottalized, 31: faa^{6} - sky

Checked syllables (those ending in p - t - k) with short vowels exhibit tones phonetically similar to tones 2 and 5 of open syllables: sat^{2} 'animal', mot^{5} 'ant'. Checked syllables with long vowels have tones phonetically similar to tones 2 and 5 of open syllables: ʔaap^{2} 'to bathe', laat^{5} 'market'.

The six tones of Black Tai had their origin in an earlier system of three tones on open syllables and no tonal contrast on checked syllables. Those tones on open syllables have been conventionally designated as A - B - C and the fourth category, the checked syllables, as D. The tones in each of these categories underwent phonemic splits, conditioned by the phonetic nature of the initial consonant of each syllable. With the D category, the splits were further conditioned by vowel length. Table 1 shows the patterns of these splits in Black Tai.

Table 1
Pattern of Tonal Splits in Black Tai

Initial\Tone	A	B	C	D-short	D-long
Voiceless friction sounds	1	2	3	2	2
Voiceless unaspirated stops	1	2	3	2	2
Glottal sounds	1	2	3	2	2
Voiced sounds	4	5	6	5	5

Consonants

Black Tai has the following initial consonants:

Voiceless unaspirated stops. p - t - c - k - ʔ: paa^{1} - fish, taa^{5} - landing, caam^{4} - indigo, kin^{1} - to eat, ʔaaŋ^{2} - basin.

Voiceless aspirated stops. th - kh: thua^{2} - bean, khaw^{3} - rice.

Voiced stops. b - d: bɯan^{1} - month, daaw^{1} - star.

Nasals. m - n - ɲ - ŋ: maa^{4} - to come, nɯŋ^{3} - to steam, ɲen^{1} - civet cat, ŋaa^{4} - tusk.

Voiceless spirants. f - s - h: fay^4 - fire, san^2 - to shake, hɔm^1 - fragrant.

Sonorants. v - l - y: vaaŋ^1 - thin, lin^3 - to play, yaaw^3 - house. In slow, careful speech, initial [y] is often pronounced as [z] through Vietnamese influence: yɔŋ^2 or zɔŋ^2 'on tiptoe'. Depending upon the locality, there are also fluctuations between [d] and [l], di^1 or li^1 'good', as well as [b] and [v], baan^1 or vaan^1 'sweet'. Gedney groups the spirant (fricative) [v] with the sonorants because of its sonority and low level of friction. In addition, [v] and [w] are in complementary distribution, with [v] appearing initially and [w] after a consonant.

Initial clusters consist of a consonant plus [w]. There are no final clusters.

Clusters with [w]. kw - khw - ŋw: kwaay^4 - water buffalo, khwaa^1 - right, ŋwaa^4 - yesterday.

Final consonants include nasals m - n - ŋ and voiceless stops p - t - k -ʔ. For final w - y - ɰ, see ***Diphthongs***.

Nasals. m - n - ŋ: cɯm^4 - cool, pan^4 - thousand, kɔŋ^6 - gong.

Voiceless stops. p - t - k - ʔ: ɲaap^2 - coarse, yet^5 - to do, fak^2 - vegetable, bɔʔ^2 - flower.

Vowels

Black Tai has nine vowels, with a length distinction only in [a]. All vowels are phonetically long in final position, although written with a single vowel with the exception of [a] which is written with a double vowel.

High. i - ɯ - u: bi^1 - comb, mɯ^4 - hand, thuŋ^4 - pail.

Mid. e - ɤ - o: ten^3 - short, sɤk^2 - enemy, fon^1 - rain.

Low. ɛ - a, aa - ɔ: kɛ^2 - old, cam^1 - near, ʔaan^2 - to read, nɔn^4 - to sleep.

Diphthongs

Diphthongs include ia - ɯa - ua: siaŋ^1 - sound, sɯa^3 - shirt, nuat^2 - beard.

Other diphthongs may be analyzed as a vocalic nucleus plus a final w - y - ɰ.

Diphthongs with final [w]. iw - iaw - ew - ɛw - aw - aaw: siw^1 - pimple, niaw^1 - tough, sticky, pay^1 ʔew^2 paa^2 - to go hunting, khɛw^1 - green, kaw^3 - nine, daaw^1 - star.

Diphthongs with final [y]. ɯay - uy - uay - ɤy - oy - ay - aay - ɔy: mɯay^{5} - stiff and tired, cuy^{1} kan^{1} - to box, kuay^{3} - banana, fɤy^{4} - yard of a house, koy^{1} - hip, lay^{1} - to flow, laay^{1} - many, hɔy^{1} - mollusk.

Diphthongs with final [ɰ]. aɰ: baɰ^{1} - leaf.

Shan — Sh

Shan belongs to the Southwestern branch of the Tai language family. Gedney obtained his Shan data list from Cushing's 1881 Shan-English dictionary (2nd edition 1914; edited and republished in Hudak 2000) in which Cushing used Burman Shan from the principalities of Laihka and Mongnai as the basis for the dictionary. In their background and history of the dialects known as Shan, Edmondson and Solnit (1997a:339) note that the Shan are believed to be one of the first Tai groups to leave China for Southeast Asia and are therefore referred to as Tai Long 'the great Tai'. Those groups leaving later came to be know as Tai Noy 'the lesser Tai'. Additional sources of Shan data include Mix (1920), Egerod (1957, 1960, 1961), and Young (1985). Moeng (1995) has published the original Cushing dictionary with the updated spelling system. Gedney's own work with a variety of Shan dialects can be found in Hudak (1994). These dialects include Hsi Paw Shan, Tai Maaw Shan, Che Fang Shan, Muong Khawn Shan, and Keng Tung Shan.

Phonology

As in other dialects and languages of the Tai family, the phonological pattern of Shan is based on the syllable. Each syllable has distinctions in tone, initial (consonant or consonant cluster), nucleus (vowel or diphthong), and optional final consonant.

Tones

On open syllables (those ending with vowel, semivowel, or nasal), Shan has five tones. Here pitch levels are based on the Chao 5-pitch scale and taken from Li (1977:15) and Egerod (1957:121–22). Cushing's descriptions of the tones (1914:9) appear in parentheses. Italics are Cushing's.

1 - rising, 35, (the natural pitch of the voice with a slight rising inflection at the end; may be called the *natural* tone): taw^{1} - to search for

2 - low level, glottalized, 11 or 21, (deep bass tone; may be called the *grave* tone): taw^{2} - turtle

3 - mid level, 33, (even tone, in pitch, between the first and second tones; may be called the *straight forward* tone): taw^{3} - to come

4 - high level, glottalized, 55, (a more elevated pitch than the first tone; may be called the *high* tone): taw^4 - moss
5 - falling, glottalized, 53, (an abrupt, explosive tone; may be called the *emphatic* tone): taw^5 - to support with something

A sixth tone, which tends to be emphatic and prolonged with a slight drop at the end, is recognized by some speakers. Cushing describes this tone as slightly circumflex with a falling inflection at the end.

Checked syllables (those ending in p - t - k) with short vowels exhibit tones phonetically similar to tones 4 and 5 of open syllables: tap^4 'liver', nok^5 'bird'. Checked syllables with long vowels have tones phonetically similar to tones 2 and 3 of open syllables: ʔaap^2 'to bathe', mit^3 'knife'.

The five tones of Shan had their origin in an earlier system of three tones on open syllables and no tonal contrast on checked syllables. Those tones on open syllables have been conventionally designated as A - B - C and the fourth category, the checked syllables, as D. The tones in each of these categories underwent phonemic splits, conditioned by the phonetic nature of the initial consonant of each syllable. With the D category, the splits were further conditioned by vowel length. Table 1 shows the patterns of these splits in Shan.

Table 1
Pattern of Tonal Splits in Shan

Initial\Tone	A	B	C	D-short	D-long
Voiceless friction sounds	1	2	3	4	2
Voiceless unaspirated stops	1	2	3	4	2
Glottal sounds	1	2	3	4	2
Voiced sounds	4	3	5	5	3

Consonants

Shan has the following initial consonants:

Voiceless unaspirated stops. p - t - k - ʔ: pɔ^3 - father, taa^4 - to smear, kay^2 - chicken, ʔen^1 - muscle.

Voiceless aspirated stops. ph - th - kh: phi^1 - spirit, thaam^1 - to ask, khet^2 - frog.

Nasals. m - n - ɲ - ŋ: maa^1 - dog, naa^4 - rice field, ɲɔp^4 - to grab, ŋam^1 - to grasp.

Voiceless spirants. s - sh - h: saaŋ^5 - elephant, shon^1 - garden, haa^3 - five. The [s] is unaspirated and slightly palatalized while the [sh] is aspirated and slightly palatalized (Li 1977:152, 164).

> Sonorants. l - r - w - y: laaw^{1} - star, raap^{3} - place, win^{3} - broken off, yaak^{3} - difficult.

Initial clusters consist of a consonant plus [r], [w], or [y]. There are no final clusters.

> Clusters with [r]. pr - phr - tr - kr - khr - mr - sr: praat^{3} - to slip, phraa^{3} - god, traa^{4} - law, kraaη^{3} - with a body in violent motion, khraa^{2} - useful, mraat^{3} - to exceed, sraaw^{1} - to leap.

> Clusters with [w]. pw - tw - thw - kw - khw - sw - shw - lw: pwaaη^{4} - to open, twaa^{4} - unable to walk, thwaak^{3} - to leave the monkhood, kwaa^{2} - to go, khwaa^{1} - right side (not left), swaa^{1} - to have a bad odor, shwaaη^{2} - to rejoice, lwaaη^{5} - to run.

> Clusters with [y]. py - phy - ky - khy - my: pyɔ^{2} - happy, phyɔ^{2} - to dilute, kyaa^{1} - to cook rice and things together, khyɔη^{2} - to fear, myaaη^{5} - in bad condition.

Final consonants include nasals m - n - η and voiceless stops p - t - k. For final w - y - ɰ, see ***Diphthongs***.

> Nasals. m - n - η: phom^{1} - hair, pun^{5} - yonder, phɤη^{4} - straw.

> Voiceless stops. p - t - k: haap^{2} - to carry on the shoulder, khot^{5} - to scoop out, hak^{4} - to break.

Vowels

Shan has nine vowels, with a length distinction only in [a]. All vowels are phonetically long in final position, although written with a single vowel except [a] which is written with a double vowel. In the fifth tone, [aa] tends to be somewhat shorter and is therefore written with a single vowel: ma^{5} - horse.

> High. i - ɯ - u: hi^{4} - long, kɯm^{4} - firm, lu^{1} - rat.

> Mid. e - ɤ - o: khe^{2} - to scratch the earth, nɤ^{5} - flesh, ho^{1} - head. Edmondson (2000a) reports that with a number of Shan dialects he has studied, [ɤ] is closer to [ə].

> Low. ɛ - a, aa - ɔ: mɛ^{3} - mother, pan^{1} - to give, paan^{1} - birthmark, ηɔn^{1} - to howl.

Diphthongs

Diphthongs may be analyzed as a vocalic nucleus plus a final w - y - ɰ.

> Diphthongs with final [w]. iw - ew - ɛw - aw - aaw: niw^{5} - finger, sew^{4} - quick, thɛw^{1} - a row, khaw^{3} - rice, phaaw^{2} - to scatter.
>
> Diphthongs with final [y]. uy - oy - ay - aay - ɔy: huy^{1} - to open, woy^{1} - a dipper, pay^{1} - to step, khwaay^{1} - to turn around, mɔy^{1} - body hair.
>
> Diphthongs with final [ɰ]. aɰ: kaɰ^{3} - near.

The Tai Dialect of Nong Khai — LNK

Belonging to the Southwestern branch of the Tai language family, the Tai dialect of Nong Khai, also referred to as a Lao dialect, is spoken in and around the city of Nong Khai on the border of Laos in northeastern Thailand. Gedney obtained his data from a student at the University of Michigan in 1967 and can be found in Hudak (1997).

Phonology

As in other dialects and languages of the Tai family, the phonological pattern of the Tai dialect of Nong Khai is based on the syllable. Each syllable has distinctions in tone, initial (consonant or consonant cluster), nucleus (vowel or diphthong), and optional final consonant.

Tones

On open syllables (those ending with vowel, semivowel, or nasal), Nong Khai has six tones. Here pitch levels are based on the Chao 5-pitch scale.

> 1 - low-rising, 24: naa^{1} - thick
> 2 - low, with a slight drop at the end, 11: ʔaa^{2} - father's younger sister
> 3 - mid-high, 44: thaa^{3} - landing
> 4 - mid-low, glottalized, 22: naa^{4} - face
> 5 - falling, sometimes glottalized, 42: naa^{5} - mother's younger sibling
> 6 - high level, 55: naa^{6} - field

Checked syllables (those ending in p - t - k) with short vowels exhibit tones phonetically similar to tones 1 and 3 of open syllables: sip^{1} 'ten', mot^{3} 'ant'. Checked syllables with long vowels have tones phonetically similar to tones 2 and 5 of open syllables: ʔaap^{2} 'to bathe', faak^{5} 'bamboo flooring'.

The six tones of Nong Khai had their origin in an earlier system of three tones on open syllables and no tonal contrast on checked syllables. Those tones on open syllables have been conventionally designated as A - B - C and the fourth category, the checked syllables, as D. The tones in each of these categories underwent phonemic splits, conditioned by the phonetic nature of the initial consonant of each syllable. With the D category, the splits were further conditioned by vowel length. Table 1 shows the patterns of these splits in Nong Khai.

Table 1
Pattern of Tonal Splits in Nong Khai

Initial\Tone	A	B	C	D-short	D-long
Voiceless friction sounds	1	3	4	1	2
Voiceless unaspirated stops	2	3	5	1	2
Glottal sounds	2	3	5	1	2
Voiced sounds	6	3	5	3	5

Consonants

Nong Khai has the following initial consonants:

> Voiceless unaspirated stops. p - t - c - k - ʔ: puak^2 - white ant, taw^3 - turtle, con^2 - poor, kay^3 - chicken, ʔaw^2 - to take.
>
> Voiceless aspirated stops. ph - th - ch - kh: phaat^5 - to lay across, tham^4 - cave, choo^1 - part of a name, khaam^6 - indigo.
>
> Voiced stops. b - d: baat^2 - wound, dɤɤn^2 - to walk.
>
> Nasals. m - n - ɲ - ŋ: mɯɯ^5 - day, naa^1 - thick, ɲay^3 - big, ŋaay^3 - easy.
>
> Voiceless spirants. f - s - h: fon^1 - rain, sin^4 - skirt, het^1 - mushroom.
>
> Sonorants. l - w - y: lɛɛm^1 - sharp-pointed, waan^1 - sweet, yen^2 - cool.

There are no initial or final clusters.

Final consonants include nasals m - n - ŋ and voiceless stops p - t - k - ʔ. For final w - y, see ***Diphthongs***.

> Nasals. m - n - ŋ: ʔum^5 - to carry in the arms, ʔun^3 - warm, khaŋ^1 - to imprison.
>
> Voiceless stops. p - t - k - ʔ: haap^2 - to carry on the shoulders, khut^1 - to dig, kaak^2 - ringworm, khuʔ^3 - water container.

Vowels

Nong Khai has nine vowels, with distinction in length undetermined. All vowels are phonetically long in final position and written with a double vowel.

High. i - ɯ - u: bii^{2} - gallbladder, fɯɯn^{6} - firewood, fun^{3} - dust.

Mid. e - ɤ - o: kep^{2} - to keep, kɤɤt^{2} - to be born, hom^{3} - shade.

Low. ɛ - a - ɔ: nɛɛ^{6} - to aim, dap^{1} - to extinguish, dɔɔk^{2} - flower.

Diphthongs

In Nong Khai, the diphthongs include ia - ɯa - ua: khian^{1} - to write, dɯan^{2} - month, khua^{1} - bridge.

Other diphthongs may be analyzed as a vocalic nucleus plus a final w - y.

Diphthongs with final [w]. iw - iaw - eew - ɛɛw - aw - aaw: kiw^{3} - narrow, ʔiaw^{5} - to turn aside, heew^{1} - chasm, kɛɛw^{5} - glass, khaw^{4} - rice, khaaw^{1} - white.

Diphthongs with final [y]. uy - uay - ɤɤy - oy - ooy - ay - aay - ɔy - ɔɔy: khuy^{3} - reed flute, khuay^{6} - buffalo, ʔɤɤy^{1} - vocative particle, ʔoy^{6} - exclamation of annoyance, booy^{2} - to flog, khay^{1} - to open, khaay^{1} - to sell, hɔy^{1} - mollusk, khɔɔy^{6} - to wait for.

Lue — LCH and LMY

Belonging to the Southwestern branch of the Tai language family, Lue, or Tai-Lue, can be found in a number of different regions: 1) in Chieng Hung, the capital city of Sipsongpanna and throughout southern Yunnan province; 2) in Muong Yong and vicinity in northeastern Burma; 3) in the provinces of Chiengmai and Chiengrai in northern Thailand; 4) in Muong Sing and Luang Prabang in Laos; and 5) in and around Binh Lue in northwest Vietnam. Gedney obtained his data over a period of fifteen years, synthesizing much of it in 1969. This synthesis was published in Hudak (1996).

Gedney's data come from Chieng Hung (LCH) and Muong Yong (LMY). In both of these dialects, Gedney was never able to find a contrast between [x] and [kh], the two sounds fluctuating in free variation. Li (1964), however, did find such a contrast at Cheng Tung in southeastern Sipsongpanna. Later research by Gedney uncovered the fact that this dialect is in an area contiguous and continuous with the White Tai area in Vietnam which does preserve this contrast. Other Lue linguistic studies can be found in Hartmann (1984) and anthropological studies in Moreman (1965, 1988) and Davis (2005).

The origin of the ethnonym Lue, lɯɯ^{6}, is unclear. Various sources have suggested it is related to the common Tai word for 'north' (nɤɤ^{1} in Lue and nɯa^{5} in Siamese); however, this appears to be impossible since neither the initial, the vowel, nor the tone agree. The term may simply represent a combination of linguistic, cultural, and political factors. The Lue capital city is named ceη^{4} huη^{5} and means 'city of the dawn'. Nor was Gedney able to find a clear and accurate explanation for the name of the Lue-speaking area, Sipsongpanna. While sipsong meant 'twelve' and panna 'a type of administrative unit', no accurate listing of these units was ever obtained.

Phonology

As in other dialects and languages of the Tai family, the phonological patterns of the Lue dialects at Chieng Hung and Muong Yong are based on the syllable. Each syllable has distinctions in tone, initial (consonant or consonant cluster), nucleus (vowel or diphthong), and optional final consonant.

Tones

On open syllables (those ending with vowel, semivowel, or nasal), Chieng Hung Lue has six tones. Here pitch levels are based on the Chao 5-pitch scale.

1 - high level, 55: haa^{1} - to seek
2 - low-rising, 12: haa^{2} - rain shower
3 - low level, glottalized, 11: haa^{3} - five
4 - low-falling, 21: haa^{4} - mold
5 - mid level, 33: haa^{5} - epidemic
6 - falling, glottalized, 31: haa^{6} - to ferment

Checked syllables (those ending in p - t - k) with short vowels exhibit tones phonetically similar to tones 1 and 5 of open syllables: sip^{1} 'ten', mot^{5} 'ant'. Checked syllables with long vowels have tones phonetically similar to tones 2 and 5 of open syllables: ʔaap^{2} 'to bathe', faak^{5} 'split bamboo'.

The six tones of Chieng Hung Lue had their origin in an earlier system of three tones on open syllables and no tonal contrast on checked syllables. Those tones on open syllables have been conventionally designated as A - B - C and the fourth category, the checked syllables, as D. The tones in each of these categories underwent phonemic splits, conditioned by the phonetic nature of the initial consonant of each syllable. With the D category, the splits were further conditioned by vowel length. Table 1 shows the patterns of these splits in Chieng Hung Lue.

Table 1
Pattern of Tonal Splits in Chieng Hung Lue

Initial\Tone	A	B	C	D-short	D-long
Voiceless friction sounds	1	2	3	1	2
Voiceless unaspirated stops	1	2	3	1	2
Glottal sounds	1	2	3	1	2
Voiced sounds	4	5	6	5	5

The phonetics of Muong Yong tones are slightly different from those at Chieng Hung:

1 - high-rising, 45: haa^1 - to seek
2 - low-rising, 12: haa^2 - rain shower
3 - low level, glottalized, 11: haa^3 - five
4 - mid, with slight rise and fall, 342: haa^4 - mold
5 - mid level, 33: haa^5 - epidemic
6 - falling, glottalized, 31: haa^6 - to ferment

Like those in Chieng Hung Lue, checked syllables with short vowels in Muong Yong Lue have tones phonetically similar to tones 1 and 5 of open syllables: dip^1 'raw', fok^5 'swollen'. Tones 2 and 5 appear on the long checked syllables: duuk^2 'bone', hɛɛt^5 'rhinoceros'.

In both dialects, short checked syllables ending in a glottal stop frequently have the glottal stop deleted with a corresponding reduction in vowel and neutralization of the tone to tone 5. Thus, the word for door may be pronounced as paʔ^1 tuu^1 or more frequently pa-tuu^1. Syllabic [m̩] also appears with or without a tone: m̩^{2} or m̩ 'classifier for fruit'.

Gedney (Hudak 1996:xxii) notes that Muong Yong Lue has tone sandhi, where certain tones are altered when in close juncture with other tones. This involves tone 4 changing to tone 5 when following tone 5; thus kaa^5 pɛŋ^4 'price is high' can also be pronounced as kaa^5 pɛŋ^5.

As Table 2 demonstrates, the tonal splits in Muong Yong are the same as the Chieng Hung splits except that words with the Proto-Tai A tone and originally preglottalized initials have the same tone as words with originally voiced initials.

Table 2
Pattern of Tonal Splits in Muong Yong Lue

Initial\Tone	A	B	C	D-short	D-long
Voiceless friction sounds	1	2	3	1	2
Voiceless unaspirated stops	1	2	3	1	2
Glottal sounds	4	2	3	1	2
Voiced sounds	4	5	6	5	5

Consonants

The two Lue dialects have the following initial consonants. Frequently, there is an h/r variation, [h] in the spoken form, hum^5 'shade', and [r] in the literary, rum^5. In the data in this volume, Gedney also records literary variants with initial [l], lum^5. Unless noted, the examples provided occur in both dialects.

Voiceless unaspirated stops. p - t - c - k - ʔ: pii^5 - older sibling, taaŋ^4 - road, caay^4 - male, kin^1 - to eat, ʔum^3 - to hold in the arms.

Voiceless aspirated stops. ph - th - ch (LMY only): phoo^1 - husband, thaw^3 - old, suʔ^1 chit^1 - to crush.

Voiced stops. b - d: baat^2 - foot, dam^3 - handle.

Nasals. m - n - ɲ (LMY only) - ŋ: mɔɔ^3 - pot, naa^3 - face, ɲɛn^4 - to clench, ŋaay^1 - face up. In LMY, [ɲ] appears as an allophone of /ŋ/ before [i] and [ɛ].

Voiceless spirants. f - s - x - h: faa^6 - sky, sɛw^4 - sharp, xay^2 - egg, hɤɤ^2 - sweat.

Sonorants. l - r - v - y: luuk^5 - child, raak^5 - root, vay^6 - to keep, yɤɤ^2 - bait. Gedney groups the spirant (fricative) [v] with the sonorants because of its sonority and low level of friction. In addition, [v] and [w] are in complementary distribution, with [v] appearing initially and [w] after a consonant.

Initial clusters occur with a consonant followed by [r] or [w]. There are no final clusters.

Clusters with [r]. tr - thr: traa^1 - brand, thrii^4 - solder.

Clusters with [w]. kw - tw (LMY only) - thw (LMY only) - xw: kwaan^1 - axe, twip^5 - continent, thwaay^1 - to give to royalty, xwaay^4 - buffalo.

LMY also records [xl] in xlɯk^5 - the sound of bone cracking when turned slowly.

Final consonants include nasals m - n - ŋ and voiceless stops p - t - k -ʔ. For final w - y, see ***Diphthongs***.

Nasals. m - n - ŋ: nam^6 - water, nɔn^4 - to sleep, mɔŋ^4 - gong.

Voiceless stops. p - t - k - ʔ: baap^2 - sin, het^5 - to do, paak^2 - mouth, neʔ^1 - lean.

Vowels

Each of the two Lue dialects has nine vowels, occurring short and long. All vowels are phonetically long in final position and written with a double vowel.

High. i, ii - ɯ, ɯɯ - u, uu: min^1 - stink, lii^2 - to squint, thɯŋ^1 - to reach, mɯɯt^5 - dark, hum^2 - to cover, puu^4 - betel.

Mid. e, ee - ɤ, ɤɤ - o, oo: xew^1 - green, veek^5 - work, lɤm^1 - python, lɤɤ^5 - to saw, mon^5 - fun, mook^2 - hat.

Low. ɛ, ɛɛ - a, aa - ɔ, ɔɔ: nɛn^3 - solid, hɛɛ^5 - ore, san^3 - short, naaw^1 - cold, hɔŋ^6 - to call, tɔɔk^2 - bamboo strip.

Diphthongs

Diphthongs may be analyzed as a vocalic nucleus plus a final w - y.

Diphthongs with final [w]. iw - ew - ɛw - aw - aaw: xiw^2 - bad smell, ʔew^2 - business, sɛw^1 - bad smell, law^3 - liquor, faaw^6 - to hurry.

Diphthongs with final [y]. uy - ɤy - oy - ay - aay - ɔy: tuy^3 - fat, nɤy^2 - tired, koy^3 - banana, pay^6 - to snare, ʔaay^2 - to lie in wait, hɔy^6 - to string.

The Tai Dialect of Chiengmai — CM

Gedney does not list his source for the Chiengmai data in this comparative list. However, since it is close to his own research in 1964 (Hudak 1997), his tone descriptions have been added. The Tai dialect of Chiengmai belongs to the Southwestern branch of the Tai language family and is spoken in and around the city of Chiengmai in northern Thailand.

Phonology

As in other dialects and languages of the Tai family, the phonological pattern of the Tai dialect of Chiengmai is based on the syllable. Each syllable has distinctions in tone, initial (consonant or consonant cluster), nucleus (vowel or diphthong), and optional final consonant.

Tones

On open syllables (those ending with vowel, semivowel, or nasal), Chiengmai has six tones. Here pitch levels are based on the Chao 5-pitch scale.

1 - mid-high, 44: pii^{1} - fat
2 - low-rising, 14: pii^{2} - year
3 - mid-low, 22: sii^{3} - four
4 - falling, 41: pii^{4} - older sibling
5 - high-falling, (glottalized ?), 53: khii^{5} - excrement
6 - high-rising-falling (glottalized ?), 454: cii^{6} - to point

Checked syllables (those ending in p - t - k) with short vowels exhibit tones phonetically similar to tones 2 and 6 of open syllables: hap^{2} 'to close', sak^{6} 'to wash clothes'. Checked syllables with long vowels have tones phonetically similar to tones 3 and 4 of open syllables: ʔaap^{3} 'to bathe', lɯak^{4} 'to choose'.

The six tones of Chiengmai had their origin in an earlier system of three tones on open syllables and no tonal contrast on checked syllables. Those tones on open syllables have been conventionally designated as A - B - C and the fourth category, the checked syllables, as D. The tones in each of these categories underwent phonemic splits, conditioned by the phonetic nature of the initial consonant of each syllable. With the D category, the splits were further conditioned by vowel length. Table 1 shows the patterns of these splits in Chiengmai.

Table 1
Pattern of Tonal Splits in Chiengmai

Initial\Tone	A	B	C	D-short	D-long
Voiceless friction sounds	2	3	5	2	3
Voiceless unaspirated stops	2	3	5	2	3
Glottal sounds	1	3	5	2	3
Voiced sounds	1	4	6	6	4

Consonants

Chiengmai has the following initial consonants:

Voiceless unaspirated stops. p - t - c - k - ʔ: pii^{4} - older sibling, tuu^{5} - cupboard, cii^{6} - to point, kɛɛ^{3} - old, ʔuu^{3} - cradle.

Voiceless aspirated stops. ph - th - kh: phua^{2} - husband, thii^{3} - closely spaced, miserly, khii^{3} - to ride.

Voiced stops. b - d: baa^{3} - shoulder, dɯa^{1} - cockspur.

Nasals. m - n - ɲ - ŋ: mɯɯ^{6} - a turn, naw^{4} - rotten, ɲɯa^{3} - bait, ŋua^{1} - ox.

Voiceless spirants. f - s - h: fii^{2} - a boil, siaη^{2} - sound, hɯɯ^{5} - to give.

Sonorants. l - w - y: lɔɔt^{3} - spool, waan^{2} - sweet, yaa^{1} - medicine.

Initial clusters appear with a consonant followed by [w]. There are no final clusters.

Clusters with [w]. kw - khw - ʔw: kwaaη^{5} - wide, khwaaη^{4} - to throw, ʔwaay^{1} - steam, vapor.

Final consonants include nasals m - n - η and voiceless stops p - t - k -ʔ. For final w - y, see ***Diphthongs***.

Nasals. m - n - η: ʔim^{3} - full, khɯn^{5} - to go up, kiη^{3} - branch.

Voiceless stops. p - t - k - ʔ: dip^{2} - raw, cet^{2} - seven, piik^{3} - wing, pɛʔ^{6} - goat.

Vowels

Chiengmai has nine vowels, with distinction in length undetermined. All vowels are phonetically long in final position and written with a double vowel.

High. i - ɯ - u: bit^{2} - to twist, cɯɯ^{4} - name, khun^{3} - turbid.

Mid. e - ɤ - o: pen^{2} - to be, dɤk^{2} - late at night, ʔot^{2} - to endure.

Low. ɛ - a - ɔ: tɛɛη^{2} - cucumber, caaη^{6} - elephant, nɔɔk^{4} - outside.

Diphthongs

In Chiengmai, the diphthongs include ia - ɯa - ua: siam^{2} - spade, cɯak^{4} - rope, nuat^{3} - beard.

Other diphthongs may be analyzed as a vocalic nucleus plus a final w - y.

Diphthongs with final [w]. iw - iaw - ew - ɛɛw - aw - aaw: siw^{2} - pimple, khiaw^{2} - green, pew^{2} - flame, ʔɛɛw^{1} - waist, ʔaw^{1} - to take, naaw^{2} - cold.

Diphthongs with final [y]. ɯay - uay - ɤy - ay - aay - ɔy - ɔɔy: pɯay^{2} - naked, cuay^{4} - to help, kɤy^{1} - accustomed, ʔay^{1} - to cough, taay^{2} - to die, pɔy^{3} - to release, lɔɔy^{1} - to float.

CHAPTER 3: CENTRAL TAI DIALECTS

The languages and dialects of the Central branch of the Tai family can be found in southern China and in northern Vietnam. Luo (1996:78) delimits the geographical boundaries of this group as follows: from the You River (You Jiang or Yu Jiang), which forms the upper and middle reaches of the Xi River, in Guangxi in the north to the Red River in Vietnam in the south; and from the Gulf of Tonkin (Beibu Gulf) off the Vietnamese coast in the east to the Sino-Vietnamese border in Yunnan, China, in the west. As noted in the Introduction, the formation of the Central branch has remained in dispute with some (Gedney) believing it should not be separated from the Southwestern branch and others (Haudricourt) suggesting it belongs with the Northern group. With this line of reasoning, the Central branch would then form an intermediate or transitional group rather than a separate branch.

Summarizing Li, Luo (1996:78) lists the following features as the most salient characteristics for distinguishing the Central branch from the other two: 1) the proto-initial clusters *tr and *thr have merged into the voiceless aspirated stop /th/; 2) traces of proto-initial clusters *pr, *ʔbl/r, and *vl/r have been retained and realized as [phy], [by], and [py] respectively; 3) the proto-voiceless labiodental fricative *f has developed into a voiceless aspirated labial stop /ph/; 4) the proto-voiced velar fricative *ɣ has developed into a voiceless unaspirated velar stop /k/; 5) there is a set of lexical items different from the other two branches.

Cognates used to represent this group are from the dialects spoken in Guangxi at Lei Ping (LP), Lungming (LM), Lungchow (LC), Ping Siang (PS), and Ning Ming (NM). Also included are two other dialects: 1) a variety of Nung similar to those in far northeastern Vietnam but located much farther to the west and designated as Western Nung (WN) by Gedney; and 2) another variety of Nung spoken at Bac Va (BV) near Phu Lang Thuong (Bac Giang) in northeastern Vietnam.

The Tai Dialect of Lei Ping — LP

Belonging to the Central branch of the Tai language family, the Tai dialect of Lei Ping (lay^4 phiŋ^4, Pinyin Leiping) is spoken in Lei Ping in southwest Guangxi, approximately thirty mile southwest of Lungming and twenty-five miles northeast of Lungchow. Gedney obtained the data in Hong Kong in 1966 from a 62-year-old informant by the name of Liang Shao-lu (lyaaŋ^4 saaw^3 nuu^4). Dominic Yip acted as interpreter in the sessions. The informant provided the following sentence to describe his native language: ŋoo^5 caaŋ^3 poon^3 thii^5 vaa^5 ‘I speak the native language'. References to the Lei Ping dialect can be found in Gedney's individual linguistic studies (1995a, 1995b; Bickner et al. 1989) and in Sarawit (1973). Gedney's complete data appear in Hudak (1995).

Phonology

As in other dialects and languages of the Tai family, the phonological pattern of Lei Ping is based on the syllable. Each syllable has distinctions in tone, initial (consonant or consonant cluster), nucleus (vowel or diphthong), and optional final consonant.

Tones

On open syllables (those ending with vowel, semivowel, or nasal), Lei Ping has five tones. Here pitch levels are based on the Chao 5-pitch scale.

1 - high rising-falling, 454: maa^{1} - dog
2 - high level, with a final drop before pause, 44: maa^{2} - to soak
3 - rising, glottalized, 13: maa^{3} - horse
4 - low-falling, 21: maa^{4} - to come
5 - low level, 11: taa^{5} - maternal grandfather

Checked syllables (those ending in p - t - k) with short vowels exhibit tones phonetically similar to tones 2 and 4 of open syllables: khap^{2} 'step', lak^{4} 'to steal'. Tone 5 usually appears on syllables that have cognates elsewhere with a long vowel, for example, lop^{5} 'to stroke' (Siamese luup^{3}). Checked syllables with long vowels have tones phonetically similar to tones 2 and 5 of open syllables: nuuk^{2} 'deaf', byook^{5} 'flower'.

The five tones of Lei Ping had their origin in an earlier system of three tones on open syllables and no tonal contrast on checked syllables. Those tones on open syllables have been conventionally designated as A - B - C and the fourth category, the checked syllables, as D. The tones in each of these categories underwent phonemic splits, conditioned by the phonetic nature of the initial consonant of each syllable. With the D category, the splits were further conditioned by vowel length. Table 1 shows the patterns of these splits in Lei Ping.

Table 1
Pattern of Tonal Splits in Lei Ping

Initial\Tone	A	B	C	D-short	D-long
Voiceless friction sounds	1	2	3	2	2
Voiceless unaspirated stops	2	5	3	2	5
Glottal sounds	2	5	3	2	5
Voiced sounds	4	5	3	4, 5	5

Consonants

Lei Ping has the following initial consonants:

Voiceless unaspirated stops. p - t - c - k - ʔ: pii^2 - year, tɤk^2 - to shoot, cet^2 - seven, kee^5 - old, ʔaaŋ^5 - basin.

Voiceless aspirated stops. ph - th - ch - kh: pheek^2 - to explode, thɤɤ^1 - to carry, chim^4 - to taste, khap^4 - to catch.

Voiced stops. b - d: baa^3 - crazy, dik^2 - child. The [d] is pronounced with a simultaneous glottal release.

Nasals. m - n - ŋ: mii^1 - bear, noon^4 - to lie down, ŋooy^4 - to see.

Voiceless spirants. f - ɬ - s - h: fɤn^4 - firewood, ɬɤɤ^1 - tiger, sɤɤk^5 - rope, hoo^4 - person.

Sonorants. v - l - y: vaam^4 - language, laaŋ^3 - to wash, yiin^2 - tobacco. Gedney groups the spirant (fricative) [v] with the sonorants because of its sonority and low friction level. In addition, [v] and [w] are in complementary distribution, with [v] appearing initially and [w] after a consonant.

Initial clusters consist of a consonant plus [w] or [y]. There are no final clusters.

Clusters with [w]. kw - khw: kwaa^2 - melon, khwaa^2 - pants.

Clusters with [y]. py - phy - ky - khy - by - my - hy - ly: pyaa^2 - fish, phyaa^3 - orphan, kyaaŋ^2 - middle, khyay^2 - egg, byook^5 - flower, myaak^5 - slippery, hyaaŋ^2 kaaŋ^2 - Hong Kong, lyaaŋ^4 - the informant's name.

Final consonants include nasals m - n - ŋ and voiceless stops p - t - k - ʔ. For final w - y - ɰ, see ***Diphthongs***.

Nasals. m - n - ŋ: neem^1 - to paste, yin^4 - to hear, hiŋ^1 - voice.

Voiceless stops. p - t - k - ʔ: ceep^5 - chaff, phat^2 - to winnow, hok^2 - six, looʔ^5 - grammatical particle.

Vowels

In his elicitation, Gedney (Hudak 1995:119) noted that there was no distinction between [ɤ] and [ɯ], although [ɤ] is a little higher after labials such as [f] and [ph]. Nor is there a contrast between [o] and [u] as in [ok] and [uk], but [u] is very high and there is a definite long [uu] as in nuuk^{2} 'deaf' and cuuk^{5} 'white ant'. With these points in mind, Gedney posited the following vowel system:

High. i, ii - uu: ʔim^{5} - full, ciin^{5} - to spin, kuuk^{5} - hoe.

Mid. ɤ, ɤɤ: cɤŋ^{2} - to steam, chɤɤŋ^{5} - elephant.

Low. e, ee - a, aa - o, oo: ʔet^{2} - one, meeŋ^{4} - insect, ʔay^{2} - to cough, ʔaay^{2} - to lean back, foŋ^{4} - to roof, hook^{5} - shell.

In the transcription system used, [e] and [o] are phonetically more open, [ɛ] and [ɔ] respectively. Long vowels tend to be more open [kɛɛ^{2} 'old', khɛɛk^{2} - 'guest', mɔɔ^{3} 'pot', mɔɔt^{2} 'mold'] and short vowels more closed [cet^{2} 'seven', khon^{1} 'body hair']. Vowels in syllable-final position have a pronunciation close to a long vowel and are therefore written with a double vowel.

Diphthongs

Diphthongs may be analyzed as a vocalic nucleus plus a final w - y - ɰ.

Diphthongs with final [w]. iiw - eew - aw - aaw: khiiw^{1} - bad-smelling, ʔeew^{3} - to bend, ʔaw^{2} - to take, haaw^{1} - to yawn.

Diphthongs with final [y]. uuy - ay - aay - ooy: vuuy^{2} - seed, day^{3} - can, haay^{1} - to die, ʔooy^{3} - sugarcane.

Diphthongs with final [ɰ]. aɰ: daɰ^{2} - in.

The Tai Dialect of Lungming — LM

Belonging to the Central branch of the Tai language family, this Tai dialect is spoken in the town and county of Lungming (colloquial loŋ^{4} ʔiŋ^{4}, formal loŋ^{4} miŋ^{1}, Pinyin Longming) in southwestern Guangxi. Gedney obtained his data from 1966 through 1976 from an informant living in Hong Kong. The informant, a 42-year-old male named thaaŋ^{1} theen^{4} sin^{1}, was born in thiim^{1} taŋ^{3} (formal theen^{1} tɤn^{1}) about forty Chinese miles from Lungming. Born in 1924, he moved to Hong Kong in 1949 where he worked in a Chinese school. Dominic Yip acted as interpreter because the informant spoke only Cantonese. Upon questioning, the informant identified his native language simply as vaam^{4} thoo^{3} 'native language or dialect', with thoo^{3} meaning 'local or native' and not a specific ethnic group as various Western scholars and researchers have treated it.

Throughout this Tai-speaking region the question of ethnonyms remains a confusing issue. Many of the speakers refer to themselves as thoo^{3}, with kaaŋ^{3} thoo^{3} meaning 'to speak the local or native language'. On the other hand, kaaŋ^{3}

kheek^{4} has the specific meaning of 'to speak Mandarin'. Li (1977:105) notes that the Tai-speakers of Lungchow and Lungming use the term tay^{4} 'Tai' to refer to the Tai-speaking people of Vietnam and not to themselves. In contrast, the Central Tai speakers in Vietnam and in some parts of China use the term Nung (from Vietnamese noŋ or nɔŋ, depending on the dialect) for themselves. Western scholars have borrowed this term to refer to the Tai dialects of western Guangxi. Other Tai groups in Vietnam refer to themselves as Tai. In China, however, all of the Tai dialects are officially referred to as Zhuang, which appears in the Lungming expressions kaaŋ^{3} cooŋ^{5} 'to speak Zhuang' and kɤn^{4} cooŋ^{5} 'a Zhuang person'.

Specific studies of Lungming have been restricted to Gedney's massive glossary (Hudak 1991b) and to his various linguistic papers (1995a, 1995b, 1995c; Bickner et al. 1989). Sarawit (1973) has also used Lungming data.

Phonology

As in other dialects and languages of the Tai family, the phonological pattern of the Lungming dialect is based on the syllable. Each syllable has distinctions in tone, initial (consonant or consonant cluster), nucleus (vowel or diphthong), and optional final consonant.

Tones

On open syllables (those ending with vowel, semivowel, or nasal), Lungming has six tones. Here pitch levels are based on the Chao 5-pitch scale.

1 - high level, 55: laa^{1} - to seek
2 - high-rising, 45: laa^{2} - a flock
3 - mid level, glottalized, 33: laa^{3} - cracked
4 - low-falling, from mid-low to low, 21: laa^{4} - to take one's leave
5 - low level, 11: laa^{5} - epidemic
6 - falling, from mid-low to low and then rising to mid-low, glottalized, 212: laa^{6} - to snatch

Checked syllables (those ending in p - t - k) with short vowels exhibit tones phonetically similar to tones 1, 2, 3, 4, and 5 of open syllables: loʔ^{1} 'final imperative particle', loʔ^{2} 'final imperative particle', phat^{3} 'to winnow', kok^{4} 'to simmer', pik^{5} 'crowded'. Checked syllables with long vowels have tones phonetically similar to tones 1, 2, 3, and 5 of open syllables: teep^{1} 'to drink with pleasure, smacking the lips', kook^{2} 'rice husks', yiip^{3} 'to pickle in brine', laap^{5} 'to dry meat'. Tone 3 on the checked syllable is not glottalized as it is on the open syllable.

Note that the checked syllables with short vowels and tones 1, 2, or 5, and the checked syllables with long vowels and tones 1 or 3 do not reflect the historical development of the tones. These syllables with their respective tones probably resulted from the secondary shortening of the vowel, or they represent distinctive vocabulary, for example, loanwords and particles or syllables resulting from onomatopoeic processes.

The six tones of Lungming had their origin in an earlier system of three tones on open syllables and no tonal contrast on checked syllables. Those tones on open syllables have been conventionally designated as A - B - C and the fourth category, the checked syllables, as D. The tones in each of these categories underwent phonemic splits, conditioned by the phonetic nature of the initial consonant of each syllable. With the D category, the splits were further conditioned by vowel length. Table 1 shows the patterns of these splits in Lungming.

Table 1
Pattern of Tonal Splits in Lungming

Initial\Tone	A	B	C	D-short	D-long
Voiceless friction sounds	1	2	3	3	2
Voiceless unaspirated stops	1	2	3	3	2
Glottal sounds	4	2	3	3	2
Voiced sounds	4	5	6	4	5

Consonants

Lungming has the following initial consonants:

Voiceless unaspirated stops. p - t - c - k - ʔ: paak^2 - mouth, taam^3 - gallbladder, coo^3 - ancestor, kɤn^4 - person, ʔaa^4 - to crow.

Voiceless aspirated stops. ph - th - ch - kh: phaaŋ^5 - to strike, thɤn^1 - to swallow, chuu^1 - rough, khan^1 - to crow.

Nasals. m - n - ŋ: mit^3 - to pinch, naa^2 - to scold, ŋee^6 - fish barbel. Nasals are often preglottalized before the vowels [ɯɯ] and [uu].

Voiceless spirants. f - s - š - h: foon^6 - brown, sii^2 - to abandon, šop^3 - to smell, huuŋ^5 - chief.

Sonorants. v - l - w - y - ɰ: vey^4 - fence, laaŋ^5 - to unroll, pooŋ^1 moo^4-wa^4 - a herd of oxen, yiim^4 - salt, maɰ^4-ɰa^4 - a leaf. Note that [w] and [ɰ] only occur initially due to assimilation processes. Gedney groups the spirant (fricative) [v] with the sonorants because of its sonority and low friction level. In addition, [v] and [w] are in complementary distribution, with [v] appearing initially and [w] after a consonant.

Initial clusters consist of a consonant plus [w] or [y]. There are no final clusters.

Clusters with [w]. kw - khw: kwaat^2 - to rake, khwiin^1 - circle.

Clusters with [y]. py - phy - ty - thy - cy - ky - khy - my - ny - ly - sy - hy: pyom^{1} - to take down, phyaa^{1} - rocky mountain, tyook^{2} - to chop fine, thyaaw^{6} ʔuu^{1} - to dance, cyaaŋ^{6} vaa^{4} - to speak, kyaɰ^{3} - near, khyow^{4} - ball, myook^{2} - flower, nyat^{3} - very tired, lyan^{3} - to play, syow^{1} - pimple, hyaa^{6} - summer.

Final consonants include nasals m - n - ŋ and voiceless stops p - t - k - ʔ. For final w - y - ɰ, see ***Diphthongs***.

Nasals. m - n - ŋ: saam^{1} - three, nan^{3} - to itch, sooŋ^{1} - two.

Voiceless stops. p - t - k - ʔ: poop^{2} - bubble, choot^{2} - to incite, lok^{5} - child. The final glottal stop only occurs in laʔ^{3} 'final emphatic particle', leʔ^{3} 'sentence-final emphatic particle', loʔ^{1} 'final imperative particle', loʔ^{2} 'final imperative particle', loʔ^{3} 'emphatic clause-final particle', neʔ^{3} 'this, these'.

Vowels

Gedney (Hudak 1991b:xxvi) arrived at the following vowel inventory for Lungming; however, it was unclear from the data whether or not the absence of short [ɯ] and short [u] was accidental or systematic.

High. i, ii - ɯɯ - uu: kin^{1} - to eat, ʔiip^{2} - to step on something, lɯɯŋ^{5} - loose, thuu^{1} - head.

Mid. ɤ, ɤɤ: phɤn^{1} - rain, yeen^{4} sɤɤ^{4} - color.

Low. e, ee - a, aa - o, oo: neʔ^{3} - this, these, cheek^{2} - to tear, vat^{4} - to dip, thaa^{1} - eye, thoŋ^{1} - to leak, cook^{2} - cup.

The short vowels [e] and [o] are phonetically more open, [ɛ] and [ɔ] respectively. Vowels in open syllables tend to be long except for the short vowels [e] and [a] in the indefinite particle -a^{4} and in various particles. Single vowels denote a short vowel and double vowels long vowels.

Diphthongs

Diphthongs analyzed as consisting of a vocalic nucleus plus a final w - y - ɰ also occur. The diphthongs ey - ɤɰ - ow, in many cases, reflect the earlier high monophthongs ii - ɯɯ - uu, respectively: khwey^{2} 'to ride' (Siamese khii^{2}), sɤɰ^{6} 'to buy' (Siamese sɯɯ^{4}), mow^{1} 'pig' (Siamese muu^{5}).

Diphthongs with final [w]. iiw - eew - aw - aaw - ow: kiiw^{1} - to call, leew^{6} - completely, law^{3} - liquor, laaw^{1} - to fear, yow^{2} - to stay.

Diphthongs with final [y]. uuy - ey - eey - ay - aay - ooy: tuuy^{4} - person, pey^{1} - to go, ʔeey^{4} - vocative particle, khay^{1} - to open, laay^{4} - striped, nooy^{2} - little.

Diphthongs with final [ɰ]. ɤɰ - aɰ: sɤɰ^{6} - to buy, maɰ^{2} - new.

The Tai Dialect of Western Nung — WN

Western Nung, a variety of Nung, belongs to the Central branch of the Tai language family and is spoken at Muong Khuong (mɯŋ^{4} khaaŋ^{1}) in the northern Vietnamese province of Lao Kay and its vicinity. The town of Muong Khuong is located about forty kilometers north and slightly east of Lao Kay. The speakers refer to themselves and their language as nɔŋ^{4} or nuŋ^{5}, and many of them have the surname Nung. Gedney notes that this dialect clearly belongs to the group of Tai languages spoken in the extreme northeastern part of Vietnam and adjacent parts of China, variously known as Nung and Thô. This dialect, however, is a linguistic isolate located much farther to the west of the main group of languages, and for this reason, Gedney decided to refer to the dialect as Western Nung. These linguistic islands are identified on the old French ethnolinguistic map, Carte Ethnolinguistique, 1949 edition, compiled by L'École Française d'Extrême-Orient. Aside from Gedney's extensive glossary (Hudak 1995), there appears to be little published information on this particular dialect, with the exception of Tingsabadh (1976). Tingsabadh examines the speech of two informants, one from Ban Pa Kha, located about sixty kilometers northeast of Lao Kay, and the other from Ban Phak Thung, about seven kilometers north of Lao Kay.

Western Nung is of particular interest to students of Tai linguistics because it differs considerably in vocabulary from the other varieties of Nung although it is similar in other respects. The question that arises is which dialect groups made the lexical innovations.

Gedney obtained his data in the years 1964 and 1968–69 from Muong Khuong refugees living in Vientiane, Laos. The data collected represents three different localities: Muong Khuong (mɯŋ^{4} khaaŋ^{1}); Ban Lao (baan^{3} law^{5}), located twenty-two kilometers north of Lao Kay, toward Muong Khuong; and Muong Thin Na (mɯŋ^{4} thin^{5} naa^{4}), located across the border in China, an overnight journey or about thirty kilometers from Muong Khuong. The speech found in these three localities is identical in phonological structure and phonetic detail, although differences in vocabulary do occur.

Phonology

As in other dialects and languages of the Tai family, the phonological pattern of the Western Nung dialect is based on the syllable. Each syllable has distinctions in tone, initial (consonant or consonant cluster), nucleus (vowel or diphthong), and optional final consonant.

Tones

On open syllables (those ending with vowel, semivowel, or nasal), Western Nung has six tones. Here pitch levels are based on the Chao 5-pitch scale.

1 - low-rising, 14: cii^1 - to strain
2 - low-falling, 21: cii^2 - to borrow
3 - mid-low level, glottalized, 22: cii^3 - how many
4 - mid-high level, 44: cii^4 - flag
5 - mid-falling, 31: cii^5 - to soak
6 - high level, glottalized, 55: cii^6 - to point

Checked syllables (those ending in p - t - k) with short vowels exhibit tones phonetically similar to tones 6 and 4 of open syllables: bak^6 'dipnet', cak^4 'to level ground'. Checked syllables with long vowels have tones phonetically similar to tones 2 and 5 of open syllables: $dɔk^2$ 'flower', luk^5 'child'.

The six tones of Western Nung had their origin in an earlier system of three tones on open syllables and no tonal contrast on checked syllables. Those tones on open syllables have been conventionally designated as A - B - C and the fourth category, the checked syllables, as D. The tones in each of these categories underwent phonemic splits, conditioned by the phonetic nature of the initial consonant of each syllable. With the D category, the splits were further conditioned by vowel length. Table 1 shows the patterns of these splits in Western Nung.

Table 1
Pattern of Tonal Splits in Western Nung

Initial\Tone	A	B	C	D-short	D-long
Voiceless friction sounds	1	2	3	6	2
Voiceless unaspirated stops	1	2	3	6	2
Glottal sounds	1	2	3	6	2
Voiced sounds	4	5	6	4	5

Consonants

Western Nung has the following initial consonants:

Voiceless unaspirated stops. p - t - c - k - ʔ: pay^{1} - to go, tem^{3} - to light, cin^{1} - to eat, kɔn^{2} - before, ʔaan^{1} - saddle.

Voiceless aspirated stops. ph - th - ch - kh: phɯɯ^{1} - we, thii^{2} - closely spaced, chuŋ^{3} - pungent, khaw^{3} - rice.

Voiced stops. b - d: baan^{3} - village, dɯy^{1} - navel.

Nasals. m - n - ɲ - ŋ: may^{3} - to burn, nam^{6} - water, ɲii^{1} - to flee, ŋuu^{4} - snake.

Voiceless spirants. f - s - š - h: faa^{6} - sky, siw^{2} - chisel, šɔy^{4} - to swing, hoo^{2} - thing.

Sonorants. v - ð - l - y: vii^{1} - a comb, ðay^{5} - dry field, leŋ^{6} - dry, yiw^{2} - to be at. Gedney grouped the spirants (fricatives) [v] and [ð] with the sonorants because of their sonority and low friction level. In addition, [v] and [w] are in complementary distribution, with [v] appearing initially and [w] after a consonant.

The only recorded initial cluster is [kw] in kwaay^{2} - stubborn.

Final consonants include nasals m - n - ŋ and voiceless stops p - t - k - ʔ. For final w - y - ɰ, see ***Diphthongs***.

Nasals. m - n - ŋ: hom^{6} - to fence, chon^{3} - to converge, caaŋ^{5} - artisan.

Voiceless stops. p - t - k - ʔ: kaap^{2} - husk, pɛt^{2} - eight, chɔk^{6} - six. A final glottal stop appears only in the particle lɔʔ^{4}.

Vowels

Western Nung has nine vowels, with a length distinction only in a, aa. Final vowels are phonetically long and are therefore written with a double vowel.

High. i - ɯ - u: ciŋ^{1} - first, nɯŋ^{3} - to steam, ðuu^{4} - hole.

Mid. e - ɤ - o: yen^{4} - tendon, ŋɤk^{2} - gums, hoo^{4} - neck.

Low. ɛ - a, aa - ɔ: hɛɛ^{5} - to cut, sak^{6} - just, laak^{5} - root, kɔk^{6} - base.

Diphthongs

Diphthongs may be analyzed as a vocalic nucleus plus a final w - y - ɰ.

> Diphthongs with final [w]. iw - ew - ɛw - aw - aaw: šiw^{2} - wrinkle, tew^{4} - to flee, sɛw^{3} - to embroider, paw^{2} - to blow, paaw^{2} - to announce.
>
> Diphthongs with final [y]. ɯy - uy - ay - aay - ɔy: sɯy^{2} - to wash, tuy^{2} - kind of nut, ʔay^{1} - to cough, baay^{1} - to clear weeds, ʔɔy^{3} - sugarcane.
>
> Diphthongs with final [ɰ]. aɰ: naɰ^{3} - light (not heavy).

The Tai Dialect of Bac Va — BV

Belonging to the Central branch of the Tai language family, the Tai dialect of Bac Va is one variety of the dialects known as Nung. Bac Va is located near Phu Lang Thuong (Bac Giang) in northeastern Vietnam. Gedney obtained the data from Tran Phuc Ky in Dalat, Vietnam, in 1964. The complete data appear in Hudak (1997).

Phonology

As in other dialects and languages of the Tai family, the phonological pattern of the Tai dialect of Bac Va is based on the syllable. Each syllable has distinctions in tone, initial (consonant or consonant cluster), nucleus (vowel or diphthong), and optional final consonant.

Tones

On open syllables (those ending with vowel, semivowel, or nasal), Bac Va has eight tones. Here pitch levels are based on the Chao 5-pitch scale.

> 1 - low-rising, 14: ɬii^{1} - four
> 2 - high-rising, 45: mii^{2} - bear
> 3 - mid level, 33: mii^{3} - to have
> 4 - low-falling, glottalized, 21: khii^{4} - to ride
> 5 - mid-falling, glottalized, 32: pii^{5} - older sibling
> 6 - low level, glottalized, 11: khii^{6} - excrement
> 7 - low level, 11: ɬɔm^{7} - sour
> 8 - high level, 55: lin^{8} - tongue

Checked syllables (those ending in p - t - k) with short vowels exhibit tones phonetically similar to tones 3 and 8 of open syllables: nɔk^{3} 'bird', mat^{8} 'flea'. Checked syllables with long vowels have tones phonetically similar to tones 1 and 5 of open syllables: paak^{1} 'mouth', luk^{5} 'child'.

The eight tones of Bac Va had their origin in an earlier system of three tones on open syllables and no tonal contrast on checked syllables. Those tones on open syllables have been conventionally designated as A - B - C and the fourth category, the checked syllables, as D. The tones in each of these categories underwent phonemic splits, conditioned by the phonetic nature of the initial consonant of each syllable. With the D category, the splits were further conditioned by vowel length. Table 1 shows the patterns of these splits in Bac Va.

Table 1
Pattern of Tonal Splits in Bac Va

Initial\Tone	A	B	C	D-short	D-long
Voiceless friction sounds	1	4	6	3	1
	2	1	7	8	1
Voiceless unaspirated stops	2	1	6	8	1
Glottal sounds	2	4	7	8	1
Voiced sounds	3	5	8	3	5

The Tai dialect of Bac Va is unique in that it exhibits a tonal split in the voiceless friction sounds that does not occur in other dialects Gedney has studied. In this case, the proto-initials in the top row include voiceless aspirated stops and voiceless fricatives such as [f] and [h]. In the second row are the preaspirated sonorants and [s].

Consonants

Bac Va has the following initial consonants:

Voiceless unaspirated stops. p - t - c - k - ʔ: pii^5 - older sibling, taa^5 - long river, cet^8 - seven, kaw^1 - old, ʔet^8 - one.

Voiceless aspirated stops. ph - th - kh: phon^1 - rain, thin^1 - stone, khiŋ^1 - ginger.

Voiced stops. b - d: baɰ^2 - leaf, dek^8 - child.

Nasals. m - n - ɲ - ŋ: mii^3 - to have, nɔɔn^3 - to sleep, ɲii^5 - two, ŋaa^3 - sesame.

Spirants. f - ɬ - s - z (< Vietnamese?) - h: faa^8 - sky, ɬiw^1 - chisel, sim^3 - to taste, zuu^4 - to be at, hɔk^3 - six.

Sonorants. l - v - y: laay^3 - stripe, vaan^2 - sweet, yɯɯ^3 - cucumber. Gedney grouped the spirant (fricative) [v] with the sonorants because of its sonority and low level of friction.

There are no initial or final clusters in the data.

Final consonants include nasals m - n - ŋ and voiceless stops p - t - k - ʔ. For final w - y - ɰ, see ***Diphthongs***.

Nasals. m - n - ŋ: phom^{1} - hair, ŋɯn^{3} - silver, piŋ^{2} - leech.

Voiceless stops. p - t - k - ʔ: thaap^{1} - to carry on a shoulder pole, pɛɛt^{1} - eight, phuk^{3} - to tie, nɔʔ^{5} - outside.

Vowels

Bac Va has nine vowels, with distinction in length undetermined. Final vowels are phonetically long and are therefore written with a double vowel.

High. i - ɯ - u: pii^{3} - fat, tɯk^{3} - young male, nuu^{2} - rat.

Mid. e - ɤ - o: pet^{8} - duck, pɤɤk^{1} - peel, poo^{5} - male.

Low. ɛ - a - ɔ: tɛm^{2} - full, thaa^{1} - eye, nɔk^{3} - bird.

Diphthongs

Diphthongs may be analyzed as a vocalic nucleus plus a final w - y - ɰ.

Diphthongs with final [w]. iw - ew - ɛw - aw - aaw: siw^{1} - pimple, cew^{3} - to look, hɛw^{8} - to trap, ʔaw^{2} - to take, haaw^{1} - to yawn.

Diphthongs with final [y]. uy - ɤy - ɤɤy - oy - ay - aay: khuy^{7} - mountain stream, mɤy^{2} - bear, ŋɤɤy^{1} - to send, soy^{3} boo^{3} - hammer, day^{2} - good, haay^{1} - moon.

Diphthongs with final [ɰ]. aɰ: maɰ^{4} - new.

The Tai Dialect of Lungchow — LC

Belonging to the Central branch of the Tai family, this dialect is spoken in and around the city of Lungchow (Pinyin Longzhou) located in the southwestern corner of Guangxi province. Li obtained his Lungchow data in 1935 in the city of Lungchow and subsequently published it in 1940 along with folk tales, stories, and poems. Li reevaluated his data for phonemicization in his 1977 *A Handbook of Comparative Tai*. Gedney acquired the data from Li (1940) and used it in his various linguistic studies (1995a, 1995b; Bickner et al. 1989). Sarawit (1973) also used it in her study of the proto-Tai vowel system.

Phonology

As in other dialects and languages of the Tai family, the phonological pattern of the Tai dialect of Lungchow is based on the syllable. Each syllable has distinctions in tone, initial (consonant or consonant cluster), nucleus (vowel or diphthong), and optional final consonant.

Tones

On open syllables (those ending with vowel, semivowel, or nasal), Lungchow has six tones. Here pitch levels are based on the Chao 5-pitch scale.

1 - mid level, 33: haa^1 - to seek
2 - high level, 55: haa^2 - heavy shower
3 - rising, 24: haa^3 - five
4 - mid-falling, 31: naa^4 - rice field
5 - low level, 11: naa^5 - mother's younger sibling
6 - low-falling, glottalized, 21: maa^6 - horse

Checked syllables (those ending in p - t - k) with short vowels exhibit tones phonetically similar to tones 2 and 4 of open syllables: ɬip^2 'ten', kut^4 'to dig'. Checked syllables with long vowels have tones phonetically similar to tones 2 and 4 of open syllables: ʔaap^2 'to bathe', laak^4 'root'.

The six tones of Lungchow had their origin in an earlier system of three tones on open syllables and no tonal contrast on checked syllables. Those tones on open syllables have been conventionally designated as A - B - C and the fourth category, the checked syllables, as D. The tones in each of these categories underwent phonemic splits, conditioned by the phonetic nature of the initial consonant of each syllable. With the D category, the splits were further conditioned by vowel length. Table 1 shows the patterns of these splits in Lungchow. For his own comparative work, Gedney renumbered the tones as indicated below. Li's original numbering follows in parentheses.

Table 1
Pattern of Tonal Splits in Lungchow

Initial\Tone	A	B	C	D-short	D-long
Voiceless friction sounds	1	2 (5)	3	2 (5)	2 (5)
Voiceless unaspirated stops	1	2 (5)	3	2 (5)	2 (5)
Glottal sounds	1	2 (5)	3	2 (5)	2 (5)
Voiced sounds	4 (2)	5 (6)	6 (4)	4 (2)	4 (2)

Consonants

Lungchow has the following initial consonants:

Voiceless unaspirated stops. p - t - c - k - ʔ: pii^{1} - year, taay^{1} - maternal grandmother, cit^{2} - seven, kay^{2} - chicken, ʔaa^{3} - to open the mouth.

Voiceless aspirated stops. ph - th - kh: phit^{2} - spicy hot, thut^{2} - to remove, khii^{3} - excrement.

Nasals. m - n - ŋ: may^{3} - to burn, nuu^{1} - rat, ŋuu^{4} - snake.

Voiceless spirants. f - ɬ - š - h: faa^{6} - sky, ɬaɰ^{1} - clear, šiik^{2} - to tear, haa^{1} - eye.

Sonorants. v - l - y: vit^{4} - mushroom, lin^{6} - tongue, yiit^{2} - to stretch. Li (1977:9) grouped the spirant (fricative) [v] with the sonorants because of its sonority and low friction level. In addition, [v] and [w] are in complementary distribution, with [v] appearing initially and [w] after a consonant.

Initial clusters consist of a consonant plus [w] or [y]. There are no final clusters.

Clusters with [w]. kw - khw: kwaa^{2} - to pass, khwii^{2} - to ride.

Clusters with [y]. py - phy - ky - khy - by - my - hy: pyaw^{4} - late meal, phyaw^{2} - to hunt, kyaa^{3} - young rice plant, khyaw^{1} - they, other people, byook^{2} - flower, myaak^{5} - slippery, hyaaw^{3} - to compare.

One [pl] cluster exists. pl: pleet^{5} - flat and thin.

Final consonants include nasals m - n - ŋ and voiceless stops p - t - k. For final w - y - ɰ, see ***Diphthongs***.

Nasals. m - n - ŋ: mum^{5} - beard, kin^{1} - to eat, liŋ^{4} - monkey.

Voiceless stops. p - t - k: khoop^{2} - to bite, boot^{2} - blind, nak^{2} - heavy.

Vowels

Lungchow has the following vowel inventory:

High. i, ii - ɯɯ - u, uu: bit^{2} - fish hook, pii^{4} - fat, kɯɯ^{1} - salt, huk^{2} - six, nuuk^{2} - deaf.

Mid. e - ɤ, ɤɤ - o : ʔeek² - yoke, phɤn¹ - to grind, dɤɤn¹ - earthworm, mook² - fog.

Low. a, aa: mat² - flea, khaat² - torn

The mid vowels [e] and [o] are phonetically long and more open, [ɛ] and [ɔ] respectively. Vowels in open syllables tend to be long and are written with a long vowel. Here, [ɤ] is used for Li's [ə].

In *A Handbook of Comparative Tai* (1977:10–11), Li phonemicized the 1940 data and arrived at the following vowel inventory: High i - ɯ - u; Mid e - o; Low a. He made the following comments: 1) the high and low vowels may be long or short in closed syllables, but are always long in open ones; 2) the mid vowels are always long and between [e] and [ɛ] and [o] and [ɔ] in quality; 3) Short /i/ and /u/ are more open; 4) long /ɯ/ is close to a central vowel in closed syllables; and 5) short /ɯ/ is [ɤ].

Diphthongs

Diphthongs may be analyzed as a vocalic nucleus plus a final w - y - ɰ.

Diphthongs with final [w]. iiw - eew - aw - aaw: niiw⁶ - finger, toe, kheew¹ - green, kaw³ - nine, laaw¹ - to fear.

Diphthongs with final [y]. uuy - ɤɤy - ooy - ay - aay: pyuuy² - to release, khɤɤy¹ - son-in-law, cooy⁵ - to help, lay¹ - to flow, vaay⁴ - water buffalo.

Diphthongs with final [ɰ]. aɰ: baɰ¹ - leaf.

The Tai Dialect of Ping Siang — PS

Belonging to the Central branch of the Tai family, the dialect referred to as the Tai dialect of Ping Siang (phɤŋ⁴ saaŋ⁴ following the Mandarin pronunciation; phaŋ⁴ chɤɤŋ⁴ following the Cantonese pronunciation; and daɰ¹ ɬaaŋ⁴ following the local pronunciation) is spoken in and around the town of Ping Siang (Pinyin Pingxiang) in Guangxi province about twenty-five miles west of Ning Ming near the Vietnamese border. Gedney interviewed the informant, Chiuh Hahn (caaw³ hɤŋ⁴ following the Mandarin), in Hong Kong June 13–19 and July 3–15, 1966. The informant had been educated in the town of Lungchow and had lived there for seven years from about the age of twelve. He left Ping Siang at about the age of twenty. When interviewed, the informant had been living in Hong Kong for about twenty years. He referred to his language as thoo³ as in ŋoo² kyaaŋ³ thoo³ vaa⁵ 'I speak Tho'. Dominic Yip acted as interpreter during the interviews.

Gedney's complete data for this dialect can be found in Hudak (1995). Additional references appear in his linguistic studies (1995a, 1995b, 1995c; Bickner et al. 1989).

Phonology

As in other dialects and languages of the Tai family, the phonological pattern of Ping Siang is based on the syllable. Each syllable has distinctions in tone, initial (consonant or consonant cluster), nucleus (vowel or diphthong), and optional final consonant.

Tones

On open syllables (those ending with vowel, semivowel, or nasal), Ping Siang has six tones. Here pitch levels are based on the Chao 5-pitch scale.

1 - mid level, 33: maa^{1} - dog
2 - high level, 55: maa^{2} - to soak
3 - rising, 24: maa^{3} - to grow, rise
4 - low-falling, 21: maa^{4} - to come
5 - low level, 11: kaa^{5} - branch
6 - falling, glottalized, 31: maa^{6} - horse

Checked syllables (those ending in p - t - k) with short vowels exhibit tones phonetically similar to tones 2 and 4 of open syllables: dip^{2} 'raw', mɤt^{4} 'ant'. Tone 5 often appears on syllables that have cognates elsewhere with a long vowel, for example, lop^{5} 'to stroke' (Siamese luup^{3}). Checked syllables with long vowels have tones phonetically similar to tones 2 and 5 of open syllables: khuup^{2} ' year', lɤɤt^{5} 'blood'.

The six tones of Ping Siang had their origin in an earlier system of three tones on open syllables and no tonal contrast on checked syllables. Those tones on open syllables have been conventionally designated as A - B - C and the fourth category, the checked syllables, as D. The tones in each of these categories underwent phonemic splits, conditioned by the phonetic nature of the initial consonant of each syllable. With the D category, the splits were further conditioned by vowel length. Table 1 shows the patterns of these splits in Ping Siang.

Table 1
Pattern of Tonal Splits in Ping Siang

Initial\Tone	A	B	C	D-short	D-long
Voiceless friction sounds	1	2	3	2	2
Voiceless unaspirated stops	1	2	3	2	2
Glottal sounds	1	2	3	2	2
Voiced sounds	4	5	6	4, 5	5

Consonants

Ping Siang has the following initial consonants:

Voiceless unaspirated stops. p - t - c - k - ʔ: pii^{1} - year, tuu^{1} - door, caa^{4} - tea, kim^{4} - tongs, ʔaw^{1} - to take.

Voiceless aspirated stops. ph - th - kh: phyom^{1} - hair, thom^{1} - pond, khiŋ^{1} - ginger.

Voiced stops. b - d: baa^{3} - crazy, doo^{1} - enough.

Nasals. m - n - ŋ: maw^{4} - drunk, naay^{4} - dew, ŋaay^{4} - morning meal.

Voiceless spirants. f - ɬ - s - h: faa^{6} - sky, ɬiiw^{1} - pillar, siin^{1} - thousand, haay^{1} - to die.

Sonorants. v - l - y: vuuy^{3} - mountain stream, lom^{4} - to forget, yim^{1} - to borrow. Gedney groups the spirant (fricative) [v] with the sonorants because of its sonority and low friction level. In addition, [v] and [w] are in complementary distribution, with [v] appearing initially and [w] after a consonant.

Initial clusters consist of a consonant plus [w] or [y]. There are no final clusters.

Clusters with [w]. kw - khw: kwaa^{1} - melon, khwan^{1} - spirit.

Clusters with [y]. py - phy - ky - khy - by - my: pyaa^{1} - fish, phyak^{2} - vegetable, kyaaw^{3} - hairknot, khyaɰ^{3} - near, byook^{2} - flower, myaak^{5} - slippery.

A single [kl] cluster appears in klik^{2} taa^{5} taa^{5} - sound of a partridge.

Final consonants include nasals m - n - ŋ and voiceless stops p - t - k. For final w - y - ɰ, see ***Diphthongs***.

Nasals. m - n - ŋ: liim^{4} - sickle, bin^{1} - to fly, noŋ^{5} - to wear.

Voiceless stops. p - t - k: cip^{2} - to fold, bit^{2} - to pinch, luuk^{5} - to scald.

Vowels

In his elicitation, Gedney recorded seven vowels with a length distinction in each:

High. i, ii - ɯ, ɯɯ - u, uu: kim^{1} - gold, yiin^{1} - tobacco, nɯŋ^{1} - one, kɯɯ^{1} - salt, kuk^{2} phyaa^{1} - foot of a mountain, yuuk^{2} - banana stem.

Mid. ɤ, ɤɤ: ʔɤk^{2} - chest, cɤɤk^{5} - rope.

Low. e, ee - a, aa - o, oo: ʔet^{2} - one, ceen^{1} - to fry, yap^{4} - to sew, ʔaap^{2} - to bathe, kon^{3} - buttocks, noon^{1} - worm.

In the transcription system used, [e] and [o] are phonetically more open, [ɛ] and [ɔ] respectively. Final vowels are phonetically long and are written with a double vowel.

Diphthongs

Diphthongs may be analyzed as consisting of a vocalic nucleus plus a final w - y - ɰ.

Diphthongs with final [w]. iiw - eew - aw - aaw: yiiw^{1} - waist, keew^{4} - scissors, ʔaw^{1} - to take, khaaw^{1} - white.

Diphthongs with final [y]. uuy - ɤɤy - ay - aay - ooy: thuuy^{3} - bowl, khɤɤy^{1} - son-in-law, khyay^{2} - egg, kaay^{4} - shoes, ʔooy^{3} - sugarcane.

Diphthongs with final [ɰ]. aɰ: kaɰ^{5} - swollen.

The Tai Dialect of Ning Ming — NM

Belonging to the Central branch of the Tai family, the Tai dialect of Ning Ming is spoken in and around the town of Ning Ming (nɤŋ^{4} mɤŋ^{4}, Pinyin Ningming), located about twenty-five miles east of Ping Siang and twenty-five miles southeast of Lungchow in the province of Guangxi. Gedney obtained his data July 8–16, 1966, in Hong Kong, from a 52-year-old informant, Mr. Wong Gong (khwaaŋ^{4} kyaaŋ^{1} in the local dialect), who had come to Hong Kong in 1949. Dominic Yip assisted as interpreter in the interviews. Gedney's complete data can be found in Hudak (1995) with additional references in his linguistic studies (1995a, 1995b, 1995d; Bickner et al. 1989).

Phonology

As in other dialects and languages of the Tai family, the phonological pattern of Ning Ming is based on the syllable. Each syllable has distinctions in tone, initial (consonant or consonant cluster), nucleus (vowel or diphthong), and optional final consonant.

Tones

On open syllables (those ending with vowel, semivowel, or nasal), Ning Ming has six tones. Here pitch levels are based on the Chao 5-pitch scale.

1 - mid level, 33: maa^{1} - dog
2 - high level, 55: maa^{2} - to soak
3 - rising, glottalized, 25: naa^{3} - face
4 - low-falling, 21: maa^{4} - to come
5 - low level, 11: taa^{5} - river
6 - low-falling, glottalized, 21: maa^{6} - horse

Checked syllables (those ending in p - t - k) with short vowels exhibit tones phonetically similar to tone 4 of open syllables: kap^{4} 'tight'. Besides tone 4, a few morphemes with short vowels also have tones 1, 2, and 5: kop^{1} 'frog', cip^{2} 'to fold', and lok^{5} 'overgrown'. Checked syllables with long vowels have tones phonetically similar to tones 2 and 5 of open syllables: ʔook^{2} 'to go out', laak^{5} 'child'.

The six tones of Ning Ming had their origin in an earlier system of three tones on open syllables and no tonal contrast on checked syllables. Those tones on open syllables have been conventionally designated as A - B - C and the fourth category, the checked syllables, as D. The tones in each of these categories underwent phonemic splits, conditioned by the phonetic nature of the initial consonant of each syllable. With the D category, the splits were further conditioned by vowel length. Table 1 shows the patterns of these splits in Ning Ming.

Table 1
Pattern of Tonal Splits in Ning Ming

Initial\Tone	A	B	C	D-short	D-long
Voiceless friction sounds	1	2	3	4	2
Voiceless unaspirated stops	1	2	3	4	2
Glottal sounds	1	2	3	4	2
Voiced sounds	4	5	6	4	5

Consonants

Ning Ming has the following initial consonants:

Voiceless unaspirated stops. p - t - c - k - ʔ: pey^{1} - year, tey^{5} - place, caɰ^{5} - it is, kee^{2} - old, ʔaw^{1} - to take.

Voiceless aspirated stops. ph - th - ch - kh: phyaw^{5} - ashes, thuu^{2} - bean, chap^{2} - to transplant, khyoη^{2} - cage.

Voiced stops. b - d: baa^{2} -shoulder, day^{3} - can, to get.

Nasals. m - n - ɲ - ŋ: may^{3} - to burn, neew^{4} - urine, ɲaɰ^{5} - Indian corn, ŋaay^{4} - morning meal.

Voiceless spirants. f - ɬ - s - h: faa^{6} - sky, ɬaay^{4} - sand, saa^{1} - fork, haay^{4} - shoes.

Sonorants. v - l - y: vaa^{5} - to say, lɯɯ^{4} - boat, yow^{2} - to be in a place. Gedney groups the spirant (fricative) [v] with the sonorants because of its sonority and low friction level. In addition, [v] and [w] are in complementary distribution, with [v] appearing initially and [w] after a consonant.

Initial clusters consist of a consonant plus [w] or [y]. There are no final clusters.

Clusters with [w]. chw - kw - khw - ŋw: chway^{1} - to blow (?), kwiin^{4} - fist, khwii^{2} - to whistle, ŋwaa^{6} - tile.

Clusters with [y]. py - phy - ky - khy - by - my - ɬy - hy: pyaa^{1} - fish, phyaa^{1} - cliff, mountain, kyaw^{3} - hairknot, khyow^{1} - ear, byook^{2} - flower, myaak^{5} - slippery, ɬyaw^{2} taaw^{1} - small knife (< Chinese), hyooŋ^{1} - loud (< Cantonese).

Final consonants include nasals m - n - ŋ and voiceless stops p - t - k - ʔ. For final w - y - ɰ, see ***Diphthongs***.

Nasals. m - n - ŋ: hoom^{1} - fragrant, noon^{4} - to sleep, nooŋ^{6} - younger sibling.

Voiceless stops. p - t - k - ʔ: tap^{4} - liver, kat^{4} - to bite, nook^{5} - outside, pɤʔ^{4} cuʔ^{4} - centipede.

Vowels

In his elicitation, Gedney recorded seven vowels with a length distinction in five ([ɯ] and [ɤɤ] do not appear in the corpus):

High. i, ii - ɯɯ - u,uu: cip^{2} - to fold, yii^{5} - two, ŋɯɯ^{4} - snake, khup^{2} - year, luuŋ^{1} - big.

Mid. ɤ: hɤŋ^{1} - ginger.

Low. e, ee - a, aa - o, oo: ben^{1} - to fly, peen^{3} - board, dam^{1} - black, naam^{1} - thorn, lom^{4} - wind, nooŋ^{5} - calf of the leg.

In the transcription system used, [e] and [o] are phonetically more open, [ɛ] and [ɔ] respectively. Final vowels are phonetically long and are written with a double vowel.

Diphthongs

Diphthongs may be analyzed as a vocalic nucleus plus a final w - y - ɰ. In Ning Ming, the high vowels ii - ɯɯ - uu have been diphthongized: dey^{1} - good (Siamese dii^{1}), ɬaɰ^{1} - writing (Siamese sɯɯ^{5}), kow^{4} - I (Siamese kuu^{1}).

Diphthongs with final [w]. iiw - eew - aw - aaw - ow: diiw^{3} - hot, angry, kheew^{1} - green, haw^{3} - to enter, daaw^{1} - star, low^{5} - to leak.

Diphthongs with final [y]. uuy - ey - ay - aay - ooy: kuuy^{4} - son-in-law, pey^{4} - fat, kay^{2} - chicken, laay^{4} - saliva, ʔooy^{3} - sugarcane.

Diphthongs with final [ɰ]. aɰ: daɰ^{1} - in.

CHAPTER 4: NORTHERN TAI DIALECTS

The Northern branch of the Tai family forms the second largest group of Tai speakers. Luo (1996:75) describes its geographical boundaries as extending from southeastern Guizhou in the north to southern Guangxi and northern Vietnam in the south, and from northeastern Guangxi in the east to the border of Yunnan and Guangxi in the west. In addition, another northern language, Saek, forms an isolated island among Southwestern Tai languages on the border of northeastern Thailand in Nakhon Phanom province and Laos in Khammouan province.

Following Li, Luo (1966:96) lists the following salient features as characteristic of the Northern branch: 1) no distinction between the original aspirated and unaspirated consonsants; 2) regular split between etymologically voiceless and voiced initials in all tone categories: 3) the proto-voiceless velar fricative *x is realized as [x]/[h]; 4) in some dialects some proto-preglottalized items in the A column follow the voiceless pattern whereas some in the B and C category follow the voiced pattern; 5) proto *ml is realized as /f/; 6) clusters such as *nr, *dr, *thr, *xr, and *tl merge into liquids and are usually realized as [r] or [l] in modern dialects; 7) proto *tr splits into /r/, /t/, or /pr/; 8) proto-clusters *thl and *vr develop into sibilants; 9) monothongization of proto-diphthongs and triphthongs occurs; and 10) there is a set of lexical items different from the other two branches.

Cognates used to represent the Northern group have been taken from Yay (Y) in the extreme northern part of Vietnam, Saek (Sk), and the dialects spoken at Wuming (WM) in Guangxi province and Po-ai (P) in Yunnan.

Yay — Y

The Tai dialect known as Yay belongs to the Northern branch of the Tai language family and is spoken in the extreme northern part of Vietnam near the Chinese border in the area of the Hong (Red) River and the Lo River (Rivière Claire). Major Yay centers in this area include Muong Hum (mɯaŋ^{4} hum^{1}) located to the west of Lao Kay (laaw^{4} kaay^{1}) and Cha Pa (sa^{1} pa^{2}) to the southwest of Lao Kay, both in the province of Phong Tho, which until 1947 belonged to the province of Lao Kay. Other Yay villages near Muong Hum include baan^{6} θew^{4}, seven kilometers from Muong Hum; daɰ^{1} mɯaŋ^{4}, nine kilometers from baan^{6} θew^{4}; paak^{2} θaat^{2}, eight kilometers from daɰ^{1} mɯaŋ^{4}; and pom^{2} θiaŋ^{5}, one kilometer from daɰ^{1} mɯaŋ^{4}. Also in the vicinity to the west and southwest are mɯaŋ^{4} θo^{1} (Phong Tho), ram^{6} θe^{1}, baan^{6} maw^{4}, na^{4} kuŋ^{6}, na^{4} vaaŋ^{5}, mɯaŋ^{4} lɯ^{5}, ko^{1} la^{3}, caw^{3} na^{4}, toŋ^{5} pan^{2}, daan^{2} haaw^{1}, and ram^{6} bon^{1}. Northeast of Lao Kay are baan^{2} law^{5} and na^{4} siŋ^{4}. In the village of θaan^{1} thaaŋ^{5}, north of mɯaŋ^{4} lɯ^{5}, Yay is mixed with na^{5}, the dialect of another group of Tai speakers. In China, Yay speakers can be found in ciw^{6} faaŋ^{5} and θaan^{1} ca^{1} ma^{6} ten^{2}. Yay speakers are also said to live in the Vietnamese area of Ha Giang (ha^{5} yaaŋ^{1}), although this dialect has a different tonal system.

Yay speakers refer to themselves as pu^{6} yay^{6} 'Yay person' and to their language as san^{4} yay^{6}. In linguistic literature and on linguistic maps, however, the terms used include Nhang or Yang, Nhang deriving from the older Vietnamese term Nhắng, and Yang from the pronunciation of the official Vietnamese name in other Tai languages, yaŋ^{5} in White Tai, for example. The current official name in Vietnamese is Gíay. Other Vietnamese spellings include Giậy and Gíây. References to Yay and other cognate northern dialects by early French scholars include Dioi or Dioy (ʔyoy^{4} or ʔjoy^{4}) where 'di' was an attempt to reproduce [ʔy] or [ʔj]. In Vietnamese, orthographic 'd' has the value of a palatal glide [y] in central and southern Vietnam and [z] in northern Vietnam. This same ethnonym occurs as Jui in the Po-ai dialect recorded by Li (see this volume) and as Yi in the Bouyei material recorded by Chinese scholars in Guizhou.

The following description and examples have been taken from Gedney's studies of Yay (1965; Hudak 1991a.; Bickner et al. 1989). Gedney obtained his data between 1964 and 1969 from two informants, nuŋ^{5} to^{5} faaŋ^{1} from Muong Hum living in Vientiane, Laos, and lu^{5} ʔa^{1} faaŋ^{1} from Cha Pa in Tung Nghia, Vietnam.

Other than Gedney's work, studies of Yay are few. Bonifacy (1907) probably has the earliest recording with a list of 146 words in six Tai languages, one of which is labeled Giây. In 1908 Esquirol and Williatte produced a Yay dictionary based on a Pu-Yi dialect in southwestern Guangxi. A 1938 French survey by L'École Française d'Extrême-Orient lists three dialect points as Giay or Nhăng. Part of this survey appears in Haudricourt 1960 and 1972. In a 1952 study, Durand lists about 400 topically arranged words in two Tai languages, one identified as Nhang. More recent treatments of Yay can be found in Sarawit (1973), Edmondson (2000b), and Edmondson and Gregerson (2001).

Phonology

As in other dialects and languages of the Tai family, the phonological pattern of Yay is based on the syllable. Each syllable has distinctions in tone, initial (consonant or consonant cluster), nucleus (vowel or diphthong), and optional final consonant.

Tones

On open syllables (those ending with vowel, semivowel, or nasal), Yay has six tones. Here pitch levels are based on the Chao 5-pitch scale.

1 - level, slightly lower than mid, 33: hun^{1} - rain
2 - low level, 22: hun^{2} - a tracing copy
3 - rising, 13: hun^{3} - hardened, solidified
4 - high, with a slight rise and fall toward the end, 454: hun^{4} - person

5 - falling, 41: hun^{5} - to seek, search
6 - higher than mid, with a slight rise toward the end, 45: hun^{6} - very hungry

Checked syllables (those ending in p - t - k) with short vowels exhibit tones phonetically similar to tones 3 and 1 of open syllables: rok^{3} 'six', rok^{1} 'bird'. Those with long vowels are similar to tones 2 and 5 of open syllables: rok^{2} 'a loom', rok^{5} 'outside'. Although infrequent, tones 4 and 6 may also appear on checked syllables: ʔaap^{4} ʔaap^{4} or ʔaap^{2} ʔaap^{2} 'sound of a duck quacking'; fik^{6} or fik^{3} 'vacuum bottle' (Gedney1965:181). The appearance of these two tones on checked syllables has probably resulted from loans or onomatopoeia processes.

The six tones of Yay had their origin in an earlier system of three tones on open syllables and no tonal contrast on checked syllables. Those tones on open syllables have been conventionally designated as A - B - C and the fourth category, the checked syllables, as D. The tones in each of these categories underwent phonemic splits, conditioned by the phonetic nature of the initial consonant of each syllable. With the D category, the splits were further conditioned by vowel length. Table 1 shows the patterns of these splits in Yay.

Table 1
Pattern of Tonal Splits in Yay

Initial\Tone	A	B	C	D-short	D-long
Voiceless friction sounds	1	2	3	3	2
Voiceless unaspirated stops	1	2	3	3	2
Glottal sounds	1	2	6	3	2
Voiced sounds	4	5	6	1	5

Consonants

Yay has the following initial consonants:

Voiceless unaspirated stops. p - t - c - k - ʔ: pu^{6} - person, tu^{1} - door, ca^{3} - young rice plants, ka^{1} - leg, ʔe^{3} - infant.

Voiceless aspirated stops. ph - th - ch - kh: pha^{5} - to mate (of animals), tho^{2} - rabbit, cha^{1} - to despise, khu^{1} - rotten (of wood). Gedney notes that the aspirated sounds appear far less frequently than the unaspirated ones and that the informants often identify these forms as loanwords. In his 1965 study (pp. 181–82), Gedney records variant forms with and without the aspiration: phaaw^{5} or paaw^{5} 'to plane wood', thiaw^{5} kɯn^{1} or tiaw^{5} kɯn^{1} 'a spoon for eating'.

Voiced stops. b - d - g: be^{2} - water dipper, di^{1} - good, gallbladder, (g or ɣ) gek^{3} - to draw or sketch a line. In his Yay glossary (Hudak 1991a), Gedney lists [g] only in the Vietnamese loan gek^{3}.

Nasals. m - n - ɲ - ŋ: mo^5 - grave, nu^1 - rat, mouse, ɲu^5 - to urinate, ŋo^2 - hungry.

Voiceless spirants. f - θ - s - h: fa^4 - iron, θi^2 - four, sa^4 - tree, plant, hɯ^1 - market.

Sonorants. v - r - l - y: va^2 - trousers, ri^5 - dry field, law^3 - liquor, ya^5 - paternal grandmother, wife, woman. Gedney notes that in careful speech and words in isolation, speakers often substitute [z] or [ž] for initial [y], a result of Vietnamese influence. He further notes that this substitution also appears among educated speakers of other Tai languages in northern Vietnam (Hudak 1991:xxiii). More recent research by Edmondson (2000b: 144) and Edmondson and Gregerson (2001) suggests that with some speakers [z] is now an inheritance in the phonological system. Gedney groups the spirant (fricative) [v] with the sonorants because of its sonority and low friction level. In addition, [v] and [w] are in complementary distribution, with [v] appearing initially and [w] after a consonant.

The most common clusters consist of a consonant plus [w] or [y]. There are no final clusters.

Clusters with [w]: kw - ʔw - ŋw - yw - hw: kwe^4 - bent, ʔwa^6 - stupid, ŋway^1 - to stagger, ywaay^5 or ywuay^5 - soft and rotten, hwa^2 - to melt.

Clusters with [y]. py - by - my: pya^1 - fish, byan^6 - to grumble, myaak^5 - slippery.

Rare clusters include kl - lw - θw: kluk^1 paak^2 - to rinse the mouth vigorously to remove things from the teeth, lwet^5 - to spread or smear on thinly and lightly, yu^2 θwaaŋ^2 - comfortable.

Final consonants include nasals m - n - ŋ and voiceless stops p - t - k. For final w - y - ɰ, see ***Diphthongs***.

Nasals. m - n - ŋ: nuam^1 - python, tin^1 - foot, neŋ^4 - insect.

Voiceless stops. p - t - k: ʔup^3 - to close, bit^3 - to pinch, tɯk^3 - to shoot. In Gedney's Yay glossary (Hudak 1991a.), a final glottal stop appears only once in pɤʔ^3 'nothing left, there isn't any'. Gedney believes that the word is probably a loan from another Tai language, with the native Yay word being θaɰ^1.

Vowels

Yay has seven vowels, three high: i - ɯ - u and three low: e - a - o; the seventh vowel, unrounded mid back [ɤ], appears in final position but rarely with a final consonant. Distinction in length only appears with the vowel [a] and only before a final consonant. All vowels are phonetically long in final position, although written with a single vowel, and of indeterminate length and duration in medial position. The vowels e - o are more open, [ɛ] and [ɔ], respectively.

High. i - ɯ - u: mi^{4} - to have, fɯ^{6} - a meal, mu^{1} - pig.

Mid. ɤ: chɤ^{1} - car.

Low. e - a, aa - o: cem^{3} - cheek, taŋ^{2} - chair, taaŋ^{2} - to differ, mo^{2} - new.

Diphthongs

Three centering diphthongs include ia - ɯa - ua: ɲia^{1} - river, nɯa^{3} - crossbow, kua^{1} - salt.

Other diphthongs may be analyzed as a vocalic nucleus plus a final w - y - ɰ.

Diphthongs with final [w]. iw - iaw - ew - aw - aaw: kiw^{3} - mother's younger brother, yiaw^{1} - to reach, hew^{4} - to swim, ʔaw^{1} - to take, taaw^{2} - to return.

Diphthongs with final [y]. ɯay - uy - uay - ɤy - ay - aay - oy: θɯay^{2} - to wash, luy^{2} - to mill rice, ʔuay^{6} - dirty, ʔɤy^{5} - a grammatical particle, cay^{2} - egg, ʔaay^{1} - goiter, coy^{3} - banana.

Diphthongs with final [ɰ]. aɰ: baɰ^{1} - leaf.

Saek — Sk

Spoken in Nakhon Phanom province in Northeastern Thailand and directly across the river in Khammouan province in Laos, Saek is a member of the Northern branch of the Tai language family. Four Saek villages are generally identified in Thailand, all located in Nakhon Phanom province: 1) baan^{3} ʔaat^{6} saa^{1} maat^{5} (or baan^{3} khɔɔŋ^{2}), five kilometers north of the city of Nakhon Phanom in Nakhon Phanom district on the banks of the Mekong River on the road to Uthen; 2) baan^{3} phay^{6} lɔɔm^{3} (probably the same as baan^{3} saw^{1} law^{3}), located in Nakhon Phanom district one mile inland from Ban At Samat; 3) baan^{3} dɔŋ^{1} sa^{6} mɔɔ^{4} in sii^{1} soŋ^{1} khraam^{4} district; and 4) baan^{3} baa^{1} vaa^{3} in kiŋ^{6} naa^{4} vaa^{3} district. Two other Saek villages, apparently abandoned, include baan^{3} thaa^{5} vaay^{4}, located between the city of Nakhon Phanom and Ban At Samat, and baan^{3} naa^{4} laʔ^{6} vaay^{4} on the road to Sakol Nakhon. In his study of Saek (1988:9), Morev lists the same four villages.

In the same study (p. 9), Morev claims that there are about ten Saek villages in Khammouan province in the districts of Nhommarat, Mahaxay, Kham Khet, and Tha Khek. *Ethnologue* cites the village of Na Kadok in Khamkeut district, Borikhamxay province. These speakers claim to have originated in Phu Quan and Ban Pho Quang in Duc Tho district, Ha Tinh province, Vietnam. In texts collected by Gedney, the villages of baan^{3} thɔɔk^{5}, baan^{3} phoo^{4} kham^{3}, and baan^{3} thaa^{5} khɛɛ^{4} are listed as Saek-speaking. In one of his notebooks, Gedney also lists baan^{3} phaa^{5} thuŋ^{1} (in Siamese) as having a true Saek population and baan^{3} phoon^{3} ŋaam^{1} with a half-Saek and half-Lao one. In Vietnam, he notes, the villages of baan^{3} trɤɤŋ^{3} and baan^{3} tɛɛn^{1} are said to have Saek speakers.

Two different histories appear in texts collected by Gedney and Morev. Gedney's texts place the Saek in northern Vietnam where, because of the scarcity of food, they killed and ate a white elephant owned by a local ruler. Faced with a heavy fine, they fled to Laos and Thailand. Morev cites a story that describes the Saek as forced by the Thai to the Bangkok region to construct a canal around the city sometime in the nineteenth century. Upon completion of the canal, they settled in the region. Abandoned Saek villages in Vietnam include baan^{3} bɤk^{4} naa^{4} tɤɤ^{3}, baan^{3} sin^{4} naa^{4} mɤɤy^{4}, baan^{3} trɤɤŋ^{1}, baan^{3} thruu^{3}, and the city of sɔɔŋ^{4}.

In the late nineteenth and early twentieth centuries, Saek was noted by French travelers and researchers in Indochina. Some of their largely impressionistic word lists and brief grammars can be found in Aymonier (1895), Rivière (1902), Macy (1905), Maspero (1912), and Bonifacy (1919). Seidenfaden (1930), Creder (1935), Blanchard (1957), and Lebar, Hickey, and Musgrave (1964) all identify Saek as a Mon-Khmer language. In a series of papers in the 1950s and 60s, however, Haudricourt (1958, 1963a, 1963b, 1976) concludes that Saek is a Tai language belonging to the Northern branch. Fraisse (1950:338) also lists Saek as a Tai language. Then in 1970, based on his own field work, Gedney confirms this placement.

The most extensive treatment of Saek has been done by Gedney (1970; Hudak 1993) with an extensive glossary and collection of texts. References can be found throughout his linguistic studies (1993a, 1993b, 1997; Bickner et al. 1989) and in Sarawit (1973), Khanitthanan (1975, 1976), Thongkum (1976), and Benedict (1997). Most of his data come from a wide range of informants in a series of interviews that span the years from 1964 to 1976. In the course of the fieldwork, Gedney discovered significant differences between the older and younger generations, differences that have probably disappeared under the hegemony of Lao and Thai. Among the cognates in this volume, lexical items from the older generation are marked as (OG) and those from the younger generation as (YG). Speakers of both generations refer to themselves and their language as thrɛɛk^{6} (Siamese sɛɛk^{2}): thay^{5} thrɛɛk^{6} 'Saek people', cian^{5} thrɛɛk^{6} 'Saek language'. The following phonological description and examples are based on Gedney's extensive fieldwork.

Phonology

As in other dialects and languages of the Tai family, the phonological pattern of Saek is based on the syllable. Each syllable has distinctions in tone, initial (consonant or consonant cluster), nucleus (vowel or diphthong), and optional final consonant.

Tones

On open syllables (those ending with vowel, semivowel, or nasal), Saek has six tones. Here pitch levels are based on the Chao 5-pitch scale.

1 - mid level, with rise on the end, 34: pii¹ - year
2 - low level, 11: maa² - dog
3 - mid, falling to low, with glottal constriction, 31: rii³ - stream
4 - high rising-falling, 454: naa⁴ - rice field
5 - high-falling, 52: phii⁵ - older sibling
6 - mid level, with a slight fall, with glottal constriction, 32: nii⁶ - this

Checked syllables (those ending in p - t - k) with short vowels exhibit tones phonetically similar to tones 4 and 6 of open syllables: kap⁴ 'frog', mɛk⁶ 'ant'. Those with long vowels exhibit tones 6 and 5: riit⁶ 'sunshine', lɔɔk⁵ 'outside'. Although infrequent, tone 2 may also appear on short checked syllables as well as on long checked syllables: phat² 'and then', muak² 'hat'. Only in rare occurrences does tone 4 appear on long checked syllables: ʔiit⁴ ʔɔɔy⁵ 'a little'.

The six tones of Saek had their origin in an earlier system of three tones on open syllables and no tonal contrast on checked syllables. Those tones on open syllables have been conventionally designated as A - B - C and the fourth category, the checked syllables, as D. The tones in each of these categories underwent phonemic splits, conditioned by the phonetic nature of the initial consonant of each syllable. With the D category, the splits were further conditioned by vowel length. Table 1 shows the patterns of these splits in Saek.

Table 1
Pattern of Tonal Splits in Saek

Initial\Tone	A	B	C	D-short	D-long
Voiceless friction sounds	2, 1	6	3	4	6
Voiceless unaspirated stops	1	6	3	4	6
Glottal sounds	1	6	3	4	6
Voiced sounds	4	5	6	6	5

Saek exhibits a simple two-way split between proto-voiceless and proto-voiced initials; however, there are two tones in the top box of column A, where normally a single tone appears (original tone A with a voiceless friction sound as in Siamese maa⁵ 'dog' and khaa⁵ 'leg'). Gedney (Hudak 1993:xxiv–xxv) explains that tone 2 seems to be the normal development, as in Saek maa^{2} 'dog'. In contrast, Saek has tone 1 for kwaa^{1} 'leg'. Gedney further explains that this word along with others lost their aspiration before the time of the tonal splits so that they then fell together with other words having unaspirated initials.

Consonants

Saek has the following initial consonants:

> Voiceless unaspirated stops. p - t - c - k - ʔ: pan^{1} - to divide, tit^{4} - attached, caŋ^{3} - to stop, keeŋ^{1} - curry, ʔay^{1} - to cough.
>
> Voiceless aspirated stops. ph - th - ch (rare) - kh: phiap^{5} - full to the brim, thop^{6} - to fold, chom^{4} phuu^{4} thiip^{5} - name of a mythical continent, khwaan^{3} - to wind into a coil.
>
> Voiced stops. b - d - (g): bɯl^{1} - to fly, deem^{3} - to taste, gaw^{6} - rice. The initial voiced velar stop [g] is usually pronounced by the younger generation with the older generation favoring the voiced velar spirant [ɣ].
>
> Nasals. m - n - ɲ - ŋ: mɯaŋ^{1} - a ditch, naŋ^{5} - to sit, ɲɛl^{2} - civet cat, ŋat^{6} - to pry.
>
> Voiceless spirants. f - s - h: fɔɔŋ^{3} - to bring a lawsuit, saak^{5} - to wake up, haŋ^{3} - fence. The spirant [f] does not appear in native Saek words, but only in loans from Lao or Thai and thus may have either a [f] or [ph] initial: fɔɔŋ^{3} or phɔɔŋ^{3} 'to bring a lawsuit'.
>
> Voiced spirants. ɣ: ɣaw^{6} - rice. The voiced velar spirant [ɣ] is favored by the older generation. Compare the voiced velar stop [g].
>
> Sonorants. v - r - l - w - y: viaŋ^{1} - rice straw, rɔk^{4} - six, luan^{4} - to crawl, yaa^{5} thaw^{3} wan^{6} - that old lady there, yuaŋ^{6} - a step. Gedney groups the spirant (fricative) [v] with the sonorants because of its sonority and low friction level. In addition, [v] and [w] are in complementary distribution, with [v] appearing initially and [w] after a consonant. Initial [r] is pronounced by apparently all speakers at all Saek localities with an initial alveolar stop release, [^{d}r]. Initial [w] occurs only as a result of assimilation with the final consonant of the preceding word.

Saek exhibits a wide range of initial clusters, some of which appear in no other Tai languages. There are no final clusters.

> Clusters with [w]: thw - kw - khw - ʔw - ŋw - sw - hw - lw: thwaay^{2} - to give, kway^{1} - to stir, khwɤɤ^{6} - daughter-in-law, ʔwaay^{6} - to turn around,

ŋwaak^5 - to turn the head to look, swaa^5 - to be famous, hwaaŋ^3 - to be worried, lwaat^5 - overly full.

Clusters with [l]. pl - phl - tl - thl - bl - ml: plaa^1 - fish, phluu^4 - betel, tlua^1 - salt, thlaa^2 - tray, blian^1 - month, moon, mlɔɔ^5 - meat.

Clusters with [r]. pr - phr - tr - thr: praa^1 - eye, phrak^4 - vegetable, trɛɛŋ^4 - sharp (of a knife), thruu^4 - similar.

Final consonants include nasals m - n - ŋ, voiceless stops p - t - k - ʔ, and -l, characteristic of the older generation. For final w - y, see ***Diphthongs***.

Nasals. m - n - ŋ: liam^4 - sickle, keen^1 - arm, saaŋ^2 - high.

Voiceless stops. p - t - k - ʔ: ʔaap^6 - to bathe, vuat^6 - the waist, suk^4 - happy, khɛʔ^6 - tired of.

Final -l: thual^5 - forest.

Vowels

Saek has nine vowels, three high: i - ɯ - u, three mid: e - ɤ - o, and three low: ɛ - a - ɔ. All nine show distinctions in length. Long vowels frequently reduce to a short vowel in fast speech without any change in tone: hɔɔy^2 and hɔy^2 'to comb'.

High. i, ii - ɯ, ɯɯ - u, uu: rip^4 - raw, kii^3 - how many, bɯk^4 - big, mɯɯ^4 - hand, suk^6 - cooked, kuu^1 - I.

Mid. e, ee - ɤ, ɤɤ - o, oo: kheŋ^1 - kind of fish, lee^5 - to choose, tɤp^6 tɤp^6 - sound of people walking barefoot, rɤɤ^1 - in, cok^4 - a hoe, ʔook^6 - snail.

Low. ɛ, ɛɛ - a, aa - ɔ, ɔɔ: tlɛl^1 - to snore, lɛɛt^5 - to paint, nan^6 - that, baat^6 - time, rɔk^4 - six, ʔɔɔk^6 - to go out.

Diphthongs

Three centering diphthongs include ia - ɯa - ua: cia^5 - paper, rɯa^4 - formerly, kua^1 - leg. The diphthong [ua] is characteristic of the speech of the younger generation. Other diphthongs may be analyzed as a vocalic nucleus plus a final w - y.

Diphthongs with final [w]. iw - iiw - iaw - uaw - eew - ɛɛw - aw - aaw: riw^3 - to carry by hand, as a suitcase, siiw^2 - spoiled (of food), riaw^4 - charcoal, ruaw^2 - to laugh, heew^2 - green, lɛɛw^6 - finished, haw^3 - to enter, haaw^2 - white.

Diphthongs with final [y]. ɯay - uy - uuy - uay - ɤɤy - ooy - ay - aay - ɔɔy: pɯay^{1} - naked, muy^{6} - to sneeze, muuy^{4} - blue, muay^{4} - to box, dɤɤy^{1} - free, idle, rooy^{2} - bee, yay^{4} - fish trap, kwaay^{1} - to sell, hɔɔy^{6} - I.

Notable Sociolinguistic Features

During his fieldwork, Gedney found pronunciation differences between the older generation of speakers (OG, aged fifty or more) and the younger (YG). As noted earlier, many of these differences have probably disappeared with the growing hegemony of Lao and Thai.

1) OG speakers keep a clear distinction between final [-l] and final [-n]. YG speakers, on the other hand, have merged the two. OG speakers, thus, distinguish between bɯl^{1} 'to fly' and bɯn^{1} 'sky' whereas YG speakers have the single form bɯn^{1} for both meanings.

2) OG speakers retain clear distinctions between clusters such as [pl-] and [pr-], [phl-] and [phr-], [tl-] and [tr-], [thl-] and [thr-]. Thus OG speakers distinguish between plaa^{1} 'fish' and praa^{1} 'eye, cockspur' whereas YG speakers use praa^{1} for both meanings.

3) OG speakers keep clusters with an initial consonant plus [w] and long [aa]: kwaay^{1} 'to sell'. Through Lao influence, YG speakers, especially those in their twenties and younger, replace the long vowel with the diphthong [ua]: kuay^{1} 'to sell'.

4) OG speakers have a voiced velar spirant as an initial: ɣaw^{6} 'rice'. YG speakers have replaced this spirant with a voiced velar stop: gaw^{6}. Most of Gedney's work was done with OG speakers so forms with the spirant rather than with the stop are listed in the cognate section.

5) OG speakers show no contrast between short [-iw] and long [-iiw] or between short [-uy] and long [-uuy], using the phonetically long sequences in both cases: ŋiiw^{3} 'kapok', muuy^{6} 'to sneeze'. For the YG speakers, there is a clear contrast between the short and long sequences. This situation suggests that Saek originally had no such distinctions and that the contrasts have arisen from Lao and Thai loanwords. In the cognate section, both forms are listed.

6) OG speakers have relatively few Lao and Thai loanwords.

The Tai Dialect of Wuming — WM

The Tai dialect of Wuming belongs to the Northern branch of the Tai language family and is spoken in and around the city of Wuming (Pinyin Wuming) in central Guangxi. A notable glossary with texts was produced by Li (1956), and it is from this publication that Gedney obtained his data for this and other research (1995c). Li also discusses the dialect in his 1977 *A Handbook of Comparative Tai.* A more recent discussion of Wuming tone sandhi can be found in Snyder and Tianqiao (1997).

Phonology

As in other dialects and languages of the Tai family, the phonological pattern of the Tai dialect of Wuming is based on the syllable. Each syllable has distinctions in tone, initial (consonant or consonant cluster), nucleus (vowel or diphthong), and optional final consonant.

Tones

On open syllables (those ending with vowel, semivowel, or nasal), Wuming has six tones. Here pitch levels are based on the Chao 5-pitch scale.

1 - mid level, 33: maa^1 - dog
2 - low-falling, 31: naa^2 - rice field
3 - high level, 55: naa^3 - face
4 - high-falling, 51: maa^4 - horse
5 - mid-rising, 24: naa^5, arrow of crossbow
6 - low-rising, 13: taa^6 - river

Checked syllables (those ending in p - t - k) with short vowels exhibit tones phonetically similar to tones 5 and 6 of open syllables: $ʔak^5$ 'chest', mak^6 'ink'. Checked syllables with long vowels also exhibit tones phonetically similar to tones 5 and 6 of open syllables: $paak^5$ 'mouth', $raak^6$ 'root'.

The six tones of Wuming had their origin in an earlier system of three tones on open syllables and no tonal contrast on checked syllables. Those tones on open syllables have been conventionally designated as A - B - C and the fourth category, the checked syllables, as D. The tones in each of these categories underwent phonemic splits, conditioned by the phonetic nature of the initial consonant of each syllable. With the D category, the splits were further conditioned by vowel length. Table 1 shows the patterns of these splits in Wuming.

Table 1
Pattern of Tonal Splits in Wuming

Initial\Tone	A	B	C	D-short	D-long
Voiceless friction sounds	1	5	3	5	5
Voiceless unaspirated stops	1	5	3	5	5
Glottal sounds	1	5	3	5	5
Voiced sounds	2	6	4	6	6

Consonants

Wuming has the following initial consonants:

Voiceless unaspirated stops. p - t - k - ʔ: pi^2 - fat, tu^6 - bean, ke^3 - to undo, untie, $ʔaa^1$ - crow.

Glottalized. ʔb - ʔd - ʔw - ʔy: ʔbaa^5 - shoulder, ʔdew^1 - single, same, ʔwuan^3 - bowl, ʔyɯak^5 - hungry.

Nasals. m - n - ɲ - ŋ: mi^2 - to have, naw^1 - rat, mouse, ɲɯ^3 - grass, ŋɯ^2 - snake.

Voiceless spirants. f - θ - š - x - h: faa^1 - wall, lid, θaaw^1 - young unmarried woman, šaa^2 - tea, xum^2 - to itch, haa^3 - five.

Sonorants. l - r - w - y: luŋ^2 - uncle, raa^1 - to seek, wen^3 - to hang up, yaa^6 - paternal grandmother.

Initial clusters consist of a consonant plus [l], [w], or [y]. There are no final clusters.

Clusters with [l]. pl - kl - ml: plaa^3 - thunder, klaa^3 - young rice plant, mlaay^2 - saliva.

Clusters with [w]. kw - klw - ʔdw - nw - ŋw - θw - šw - xw - lw: kwaa^2 - right (hand), klwe^3 - a small frog, ʔdway^1 - negative, nwaay^5 - tired, ŋwaa^2 - tile, θwaaŋ^3 - comfortable, cool, šwi - to blow a musical pipe, xwaay^2 - water buffalo, lwet^6 - to spread, smear.

Clusters with [y]. ky: kyaa^1 - home.

There is also one cluser with [r] in praɰ^2 - who.

Final consonants include nasals m - n - ŋ and voiceless stops p - t - k. For final w - y - ɰ, see ***Diphthongs***.

Nasals. m - n - ŋ: θaam^1 - three, tin^1 - foot, ʔdiŋ^1 - red.

Voiceless stops. p - t - k: šip^6 - ten, dit^5 - sunshine, kuk^2 - tiger.

Vowels

Wuming has seven vowels: three high, i - ɯ - u; three mid, e - ɤ - o; and one low a,aa. Distinction in length only appears with the vowel [a] and only before a final consonant. All vowels are phonetically long in final position, although written with a single vowel except for [a], and of indeterminate length and duration in medial position. The vowels e - o are more open, [ɛ] and [ɔ], respectively. In his publications Li used [ø] (1940) and [ö] (1977) for [ɤ]. Mark and Li (1966:167) appear to identify it mistakenly as a front rounded vowel. Here, [ɤ] is used for Li's [ø] and [ö].

High. i - ɯ - u: pliŋ^{1} - leech, hɯn^{3} - to go up, klu^{1} - salt.

Mid. e - ɤ - o: heŋ^{1} - chopping board, kɤ^{1} - tree, plant, roŋ^{2} - to go down.

Low. a, aa: haw^{1} - to smell bad, haaw^{1} - white.

Diphthongs

Three centering diphthongs that occur with a final consonant include ia - ɯa - ua: kiaŋ^{2} - tripod, hɯat^{5} - the waist, ruak^{6} - to vomit.

Other diphthongs may be analyzed as a vocalic nucleus plus a final w - y - ɰ.

Diphthongs with final [w]. iw - iaw - ew - aw - aaw: niw^{3} - scab, riaw^{1} - to laugh, hew^{1} - green, law^{3} - liquor, ʔbaaw^{5} - young unmarried man.

Diphthongs with final [y]. ɯy - uy - ɤy - oy - ay - aay: mɯy^{1} - bear, ruy^{3} - mountain stream, ʔdɤy^{1} - hill, mountain, ʔdoy^{1} - good, klay^{2} - to desire, plaay^{3} - to walk.

Diphthongs with final [ɰ]. aɰ: ʔbaɰ^{1} - leaf.

The Tai Dialect of Po-ai — P

The Tai dialect of Po-ai belongs to the Northern branch of the Tai language family and is spoken in and around the town of Po-ai (Pinyin Bo'ai), located in the southeastern corner of Yunnan province near the Guangxi border. Speakers of the dialect use the term Jui to refer to the dialect. Gedney obtained his data from studies of the dialect made by Li (1944, 1957a, 1957b). Li also uses Po-ai data to illustrate the Northern branch of the Tai language family in his 1977 *A Handbook of Comparative Tai*.

Phonology

As in other dialects and languages of the Tai family, the phonological pattern of the Tai dialect of Po-ai is based on the syllable. Each syllable has distinctions in tone, initial (consonant or consonant cluster), nucleus (vowel or diphthong), and optional final consonant.

Tones

On open syllables (those ending with vowel, semivowel, or nasal), Po-ai has six tones. Here pitch levels are based on the Chao 5-pitch scale.

1 - rising, from mid-low to mid-high, 24: maa^{1} - dog
2 - high level, 55: maa^{2} - to soak
3 - mid-high level, 44: maa^{3} - to increase
4 - mid level, 33: maa^{4} - horse
5 - mid-low, 22: maa^{5} - shoulder
6 - falling, from mid to low, 31: taa^{6} - river

Checked syllables (those ending in p - t - k) with short vowels exhibit tones phonetically similar to tones 2 and 3 of open syllables: mat^{2} 'flea', mɔt^{3} 'ant'. Those with long vowels exhibit tones similar to tones 5 and 6: kaat^{5} 'torn', look^{6} 'outside'. Tone 4 occurs rarely on checked syllables with short vowels and tone 2 on checked syllables with long vowels (Li 1977:14).

The six tones of Po-ai had their origin in an earlier system of three tones on open syllables and no tonal contrast on checked syllables. Those tones on open syllables have been conventionally designated as A - B - C and the fourth category, the checked syllables, as D. The tones in each of these categories underwent phonemic splits, conditioned by the phonetic nature of the initial consonant of each syllable. With the D category, the splits were further conditioned by vowel length. Table 1 shows the patterns of these splits in Po-ai.

Table 1
Pattern of Tonal Splits in Po-ai

Initial\Tone	A	B	C	D-short	D-long
Voiceless friction sounds	1	5	3	2	5
Voiceless unaspirated stops	1	5	3	2	5
Glottal sounds	6	5	3	3	5
Voiced sounds	2	6	4	3	6

Consonants

Po-ai has the following initial consonants:

Voiceless unaspirated stops. p - t - c - k - ʔ: pii^{1} - year, tuu^{1} - door, cee^{3} - to undo, untie, kay^{5} - chicken, ʔay^{6} - to cough.

Voiceless aspirated stops. ph - th - ch - kh: Aspirated stops have only occurred on recent Chinese loans and are therefore omitted in this study.

Nasals. m - n - ŋ: may^{4} - wood, neeŋ^{2} - insect, ŋɔn^{2} - day.

Voiceless spirants. f - ɬ - š - h: fɯɯn^{2} - firewood, ɬooŋ^{1} - two, šiiŋ^{4} - to tend animals, hut^{3} - to dig.

Sonorants. v - l - y: vii^{3} - mountain stream, lii^{2} - to lick, yii^{5} - don't. Li (1977:12) groups the spirant (fricative) [v] with the sonorants because of its low friction level and sonority, In addition, [v] and [w] are in complementary distribution, with [v] appearing initially and [w] after a consonant.

Initial clusters consist of a consonant plus [w] or [y]. There are no final clusters.

Clusters with [w]. tw - cw - kw - ʔw - nw - ŋw - ɬw - šw - hw - lw - yw: kwaa^{5} - to pass, ʔween^{5} - swallow (the bird), nway^{1} - snow, ɬwii^{1} - to follow, lwii^{2} - track, footprint, ywaay^{6} - soft and rotten. Li provides no examples for the remaining clusters: tw - cw - ŋw - šw.

Clusters with [y]. py - cy - ky - my - ny - ɬy - šy - ly: pyaw^{1} - to burn, kway^{3} kyaa^{6} - helmet and armor, myaak^{6} - slippery, lyuu^{2} - to laugh. Li provides no examples for the remaining clusters: cy - ny - ɬy - šy.

Final consonants include nasals m - n - ŋ and voiceless stops p - t - k. For final w - y - ɰ, see ***Diphthongs***.

Nasals. m - n - ŋ: lam^{2} - bran, man^{2} - potato, piŋ^{1} - leech.

Voiceless stops. p - t - k: šip^{3} - ten, pɯt^{2} - lung, mit^{3} - knife.

Vowels

Po-ai has nine vowels, three high: i - ɯ - u and three low: ɛ - a - ɔ, all of which may be either short or long. There are also three mid vowels, e - ɤ - o, which are always long. All vowels are phonetically long in final position and written with a double vowel. Here, [ɤ] is used for Li's [ə].

High. i, ii - ɯ, ɯɯ - u, uu: yip^{3} - to sew, yiik^{5} - hungry, ŋɯk^{2} - gills, ŋɯɯk^{5} - palate, tup^{3} - to beat, nuuŋ^{4} - younger sibling.

Mid. e - ɤ - o: peet^{5} - eight, khyɔɔ^{6} tɤɤ^{6} - to feel, ʔook^{5} - to go out.

Low. ɛ, ɛɛ - a, aa - ɔ, ɔɔ: nɛt^{3} - seed, mɛɛŋ^{6} - thin, not thick, tap^{2} - liver, kaat^{5} - torn, lɔk^{2} - six, ɬɔɔy^{1} - cursed.

Diphthongs

Diphthongs may be analyzed as a vocalic nucleus plus a final w - y - ɰ.

Diphthongs with final [w]. iiw - eew - ɛɛw - aw - aaw: ɬiiw^5 - chisel (ɬiw^5?), leew^5 - withered, mɛɛw^4 - cat, kaw^1 - horn of an animal, haaw^2 - fishy smell.

Diphthongs with final [y]. ɯɯy - uuy - ooy - ay - aay - ɔɔy: kɯɯy^2 - son-in-law, tuuy^4 - bowl, cup (tuy^4?), ʔooy^3 - sugarcane, lay^6 - to chase, taay^1 - to die, ɬɔɔy^1 - cursed.

Diphthongs with final [ɰ]. aɰ: maɰ^6 - leaf.

CHAPTER 5: COGNATES

The following Tai cognates are listed in the three branches of the Tai family: the Southwestern (SW), the Central (CN), and the Northern (N). Representing the Southwestern branch are Siamese (S), White Tai (W), Black Tai (B), Shan (Sh), the Tai dialect of Nong Khai (LNK), the Lue dialect of Chieng Hung (LCH), the Lue dialect of Muong Yong (LMY), and the Tai dialect of Chiengmai (CM). The Central branch includes the Tai dialects of Lei Ping (LP), Lungming (LM), Western Nung (WN), Bac Va (BV), Lungchow (LC), Ping Siang (PS), and Ning Ming (NM). Within the Northern branch are Yay (Y), Saek (Sk), the Tai dialect of Wuming (WM), and the Tai dialect of Po-ai (P). Detailed explanations of the phonology and the symbols used for each dialect can be found in the phonological descriptions. The Proto-Tai category for each cognate follows its gloss.

Southwestern, Central, and Northern Tai Cognates

0001 - to bathe, DL3
SW - S, W, B, Sh, LNK, LCH, LMY ʔaap^{2}; CM ʔaap^{3}
CN - LP ʔaap^{5}; LM, WN, LC, PS ʔaap^{2}
N - Y ʔaap^{2}; Sk ʔaap^{6}; P ʔaap^{5}

0002 - to take, A3
SW - S, W, B, Sh ʔaw^{1}; LNK ʔaw^{2}; LCH ʔaw^{1}; LMY ʔaw^{4}; CM ʔaw^{1}
CN - LP ʔaw^{2}; LM ʔaw^{4}; WN ʔaw^{1}, BV ʔaw^{2}; LC, PS, NM ʔaw^{1}
N - Y, Sk, WM ʔaw^{1}; P ʔaw^{6}

0003 - to cough, A3
SW - S, W, B, Sh ʔay^{1}; LNK ʔay^{2}; LCH ʔay^{1}; LMY ʔay^{4}; CM ʔay^{1}
CN - LP ʔay^{2}; LM ʔay^{4}; WN, LC, PS, NM ʔay^{1}
N - Y, Sk, WM ʔay^{1}; P ʔay^{6}

0004 - steam, vapor, A3
SW - S ʔay^{1}; W, B, Sh ʔaay^{1}; LNK ʔaay^{2}; LCH ʔaay^{1}; LMY ʔaay^{4}; CM ʔwaay^{1}
CN - LP yaay^{2}; LM yaay^{4}; WN, LC, PS, NM yaay^{1}
N - Y θɯay^{1}; Sk sooy^{2} (A1)

0005 - waist, A3, (cf. 0793)
SW - S ʔew^{1}; W, B, Sh ʔɛw^{1}; LNK ʔɛɛw^{2} (modern pron. by some ʔeew^{2}); LCH ʔɛw^{1}; LMY ʔɛw^{4}; CM ʔɛɛw^{1}
CN - LP yiiw^{2}; LM yiiw^{1}, ʔiiw^{4}; LC yiiw^{1} ‘kidney’ (Li says < Chinese); PS, NM yiiw^{1}
N - Y ʔew^{1} ‘narrow waist’; Sk ʔɛɛw^{1}

0006 - yoke, DL3
SW - S ʔɛɛk^{2}; W, B ʔɛʔ^{2}; Sh ʔɛk^{2}; LNK, LMY ʔɛɛk^{2}; CM ʔɛɛk^{3}
CN - LP ʔeek^{5}; LM ʔeek^{2}; WN ʔɛk^{2}; LC, PS, NM ʔeek^{2}
N - Y ʔek^{2}; Sk ʔɛɛk^{6}

0007 - full (after eating), B3
SW - S, W, B, Sh ʔim^{2}; LNK ʔim^{3}; LCH, LMY ʔim^{2}; CM ʔim^{3}
CN - LP ʔim^{5}; LM, WN, LC, PS ʔim^{2}; NM ʔom^{2}
N - Y ʔim^{2}; Sk ʔiim^{6}; WM, P ʔim^{5}

0008 - the chest, DS3
SW - S ʔok^{2}; W, B ʔɤk^{2}; Sh ʔok^{4}, ʔɯk^{4}; LNK, LCH, LMY ʔɤk^{1}, ʔok^{1}; CM ʔok^{2}
CN - LP ʔɤk^{2}; LM ʔɤk^{3}; WN ʔak^{6}; LC, PS ʔɤk^{2}; NM ʔɯk^{4}
N - Y ʔak^{3}; WM ʔak^{5}

0009 - to go hungry, DS3, (cf. 0727)
SW - S ʔot^{2}; W, B ʔɯt^{2}; LNK ʔɯt^{1}; LCH ʔɯp^{1}; LMY ʔot^{1} ‘to endure’; CM ʔot^{2} ‘to endure’
N - Sk ʔot^{4}

0010 - to go out, DL3
SW - S ʔɔɔk^{2}; W, B ʔɔʔ^{2}; Sh ʔɔk^{2}; LNK, LCH, LMY ʔɔɔk^{2}; CM ʔɔɔk^{3}
CN - LP ʔook^{5}; LM ʔook^{2}; WN ʔɔk^{2}; LC, PS, NM ʔook^{2}
N - Y ʔok^{2}; Sk ʔɔɔk^{6}; WM ʔɤk^{5}; P ʔook^{5}

0011 - young; soft, B3
SW - S ʔɔɔn^{2}; W, B, Sh ʔɔn^{2}; LNK ʔɔɔn^{3}; LCH, LMY ʔɔn^{2}; CM ʔɔɔn^{3}
CN - LP ʔoon^{5}; LM ʔoon^{2}; WN ʔɔn^{2}; LC, PS, NM ʔoon^{2}
N - Y ʔun^{2}; Sk ʔuun^{6}; WM ʔun^{5}

0012 - sugarcane, C3
SW - S, W, B, Sh ʔɔy^{3}; LNK ʔɔɔy^{5}; LCH, LMY ʔɔy^{3}; CM ʔɔɔy^{5}
CN - LP, LM ʔooy^{3}; WN ʔɔy^{3}; LC, PS, NM ʔooy^{3}
N - Y ʔoy^{6}; Sk ʔɔɔy^{3}; P ʔooy^{3}

0013 - to carry in the arms, C3
SW - S, W, B, Sh ʔum^{3}; LNK ʔum^{5}; LCH, LMY ʔum^{3}; CM ʔum^{5}
CN - LP, LM ʔom^{3}; WN, LC ʔum^{3}
N - Y ʔum^{6}; Sk ʔuum^{3}; WM, P ʔum^{3}

0014 - to plug (a hole), DS3, (cf. 1007)
SW - S ʔut^{2}; W, B ʔot^{2}; Sh ʔut^{4}; LNK ʔut^{1}; LMY ʔɯt^{1}; CM ʔɯt^{2}
CN - LP ʔot^{2}; LM ʔot^{3}; WN ʔɔt^{6}; LC ʔut^{2}; PS ʔot^{2}; NM ʔot^{4}
N - Sk ʔɔt^{4}

0015 - crazy, C3, (cf. 0877)
SW - S, W, B baa^{3}; Sh maa^{3}; LNK baa^{5}; LCH, LMY baa^{3}; CM baa^{5}
CN - LP baa^{3}; LM maa^{3}; WN vaa^{3} 'dumb' (perhaps not cognate); LC, PS baa^{3}
N - Sk kwaa^{3} (OG), kua^{3} (YG) (probably not cognate)

0016 - not, B3
SW - W, B baw^{2}; Sh maw^{2}; LNK bɔɔ^{3}; LCH, LMY baw^{2} (but usually syllabic [m] in ordinary speech); CM bɔɔ^{3}
CN - WN boo^{2}, bɔɔ^{2}; LC baw^{2}, boo^{2} (current in the countryside)
N - Y baw^{2}, bo^{2}; Sk boo^{6}; WM ʔbaw^{3} (C3)

0017 - dumb, mute, C3
SW - S bay^{3}; W, B baɰ^{3} 'stupid'; Sh maɰ^{3} 'silly, foolish'; LNK bay^{5}; LCH, LMY bay^{3} (also, 'stupid'); CM bay^{5}

0018 - leaf, A3
SW - S bay^{1}; W, B baɰ^{1}; Sh maɰ^{1}; LNK bay^{2}; LCH bay^{1}; LMY bay^{4}; CM baɰ^{1}
CN - LP baɰ^{2}; LM maɰ^{4}; WN, LC, PS, NM baɰ^{1}
N - Y baɰ^{1}; Sk bɤɤ^{1}; WM ʔbaɰ^{1}; P maɰ^{6}

0019 - fish hook, DS3
SW - S, W, B bet^{2}; Sh met^{4}, wet^{4}; LNK, LCH, LMY bet^{1}; CM bet^{2}
CN - LP bit^{2}; LM myat^{3}; WN bɔt^{6}, bat^{6}; LC, PS bit^{2}

0020 - to fly, A3
SW - S, W, B bin^{1}; Sh min^{1}; LNK bin^{2}; LCH bin^{1}; LMY bin^{4}; CM bin^{1}
CN - LP bin^{2}; LM min^{4}; WN ban^{1}; LC, PS bin^{1}; NM ben^{1}
N - Y bin^{1}; Sk bɯl^{1} (OG), bɯn^{1} (YG); WM ʔbin^{1}; P min^{6}

0021 - master, owner; you, C2
SW - S caaw^{3} 'master', caw^{3} 'you'; W, B caw^{3}; Sh saw^{3}; LNK caw^{5} 'you (polite), royal personage'; LCH, LMY caw^{3}; CM caw^{5}
CN - LP, LM, WN, LC, PS caw^{3}
N - Y θu^{3}; Sk caw^{3} in many expressions, but phɔɔ^{5} suu^{3} 'owner'

0022 - heart, breath, A2, (cf. 1106)
SW - S cay^{1}; W, B caɰ^{1}; Sh saɰ^{1}; LNK cay^{2}; LCH, LMY cay^{1}; CM cay^{2}
CN - LP caɰ^{2}; WN, LC caɰ^{1}
N - Y sɯ^{1}; Sk cɯɯ^{1}; WM šaɰ^{1}

0023 - to hurt, DS2
SW - S, W, B cep^{2}; Sh sep^{4}; LNK, LCH, LMY cep^{1}; CM cep^{2}
CN - LP cip^{2}; LM cap^{3}; LC, PS cip^{2}

0024 - seven, DS2
SW - S, W, B cet^{2}; Sh set^{4}; LNK, LCH, LMY cet^{1}; CM cet^{2}
CN - LP cet^{2} (cit^{2}?); LM cat^{3}; WN cεt^{6}; LC, PS cit^{2}; NM cet^{4}
N - Y sat^{3}; Sk cεt^{4}; WM šat^{5}; P šεt^{2}

0025 - to lead by the hand, A2
SW - S cuuŋ^{1}; W, B cuŋ^{1}; Sh suŋ^{1}; LNK cuuŋ^{2}; LMY cuŋ^{1}; CM cuuŋ^{2}
CN - LP coŋ^{2}; LM coŋ^{1}; WN, LC cuŋ^{1}; PS, NM coŋ^{1}
N - Sk ciiŋ^{1}

0026 - tea, A4
SW - S chaa^{1}; W, B cε^{4}; LNK saa^{6}; LCH, LMY saa^{4} (more frequent laa^{6}); CM chaa^{1}, saa^{1}
CN - LP chaa^{4}; LM, WN, LC, PS caa^{4}; NM saa^{4}
N - Y sa^{4}; Sk saa^{4}; WM, P šaa^{2}

0027 - spider, A1
SW - W (chiŋ^{2}) chaaw^{1} (A?); B (siŋ^{2}) saaw^{1}; Sh (koŋ^{2}) kaaw^{1}; LCH (mεŋ^{4} buŋ^{3}) kwaaw^{1}; LMY (koŋ^{3}) kwaaw^{1}
CN - LP -haaw^{1}; LM -laaw^{1}; WN chaaw^{1}; LC (khyaaŋ^{3}) khyaaw^{1}; PS -khyaaw^{1}
N - Y (ciŋ^{2}) caaw^{1}; Sk (thruŋ^{6}) thraaw^{2}; WM klwaaw^{1}

0028 - morning, C4, (cf. 1038)
SW - S chaaw^{4}; W, B caw^{6}; Sh saw^{5} 'early'; LNK saw^{5}; LCH, LMY, CM caw^{6}
CN - LP chaw^{3}, saw^{3}; LM, WN caw^{6}; LC caw^{6} 'early'; PS caw^{6}; NM saw^{6}
N - Y saw^{6} 'early'; WM šaw^{4}

0029 - man, male person, A4
SW - S chaay^{1}; W, B caay^{4}; Sh saay^{4}; LNK saay^{6}; LCH, LMY caay^{4}; CM caay^{1}
CN - LM, WN, LC caay^{4}
N - Y θaay^{1}; Sk saay^{2}; WM θaay^{1}; P ɬaay^{1} (A1 in N languages)

0030 - to hate, A4
SW - S chaŋ^{1}; W, B caŋ^{4}; Sh saŋ^{4}; LNK saŋ^{6}; LCH, LMY caŋ^{4}; CM caŋ^{1}
CN - WN, LC caŋ^{4}
N - Y, Sk saŋ^{4}; WM šaŋ^{2}

0031 - skilled; an artisan, B4
SW - S chaŋ^{3}; W, B caaŋ^{5}; Sh, LNK saaŋ^{3}; LCH, LMY caaŋ^{5}; CM caaŋ^{4}
CN - LP chɤɤŋ^{5}; LM cɯɯŋ^{5}; WN caaŋ^{5}; LC cɤɤŋ^{5} (Li says < Chinese)
N - Y, Sk saaŋ^{5}; WM, P šaaŋ^{6}

0032 - to use, C4, (cf. 1077)
SW - S chay^{4}, chaay^{4}; W, B caɰ^{6} 'to employ as a servant, send on an errand'; Sh saɰ^{5} 'to commission, send'; LNK say^{5}; LCH, LMY, CM cay^{6}
CN - LP chaɰ^{3} 'to serve, wait on'; LM caɰ^{6} 'to serve, wait on'; WN caɰ^{6} 'to wait on a table'; LC caɰ^{6} 'to eat, referring to an honored person'
N - Y θaɰ^{3}; Sk say^{3} (said to be < Lao); P ɬaɰ^{3} (C1 in N languages)

0033 - to wipe, DS4
SW - S chet^{4}; W cet^{4}; B cet^{5}; Sh set^{5}; LNK set^{3}; LCH, LMY cet^{5}; CM cet^{6}
CN - WN cɛt^{4}
N - Sk sɛt^{6}

0034 - to point, C4
SW - S chii^{4}; W, B ci^{6}; Sh si^{5}; LNK sii^{5}; LCH, LMY, CM cii^{6}
CN - LP cii^{3}; LM cey^{3} (C?, cognate with 1120?); WN cii^{6}; PS, NM cii^{3} (C?)
N - Y yi^{6}, vi^{6}; Sk ɲii^{6}

0035 - to tear, DL1
SW - S chiik^{2}; W, B ciʔ^{2}; Sh shik^{2}; LMY siik^{2}; CM siik^{3}
CN - LP siik^{2}; LM cheek^{2}; LC šiik^{2}; PS siik^{2}; NM šiik^{2}
N - Sk siik^{6}; WM θik^{5} (Li says < Chinese)

0036 - to taste, A4
SW - S chim^{1}; W, B cim^{4}; Sh sim^{4}; LNK sim^{6}; LCH, LMY cim^{4}; CM cim^{1}
CN - LP chim^{4}; LM, WN, LC, PS cim^{4}
N - Y sim^{4}; WM šim^{2}

0037 - rope, cord, DL4
SW - S chɯak^{3}; W cɤ^{4}; B cɯaʔ^{5}; Sh sɤk^{3}; LNK sɯak^{5}; LCH, LMY cɤɤk^{5}; CM cɯak^{4}
CN - LP chɤɤk^{5}; LM cɯɯk^{5}; WN cik^{5}; LC cɤɤk^{4}; PS cɤɤk^{5}; NM cɯɯk^{5}
N - Y, Sk saak^{5}; WM, P šaak^{6}

0038 - crack, hole, B4, (cf. 0318, 0546)
SW - S chɔŋ^{3}; W, B cɔŋ^{5}; LNK sɔɔŋ^{3}; LCH, LMY cɔŋ^{5}; CM cɔɔŋ^{4}
CN - LM cooŋ^{5}; WN coŋ^{5}
N - Y soŋ^{5}; Sk sɔɔŋ^{5}; WM šɤŋ^{6}

0039 - to help, B4
SW - S chuay^{3}; W, B cɔy^{5}; Sh sɔy^{3}; LNK sɔɔy^{3}; LCH, LMY cɔy^{5}; CM cuay^{4}
CN - LP chooy^{5}; LM cooy^{5}; WN say^{5}; LC cooy^{5}
N - Sk sooy^{5}

0040 - handle (of a knife), C3
SW - S daam^{3}, dam^{3}; W dam^{3}; B dam^{3}, lam^{3}; Sh laam^{3} 'an oar, flat wooden spoon'; LNK daam^{5}; LCH dam^{3}; LMY dam^{3}, daam^{3}; CM daam^{5}
CN - LM naam^{3}; WN dam^{3} 'handle', daam^{3} 'wooden paddle'; LC daam^{3}; PS dam^{3}
N - Y daam^{6} 'wooden ladle'; Sk daam^{3}

0041 - star, A3
SW - S, W daaw^{1}; B daaw^{1}, laaw^{1}; Sh laaw^{1}; LNK daaw^{2}; LCH daaw^{1}; LMY daaw^{4}; CM daaw^{1}
CN - LP daaw^{2}; LM naaw^{4}; WN, LC, PS daaw^{1} dii^{2}; NM daaw^{1}
N - Y daaw^{1} di^{2}; Sk traaw^{1}; WM ʔdaaw^{1} ʔdoy^{5}; P naaw^{6} nii^{5}

0042 - can; to obtain, C3
SW - S daay^{3}; W day^{3}; B day^{3}, lay^{3}; Sh lay^{3}; LNK day^{5}; LCH, LMY day^{3}; CM day^{5}
CN - LP day^{3}; LM nay^{3}; WN, LC, PS, NM day^{3}
N - Y day^{6}; Sk day^{3}; WM ʔday^{3}; P nay^{3}

0043 - black, A3
SW - S, W dam^{1}; B dam^{1}, lam^{1}; Sh lam^{1}; LNK dam^{2}; LCH dam^{1}; LMY dam^{4}; CM dam^{1}
CN - LP dam^{2}; LM nam^{4}; WN, LC, PS, NM dam^{1}
N - Sk ram^{1}; WM ʔdam^{1}

0044 - stairs, ladder, A3
SW - S (kă^{2}) day^{1}; W day^{1}; B day^{1}, lay^{1}; Sh lay^{1} a verb 'to slope down, from lay^{1}', as in '[-lay^{1}] stairs'; LNK (kă-) day^{2}; LCH day^{1}; LMY day^{4}; CM day^{1}
CN - LP day^{2}; LM nay^{4}; WN lay^{1}; LC, PS, NM day^{1}
N - Y lay^{1}; Sk ray^{1}; WM loy^{4} (C4); P lay^{2} (A2)

0045 - sunshine, DL3
SW - S dɛɛt^{2}; W dɛt^{2}; B dɛt^{2}, lɛt^{2}; Sh lɛt^{2}; LNK, LCH, LMY dɛɛt^{2}; CM dɛɛt^{3}
CN - LP deet^{5}; LM neet^{2}; WN dɛt^{2}; LC, PS, NM deet^{2}
N - Y dit^{3} (DS3); Sk riit^{6}; WM dit^{5}

0046 - single, only one, same, A3
SW - S diaw^{1}; W dew^{1}; B diaw^{1}, liaw^{1}; Sh lew^{1}; LNK diaw^{2}; LCH dew^{1}; LMY dew^{4}; CM diaw^{1}
CN - LP deew^{5} (B3); LM neew^{4}; WN dew^{1}; LC, PS, NM deew^{2} (B3)
N - Y dew^{1}; Sk diaw^{1}; WM ʔdew^{1}; P neew^{6}

0047 - month, moon, A3
SW - S dɯan^{1}; W bɤn^{1}; B bɯan^{1}; Sh lɤn^{1}; LNK dɯan^{2}; LCH dɤn^{1}; LMY dɤn^{4}; CM dɯan^{1}
CN - LP bɤɤn^{2}; LM mɯɯn^{4}; WN dɯn^{1}; LC, PS bɤɤn^{1}; NM buun^{1}
N - Y dɯan^{1}; Sk blian^{1}; WM ʔdɯan^{1}; P nɯɯn^{6}

0048 - earthworm, A3
SW - S (say^{3}) dɯan^{1}; W dɤn^{1}; B dɯan^{1}, lɯan^{1}; LNK (khii^{4} kă-) dɯan^{2}; LCH dɤn^{1}; LMY dɤn^{4}; CM dɯan^{1}
CN - LP dɤɤn^{2}; LM nɯɯn^{4}; WN dɯn^{1}; LC, PS dɤɤn^{1}; NM dɯɯ^{1}
N - Y dɯan^{1}; Sk trual^{1} (OG), truan^{1} (YG); WM ʔdɯan^{1}

0049 - cockspur, A3
SW - S dɯay^{1}; W dɤ^{1}; B dɯa^{1}; Sh loy^{1}; LNK dɯay^{2}; LCH dɤɤ^{1}; LMY dɤɤ^{4} (cf. LCH dɤy^{1} 'Job's tears'; LMY dɤy^{4}); CM dɯa^{1}
CN - LP dɤɤ^{2}; LM nɯɯ^{4}; WN lɯy^{1}, dɯɯ^{1}; PS dɯɯ^{1}
N - Y da^{1}; Sk traa^{1}, praa^{1}

0050 - navel, A3, (cf. 0992)
SW - S (să^{2}) dɯɯ^{1}; W (saay^{1}) bi^{1}; B (saay^{1}) bɯ^{1}; LNK bɯɯ^{2}, dɯɯ^{2}; LCH bɯɯ^{1}; LMY dɯɯ^{4}; CM (să^{2}) dɯɯ^{1}
CN - WN dɯy^{1}; LC dɯa^{1}
N - Y dɯa^{1}; Sk bɯɯ^{1}, dua^{1}; WM ʔbɯ^{1}; P nɯɯ^{6}

0051 - late at night, DS3
SW - S dɯk^{2}; W dɤk^{2}; B dɯk^{2}, lɯk^{2}; Sh lɯk^{4}; LNK, LCH, LMY dɤk^{1}, dɯk^{1}; CM dɤk^{2}
CN - WN dɤk^{6}
N - Y dak^{3}; Sk dɯk^{4}

0052 - flower, DL3
SW - S dɔɔk^{2}; W, B bɔʔ^{2}; Sh mɔk^{2}; LNK, LCH, LMY dɔɔk^{2}; CM dɔɔk^{3}
CN - LP byook^{5}; LM myook^{2}; WN dɔk^{2}; LC, PS, NM byook^{2}
N - Y dok^{2}; Sk blɔɔk^{6}

0053 - to pickle, A3, (cf. 0927)
SW - S dɔɔŋ^{1}; W, B bɔŋ^{1}; Sh mɔŋ^{1}; LNK bɔɔŋ^{2}, dɔɔŋ^{2}; LCH bɔŋ^{1}; LMY dɔŋ^{4}, bɔŋ^{4}; CM dɔɔŋ^{1}
CN - WN doŋ^{1}
N - Y doŋ^{1}; Sk bɔɔŋ^{1}, dɔɔŋ^{1}; P nooŋ^{6}

0054 - classifier for round objects, A3
SW - S duaŋ^{1}; W doŋ^{1}; B duaŋ^{1}, luaŋ^{1}; LNK duaŋ^{2}; LMY doŋ^{4}; CM duaŋ^{1}

0055 - bone, DL3
SW - S (kă^{2}) duuk^{2}; W dup^{2}; B duʔ^{2}; Sh lup^{2} (also, infrequent luk^{2}); LNK (ka-) duuk^{2}; LCH, LMY duuk^{2}; CM (kă^{2}) duuk^{3}
CN - LP dok^{5}; LM nok^{3} (DS3); WN duk^{6} (DS3); LC duk^{2}; PS dok^{2}; NM duuk^{5}
N - Y dok^{2}; Sk rɔɔk^{6}; WM ʔdɤk^{5}; P nook^{5}

0056 - cloud, C1
SW - S faa^{3} 'cloudy film, as on glass'; W, B faa^{3}; Sh phaa^{3}; LNK faa^{4}; LCH, LMY faa^{3}; CM faa^{5}
CN - LP, LM, LC, PS phaa^{3}; NM phɯɯ^{3}
N - Y vɯa^{3}; Sk via^{3}; WM fɯ^{3}; P fɯɯ^{3}

0057 - sky, C4
SW - S faa^{4}; W, B faa^{6}; Sh pha^{5}; LNK faa^{5}; LCH, LMY, CM faa^{6}
CN - LP faa^{3}; LM, WN, LC, PS, NM faa^{6}
N - Sk phaa^{3} (C1?, usual word is bɯn^{1})

0058 - wall; lid, A1, (cf. 0980)
SW - S faa^{5}; W, B faa^{1}; Sh phaa^{1}; LNK, LCH, LMY faa^{1}; CM faa^{2}
CN - LP, LM, WN, BV, LC, PS, NM phaa^{1}
N - Y va^{1}; Sk vaa^{1}; WM faa^{1}

0059 - astringent in taste, DL1
SW - S, W, B faat^{2}; Sh phaat^{2}; LNK, LCH, LMY faat^{2}; CM faat^{3}
CN - WN phaat^{2}
N - Y vɯat^{2}; Sk viat^{6}

0060 - sheath; pod, DS1
SW - S, W, B fak^{2}; Sh phak^{4}; LNK, LCH, LMY fak^{1}; CM fak^{2}
CN - LP phak^{2}; LM phak^{3}; WN phak^{6}; PS phak^{2}; NM phak^{4}
N - Y hok^{3}; Sk vak^{4}; P fak^{2}

0061 - to incubate, DS4
SW - S, W fak^{4}; B fak^{5}; LNK fak^{3}; CM fak^{6}
CN - LP, LM, WN, LC, PS, NM fak^{4}
N - Y fak^{1}; P fak^{3}

0062 - to listen, obey, A4
SW - S faŋ^{1}; W, B faŋ^{4}; LNK faŋ^{6}; LCH, LMY faŋ^{4}; CM faŋ^{1}
CN - LM faŋ^{4}
N - Sk phaŋ^{4} (rare, said to be < Lao or Siamese)

0063 - fire, A4
SW - S fay^{1}; W, B fay^{4}; Sh phay^{4}; LNK fay^{6}; LCH, LMY fay^{4}; CM fay^{1}
CN - LP, LM, WN, LC, PS fay^{4}; NM fey^{4}
N - Y fi^{4}; Sk vii^{4}; WM foy^{2}; P fii^{2}

0064 - rain, A1
SW - S fon^{5}; W fɯn^{1}; B fon^{1}; Sh phon^{1}; LNK fon^{1}; LCH, LMY fun^{1}; CM fon^{2}
CN - LP, LM phɤn^{1}; WN phan^{1}; BV phon^{1}; LC, PS phɤn^{1}; NM phen^{1}
N - Y hun^{1}; Sk vɯn^{2}; WM fun^{1}; P hɯn^{1}

0065 - heavy shower, B1
SW - S, W, B, Sh haa^{2}; LNK haa^{3}; LCH, LMY haa^{2}; CM haa^{3}
CN - LP haa^{2}; LM laa^{2}; WN chaa^{2}; LC, PS haa^{2}; NM khyaa^{2}
N - Y ra^{2}; Sk raa^{6}; WM raa^{5}; P laa^{5}

0066 - five, C1
SW - S, W, B, Sh haa^{3}; LNK haa^{4}; LCH, LMY haa^{3}; CM haa^{5}
CN - LP, LM, WN, LC, PS, NM haa^{3}
N - Y ha^{3}; Sk, WM, P haa^{3}

0067 - to seek, A1
SW - S haa^{5}; W, B, Sh, LNK, LCH, LMY haa^{1}; CM haa^{2}
CN - LP haa^{1}; LM laa^{1}; WN chaa^{1}; LC, PS haa^{1}; NM khyaa^{1}
N - Y ra^{1}; Sk raa^{2}; WM raa^{1}; P laa^{1}

0068 - goose, B1, (cf. 1056)
SW - S, W, B, Sh haan^{2}; LNK haan^{3}; LCH, LMY haan^{2}; CM haan^{3}
CN - LM haan^{2} 'crane'; WN haan^{2}
N - Y haan^{2}; Sk haan^{6}; WM, P haan^{5}

0069 - tail, A1
SW - S haaŋ^{5}; W, B, Sh, LNK, LCH, LMY haaŋ^{1}; CM haaŋ^{2}
CN - LP haaŋ^{1}; LM, WN, BV thaaŋ^{1}; LC, PS, NM haaŋ^{1}
N - Y rɯaŋ^{1}; Sk ruaŋ^{2}; WM rɯaŋ^{1}; P lɯɯŋ^{1}

0070 - to carry on two ends of a shoulder pole, DL1
SW - S, W, B, Sh, LNK, LCH, LMY haap^{2}; CM haap^{3}
CN - LP haap^{2}; LM, WN thaap^{2}; LC, PS, NM haap^{2}
N - Y raap^{2}; Sk raap^{6}; WM raap^{5}; P laap^{5}

0071 - to yawn, A1
SW - S haaw^{5}; W, B, Sh, LNK, LCH, LMY haaw^{1}; CM haaw^{2}
CN - LP, LM haaw^{1}; WN ŋaaw^{1} ŋaap^{5}, chaaw^{1} ŋaap^{5}; BV haaw^{1}; LC haaw^{1}; PS haaw^{1}
N - Y raaw^{1}; Sk raaw^{2}, haaw^{2} (< Siamese)

0072 - to weep, C1
SW - S haay^{3}; W, B, Sh hay^{3}; LNK hay^{4}; LCH, LMY hay^{3}; CM hay^{5}
CN - LP, LM, WN, LC, PS, NM hay^{3}
N - Y, Sk, WM, P tay^{3}

0073 - to break (a stick, etc.) (transitive), DS1, (cf. 0355)
SW - S, W, B hak^{2}; Sh hak^{4}; LNK, LCH, LMY hak^{1}; CM hak^{2}
CN - LP tak^{2}; LM tak^{3}; WN thak^{6}; LC, PS tak^{2}; NM thak^{4}
N - Y rak^{3}; Sk rak^{4}; WM rak^{5}; P lak^{2}

0074 - to bark, B1
SW - S, W, B, Sh haw^{2}; LNK haw^{3}; LCH, LMY haw^{2}; CM haw^{3}
CN - LP, LM, WN, LC, PS, NM haw^{2}
N - Y raw^{2}; Sk haw^{6}; WM raw^{5}; P law^{5}

0075 - to give, C1
SW - S hay^{3}; W, B, Sh haɰ^{3}; LNK hay^{4}; LCH, LMY hɯɯ^{3}; CM hɯɯ^{5}
CN - LP hɤɤ^{3}; LM hɤɰ^{3}; WN haɰ^{3}; LC, PS hɯɯ^{3}; NM haɰ^{3}
N - Y haɰ^{3}; Sk hɤɤ^{3}; WM, P haɰ^{3}

0076 - to see, A1
SW - S hen^{5}; W hin^{1}; B hen^{1}; LNK hen^{1} (but han^{1} cay^{2} 'to breathe'); LCH, LMY han^{1}; CM han^{2}
CN - LP, LM han^{1}; WN than^{1}; LC, PS, NM han^{1}
N - Y ran^{1}; Sk rɛn^{2}; P han^{1}

0077 - civet cat, A1
SW - S hen^{5}; W hin^{1}; B ɲen^{1}; Sh hen^{1}; LNK hen^{1}, heen^{1}; LCH, LMY hin^{1}; CM hen^{2}
CN - LP, LM hin^{1}; WN han^{1}; LC hin^{1} 'jungle cat'
N - Y ɲan^{1}; Sk ɲɛl^{2} (OG), ɲɛn^{2} (YG); WM ɲan^{1} 'fox'

0078 - mushroom, DS1
SW - S, W, B het^{2}; Sh hep^{4}; LNK, LCH, LMY het^{1}; CM het^{2}
CN - LP viit^{2} (DS4); LM vit^{5} (DS4); WN hat^{6}; LC vit^{4} (DS4); PS vit^{5} (DS4); NM ɬap^{4} (DS4)
N - Y rat^{3}; Sk het^{4} (< Lao, usual word is daaŋ^{3}); WM rat^{5}; P lɛt^{2}

0079 - dried up, C1
SW - S hɛɛŋ^{3}; W, B, Sh hɛŋ^{3}; LNK hɛɛŋ^{4}; LCH, LMY hɛŋ^{3}; CM hɛɛŋ^{5}
CN - WN hɛŋ^{3}
N - Y reŋ^{3}; Sk hɛɛŋ^{3}

0080 - withered, B1
SW - S hiaw^{2}; W, B hɛw^{2}; Sh hew^{2}; LNK hiaw^{3}; LCH, LMY hew^{2}; CM hiaw^{3}
CN - LP, LM heew^{2}; WN šiw^{2}; LC, PS, NM heew^{2}
N - Y rew^{2}; Sk hɛɛw^{3} (C1); WM rew^{5}; P leew^{5}

0081 - stone, A1
SW - S hin^{5}; W, B, Sh, LNK, LCH, LMY hin^{1}; CM hin^{2}
CN - LP hin^{1}; LM, BV thin^{1}; LC, PS hin^{1}; NM hen^{1}
N - Y rin^{1}; Sk riil^{2} (OG), riin^{2} (YG); WM rin^{1}; P hin^{1}

0082 - six, DS1
SW - S, W, B hok^{2}; Sh hok^{4}; LNK, LCH, LMY hok^{1}; CM hok^{2}
CN - LP hok^{2}; LM lok^{3}; WN chɔk^{6}; LC huk^{2}; PS hok^{2}; NM hok^{4}
N - Y rok^{3}; Sk rɔk^{4}; WM rok^{5}; P lɔk^{2}

0083 - a spear, DL1
SW - S hɔɔk^{2}; W, B hɔʔ^{2}; Sh hɔk^{2}; LNK, LCH, LMY hɔɔk^{2}; CM hɔɔk^{3}
CN - LM hook^{2} 'to throw a spear'; WN chɔk^{2}
N - Y rok^{2}

0084 - fragrant, A1
SW - S hɔɔm^{5}; W, B, Sh hɔm^{1}; LNK hɔɔm^{1}; LCH, LMY hɔm^{1}; CM hɔɔm^{2}
CN - LP, LM hoom^{1}; WN hom^{1}; BV hɔɔm^{1}; LC, PS, NM hoom^{1}
N - Y hom^{1}; P hoom^{1}

0085 - mollusk, A1, (cf. 1142)
SW - S hɔy^{5}; W, B, Sh, LNK, LCH, LMY hɔy^{1}; CM hɔɔy^{2}
CN - LP, LM hooy^{1}; WN hɔy^{1}; LC hooy^{1} 'kind of snail'; PS hooy^{1} 'snail'; NM hooy^{1}
N - Y, WM θay^{1}

0086 - head, A1
SW - S hua^{5}; W ho^{1}; B hua^{1}; Sh ho^{1}; LNK hua^{1}; LCH, LMY hoo^{1}; CM hua^{2}
CN - LP vuu^{1}; LM, WN, BV thuu^{1}; LC, PS, NM huu^{1}

0087 - mountain stream, C1
SW - S huay^{3}; W hoy^{3}; B huay^{3}; Sh hoy^{3} 'a ravine, gully'; LNK huay^{4}; LCH, LMY hoy^{3}; CM huay^{5}
CN - LP khooy^{3}; LM luuy^{3}; WN khuy^{3}; LC vuuy^{3}, huuy^{3}; PS vuuy^{3}; NM khuuy^{3}
N - Y vi^{3}; Sk rii^{3}; WM ruy^{3}; P vii^{3}

0088 - nine, C2
SW - S kaaw^{3}; W, B, Sh kaw^{3}; LNK kaw^{5}; LCH, LMY kaw^{3}; CM kaw^{5}
CN - LP, LM, WN, LC, PS kaw^{3}; NM kow^{3}
N - Y ku^{3}; Sk kuu^{3}; WM kaw^{3}; P kuu^{3}

0089 - each other, together, A2
SW - S, W, B, Sh kan^{1}; LNK kan^{2}; LCH, LMY kan^{1}; CM kan^{2}
CN - LP kan^{2}; LC, PS kan^{1}
N - Sk kin^{1}; WM kan^{1}

0090 - chicken, B2
SW - S, W, B, Sh kay^{2}; LNK kay^{3}, kɤɤ^{3}; LCH, LMY kay^{2}; CM kay^{3}
CN - LP kay^{5}; LM kay^{2}; WN cay^{2}; LC, PS, NM kay^{2}
N - Y kay^{2}; Sk kay^{6}; WM, P kay^{5}

0091 - old (of living beings), B2, (cf. 0483, 0712)
SW - S kɛɛ^{2}; W, B kɛ^{2} 'adult and married'; Sh kɛ^{2} 'mature, firm'; LNK kɛɛ^{3}; LCH, LMY kɛɛ^{2}; CM kɛɛ^{3}
CN - LP kee^{5}; LM kee^{2}; WN cee^{2}; LC, PS, NM kee^{2}
N - Y ce^{2}; Sk kee^{6}

0092 - cheek, C2
SW - S kɛɛm^{3}; W, B, Sh kɛm^{3}; LNK kɛɛm^{5}; LCH, LMY kɛm^{3}; CM kɛɛm^{5}
CN - LP, LM, LC keem^{3}
N - Y cem^{3}; Sk keem^{3}; WM kem^{3}

0093 - how many, C2
SW - S kii^{2} (B2); W, B ki^{3}; LCH kii^{2}, kii^{3}; LMY kii^{1}, kii^{2}, kii^{3} (depending upon context); CM kii^{3}, kii^{4}
CN - LP, LM kii^{3}; WN cii^{3}; LC, PS kii^{3}; NM key^{2} (B2)
N - Y ki^{3}, ci^{3}; Sk kii^{3}; WM koy^{1} (A?); P kii^{3}

0094 - hoof (as of a horse), DL2
SW - S kiip^{2}; W kip^{2} 'hoof of a pig'; B, Sh kip^{2}; LNK, LCH, LMY kiip^{2}; CM kiip^{3}
CN - LP kip^{2} (DS2)
N - Sk liip^{5} (DL4)

0095 - middle, A2
SW - S klaaŋ^{1}; W, B, Sh kaaŋ^{1}; LNK kaaŋ^{2}; LCH, LMY kaaŋ^{1}; CM kaaŋ^{2}
CN - LP kyaaŋ^{2}; LM kyaaŋ^{1}; WN caaŋ^{1}; LC, PS, NM kyaaŋ^{1}
N - Y caaŋ^{1}; Sk tlaaŋ^{1} (OG), traaŋ^{1} (YG); WM klaaŋ^{1}; P caaŋ^{1}

0096 - near, C2
SW - S klay^{3}; W chaɰ^{3}; B saɰ^{3}; Sh kaɰ^{3}; LNK kay^{5}; LCH, LMY kay^{3}; CM kay^{5}
CN - LP caɰ^{3}; LM kyaɰ^{3}; WN chaɰ^{3}; LC, PS, NM khyaɰ^{3}
N - Y caɰ^{3}; Sk tlɤɤ^{3} (OG), trɤɤ^{3} (YG); WM klaɰ^{3}; P caɰ^{3}

0097 - fish scales, DS2
SW - S klet^{2}; W, B ket^{2}; Sh ket^{4}; LNK, LCH, LMY ket^{1}; CM ket^{2}
CN - LP kip^{2}; LM kip^{3}; WN cip^{6}; LC kit^{2}
N - Y cip^{3}, cap^{3}; Sk tlɛk^{4} (OG), trɛk^{4} (YG); WM klip^{5}; P cɛt^{2}

0098 - chaff, DL2
SW - S klɛɛp^{2}; W, B, Sh kɛp^{2}; LNK kɛɛp^{2}; CM kɛɛp^{3}
CN - LP ceep^{5}; LM leep^{5} (DL4); WN ðɛp^{5} (DL4); LC, PS, NM keep^{2}
N - Y rep^{5}; WM rip^{6} (DL4 in N languages)

0099 - salt, A2
SW - S klɯa^{1}; W kɤ^{1}; B kɯa^{1}; Sh kɤ^{1}; LNK kɯa^{2}; LCH, LMY kɤɤ^{1}; CM kɯa^{2}
CN - LP kɤɤ^{2}, cɤɤ^{2}; LM kyɯɯ^{1}; WN kɯɯ^{1}; LC, PS, NM kɯɯ^{1}
N - Y kua^{1}; Sk tlua^{1} (OG), trua^{1} (YG); WM klu^{1}; P cuu^{1}

0100 - hollow, A2
SW - S kluaŋ^{1}; W koŋ^{1} 'in, inside'; B kuaŋ^{1} 'in, inside'; Sh koŋ^{1}; LMY koŋ^{1} 'hollow object'; CM kuaŋ^{2}
CN - LM kyuuŋ^{1}; WN cuŋ^{1}

0101 - banana, C2
SW - S kluay^{3}; W koy^{3}; B kuay^{3}; Sh koy^{3}; LNK kuay^{5}; LCH, LMY koy^{3}; CM kuay^{5}
CN - LP kooy^{3}; LM kyuuy^{3}; WN kuy^{3}; LC, PS, NM kuuy^{3}
N - Y cuay^{3}, coy^{3}; WM klɤy^{3}; P cooy^{3}

0102 - to bend over, C2
SW - S kom^{3}; W kum^{3}; B, Sh kom^{3}; LNK kom^{5}; LCH, LMY kum^{3}; CM kom^{5}
CN - LP, LM kom^{3}; WN kam^{3}; LC kum^{3}; PS, NM kom^{3}
N - Sk kam^{3}

0103 - frog, DS2
SW - S, W, B kop^{2}; Sh kop^{4}; LNK, LCH, LMY kop^{1}; CM kop^{2}
CN - LP kop^{2}; LM kop^{3}; WN kap^{6}; LC kup^{2}; PS kop^{2}; NM kop^{1} (tone?)
N - Y kap^{3}; Sk kap^{4}; WM kop^{5}

0104 - also, then, C?
SW - S kɔ^{3}, kɔɔ^{3}; W kɔ^{6}; B kɔ^{3}; Sh kɔ^{3}, kɔ^{4}; LNK kɔɔ^{5}; LCH, LMY kɔɔ^{6}; CM kɔ^{4}
N - Y ko^{6}; WM kɤ^{1}; P koo^{3}

0105 - tree, plant, A2
SW - S kɔɔ^{1} 'clump, as of bamboo'; W, B, Sh kɔ^{1}; LNK kɔɔ^{2}; LCH, LMY kɔɔ^{1}; CM kɔɔ^{2} 'clump, as of bamboo'
CN - LP koo^{2}; LM, WN, LC, PS, NM koo^{1}
N - Y ko^{1}; Sk khoo^{6} (B1); WM kɤ^{1}; P koo^{1}

0106 - before, B2
SW - S kɔɔn^{2}; W kɤn^{2}; B, Sh kɔn^{2}; LNK kɔɔn^{3}; LCH, LMY kɔn^{2}; CM kɔɔn^{3}
CN - LP koon^{5}; LM koon^{2}; WN kɔn^{2}; LC, PS, NM koon^{2}
N - Y kon^{2}; Sk kɔɔn^{6}; WM kɤn^{5}; P koon^{5}

0107 - to snore, A2
SW - S kron^{1}; W (xɔ^{4}) kɯn^{1}; B (kɔ^{4}) kon^{1}; Sh khon^{1}; LNK kon^{2}; LCH, LMY xun^{1}; CM khon^{2}
CN - WN can^{1}
N - Sk tlɛn^{1} (OG), trɛn^{1}(YG)

0108 - shrimp, C2
SW - S, W, B, Sh kuŋ^{3}; LNK kuŋ^{5}; LCH, LMY kuŋ^{3}; CM kuŋ^{5}
CN - LP, LM koŋ^{3}; WN, LC kuŋ^{3}; PS, NM koŋ^{3}
N - Y kuŋ^{2}; Sk kuŋ^{6}; WM kuŋ^{5} (B2 in N languages)

0109 - deer, A2, (cf. 0782, 1034)
SW - S, W, B, Sh kwaaŋ^{1}; LNK kuaŋ^{2}; LCH, LMY kwaaŋ^{1}; CM kwaaŋ^{2}
CN - WN kaaŋ^{1}; LC kwaaŋ^{1}
N - Y vɯaŋ^{4}; Sk vuaŋ^{4} (A4 in N languages)

0110 - wide, C2
SW - S, W, B, Sh kwaaŋ^{3}; LNK kuaŋ^{5}; LCH, LMY kwaaŋ^{3}; CM kwaaŋ^{5}
CN - LP, LM kwaaŋ^{3}; WN kaaŋ^{3}; LC, PS, NM kwaaŋ^{3}
N - Y kwaaŋ^{2}; WM kwaaŋ^{5} (B2 in N languages)

0111 - to sweep, DL2
SW - S kwaat^{2}; W, B, Sh kwaat^{2} 'to rake up'; LNK kuat^{2}; LCH, LMY kwaat^{2}; CM kwaat^{3}
CN - LP kwaat^{5}; LM kwaat^{2}; WN kaat^{2}; PS, NM kwaat^{2} ('to rake up' in LP, LM, PS, NM)
N - Y kwaat^{2} 'to rake up'; Sk kwaat^{6} (OG), kuat^{6} (YG)

0112 - to kill, C1
SW - S khaa^{3}; W xaa^{3}; B, Sh khaa^{3}; LNK khaa^{4}; LCH, LMY xaa^{3}; CM khaa^{4}
CN - LP, LM, WN, LC, PS, NM khaa^{3}
N - Y ka^{3}; Sk, WM, P kaa^{3}

0113 - to engage in trade, C4
SW - S khaa^{4}; W, B kaa^{6}; Sh ka^{5}; LNK khaa^{5}; LCH, LMY, CM kaa^{6}
CN - LP khaa^{3}; LM, WN haa^{6}; PS kaa^{6}; NM haa^{6} (all 'to tell', perhaps none cognate)
N - Y ka^{6}; Sk khaa^{6}

0114 - to cross, C1
SW - S khaam^{3}; W xaam^{3}; B, Sh khaam^{3}; LNK khuam^{4} (modern khaam^{4}); LCH, LMY xaam^{3}; CM khaam^{5}
CN - LP, LM, WN, LC khaam^{3}
N - Y, Sk, WM, P haam^{3}

0115 - torn, DL1
SW - S khaat^{2}; W xaat^{2}; B, Sh, LNK khaat^{2}; LCH, LMY xaat^{2}; CM khaat^{3}
CN - LP, LM, WN, LC, PS, NM khaat^{2}
N - Y kaat^{2}; Sk kaat^{6}; WM, P kaat^{5}

0116 - rice, C1
SW - S khaaw^{3}; W, B, Sh khaw^{3}; LNK khaw^{4}; LCH, LMY xaw^{3}; CM khaw^{5}
CN - LP, LM, WN, LC, PS, NM khaw^{3}
N - Y haw^{6}; Sk ɣaw^{6}; WM xaw^{4}; P haw^{4} (C4 in N languages)

0117 - gold, A4, (cf. 0938)
SW - S kham^{1}; W xam^{4}; B kam^{4}; LNK kham^{6}; LCH, LMY xam^{4}; CM kham^{1}
N - Y cim^{1} (A2); Sk ɣam^{4}; WM kim^{1} (A2)

0118 - night, nightfall, B4, (cf. 0141)
SW - S kham^{3}; W xam^{5} 'afternoon, evening'; B kam^{5} 'afternoon, evening'; Sh, LNK kham^{3}; LCH, LMY xam^{5}; CM kham^{4}
CN - LP ham^{5}, kham^{5}; LM, WN ham^{5}; LC, PS kam^{5}; NM ŋam^{5}
N - Y ham^{5}; Sk ɣam^{5}; WM xam^{6}; P ham^{6}

0119 - to crow, A1
SW - S khan^{5}; W xan^{1}; B, Sh, LNK khan^{1}; LCH, LMY xan^{1}; CM khan^{2}
CN - LP, LM, WN, BV, LC, PS khan^{1}; NM han^{1}
N - Y han^{1}; Sk hal^{2} (OG), han^{2} (YG); WM, P han^{1}

0120 - to shut up, imprison, A1
SW - S khaŋ^{5}; W chaŋ^{1}; B saŋ^{1}; Sh, LNK khaŋ^{1}; LCH, LMY xaŋ^{1}; CM khaŋ^{2}
CN - LP haŋ^{1}; LM laŋ^{1}; WN chaŋ^{1}; BV, PS haŋ^{1}; NM khyaŋ^{1}
N - Y caŋ^{1}; Sk thraŋ^{2}; WM klaŋ^{1}; P caŋ^{1}

0121 - to chase, DS1, (cf. 0179)
SW - S khap^{2}; W chap^{2}; B sap^{2}; LNK khap^{1}; LCH, LMY xap^{1}; CM khap^{2}
CN - WN chap^{6} 'to call (someone) to come in a hurry'
N - Sk khap^{4} 'to drive (a car)'

0122 - knee, B1
SW - S khaw^{2}; W xaw^{2}; B, Sh khaw^{2}; LNK khaw^{3}; LCH, LMY xaw^{2}; CM khaw^{3}
CN - LP khaɰ^{2}; LM, WN, LC, PS khaw^{2}; NM hoo^{2}
N - Y ho^{2}; Sk kɔɔ^{6}; WM hɤ^{5}

0123 - to enter, C1
SW - S khaw^{3}; W xaw^{3}; B, Sh khaw^{3}; LNK khaw^{4}; LCH, LMY xaw^{3}; CM khaw^{5}
CN - LP, LM, WN, LC, PS khaw^{3}; NM haw^{3}
N - Y, Sk, WM, P haw^{3}

0124 - egg, B1
SW - S khay^{2}; W chay^{2}; B say^{2}; Sh khay^{2}; LNK khay^{3}; LCH, LMY xay^{2}; CM khay^{3}
CN - LP khyay^{2}; LM lay^{2}; WN chay^{2}; LC, PS, NM khyay^{2}
N - Y cay^{2}; WM ray^{5}; P cay^{5}

0125 - fever, C1
SW - S khay^{3}; W chay^{3}; B say^{3}; Sh khay^{3}; LNK khay^{4}; LCH, LMY xay^{3}; CM khay^{5}
CN - LP hay^{3}; LM lay^{3}; WN chay^{3}; LC, PS hay^{3}; NM khyay^{3}
N - Y cay^{3} 'illness'

0126 - to open, A1
SW - S khay^{5}; W, B khay^{1}; Sh khuy^{1}; LNK khay^{1}; LCH xay^{1}, xuy^{1}; LMY xay^{1}; CM khay^{2}
CN - LP, LM, WN, BV, LC, PS khay^{1}; NM hay^{1}
N - Y haay^{1}; Sk hay^{2}; WM kaay^{1} (Li says < Chinese); P haay^{1}

0127 - tallow, A1
SW - S khay^{5}; W xay^{1}; B, Sh, LNK khay^{1}; LCH, LMY xay^{1}; CM khay^{2}
CN - LM khay^{1}; WN chay^{1}
N - Sk khay^{1}

0128 - needle, A1
SW - S khem^{5}; W xim^{1}; B, Sh, LNK khem^{1}; LCH, LMY xim^{1}; CM khem^{2}
CN - LP, LM khim^{1}; WN cham^{1}; BV khem^{1}; LC, PS khim^{1}; NM hom^{4} (A4)
N - Y cim^{1}; Sk kim^{1}; WM šim^{1}; P cim^{1}

0129 - arm, A1
SW - S khɛɛn^{5}; W xɛn^{1}; B, Sh khɛn^{1}; LNK khɛɛn^{1}; LCH, LMY xɛn^{1}; CM khɛɛn^{2}
CN - LP, LM kheen^{1}; WN chen^{1}; BV khɛɛn^{1}; LC, NM kheen^{1}
N - Y cen^{1}; Sk keen^{1}; WM ken^{1}; P ceen^{1}

0130 - narrow, DL4
SW - S khɛɛp^{3}; W xɛp^{4}; B kɛp^{5}; Sh kɛp^{3}; LNK khɛɛp^{5}; CM khɛɛp^{4} 'border'
CN - LP, LM keep^{5}; LC kap^{4} keep^{4}; PS keep^{5}; NM keep^{2} (DL?)
N - Sk ɣeep^{5}

0131 - shin, lower leg, B4, (cf. 0501, 1150)
SW - S khɛη^{3}; W xɛη^{5}; B kɛη^{5}; LNK khɛɛη^{3}; LCH, LMY xɛη^{5}; CM khɛɛη^{4}
CN - LP heeη^{5}; LM, LC, PS keeη^{5}
N - Y heη^{5}; Sk ɣeeη^{5} 'foot'; WM xeη^{6}

0132 - small frog, DL1
SW - S khiat^{2}; W khet^{2}, khwet^{2}; B khiat^{2}; Sh khet^{2}; LNK khiat^{2}; LCH, LMY xeet^{2}; CM khiat^{3}
CN - LM viit^{2}; WN khit^{2}; PS, NM viit^{2}
N - Y kwe^{3}; Sk thrɛɛ^{3}; WM klwe^{3}; P kwɛɛ^{3} (C1?)

0133 - tooth, C1, (cf. 0456)
SW - S khiaw^{3} 'canine tooth'; W xɛw^{3}; B khɛw^{3}; Sh khew^{3}; LNK khɛɛw^{4}; LCH, LMY xew^{3}; CM khiaw^{5}
CN - LP, LM, LC, PS kheew^{3}; NM heew^{3}
N - Y hew^{3}; P heew^{3}

0134 - to chew, C4
SW - S khiaw^{4}; W, B kɛw^{6}; Sh kew^{5}; LNK khiaw^{5}; LCH, LMY kew^{6}; CM kiaw^{6}
CN - LP kheew^{3}; LM, PS, NM keew^{6}
N - Y cew^{6}

0135 - green, A1
SW - S khiaw^{5}; W xɛw^{1}; B khɛw^{1}; Sh khew^{1}; LNK khiaw^{1}; LCH, LMY xew^{1}; CM khiaw^{2}
CN - LP, LM kheew^{1}; WN chiw^{1}; BV khew^{1}; LC, PS, NM kheew^{1}
N - Y hew^{1}; Sk heew^{2}; WM hew^{1}; P heew^{1}

0136 - unpleasantly pungent, A1
SW - S khiaw^{5}; W, B khiw^{1}; Sh khew^{1}; LNK khiw^{1}; LCH, LMY xiw^{2} (B1?); CM khiw^{3} (B1?)
CN - LP, LM khiiw^{1}; WN chiw^{1}; BV khew^{1}; LC, PS, NM khiiw^{1}
N - Sk khiiw^{2} (OG), khiw^{2} (YG)

0137 - to ride, B1
SW - S khii^{2}; W, B khi^{2}, khwi^{2}; Sh khi^{2}; LNK khii^{3}; LCH, LMY xii^{2}; CM khii^{3}
CN - LP khwii^{2}; LM khwey^{2}; WN khii^{2}; LC, PS khwii^{2}; NM khwey^{2}
N - Y kɯay^{5} (B4); Sk khooy^{5}, khoy^{5} (fast speech) (B4); WM kɯy^{5} (B1?); P kɯɯy^{6} (B4)

0138 - pliers, tongs, A4
SW - S khiim^{1}; W, B, Sh kim^{4}; LNK khiim^{6}; LCH, LMY kim^{4}; CM kiim^{1}
CN - LP khim^{4}; LM kim^{4}; WN cim^{4}; LC, PS kim^{4}; NM kiim^{4}
N - Y kim^{4}, cim^{4}; Sk khiim^{4}; WM kim^{2}

0139 - to take hold of with tongs, claws, DL4, (cf. 0604)
SW - S khiip^{3}; W kip^{4}; B kip^{5}; Sh kip^{3}; LNK khiip^{5}; LCH, LMY kiip^{5}; CM kiip^{4}

0140 - to scratch, DL1, (cf. 0802)
SW - S khiit^{2}; W, B, Sh khit^{2}; LNK khiit^{2}; LMY xiit^{2}; CM khiit^{3}
N - Sk khiit^{6}

0141 - night, A4, (cf. 0118)
SW - S khɯɯn^{1}; W xɯn^{4}; B kɯn^{4}; Sh khɯn^{4}; LNK khɯɯn^{6}; LCH, LMY xɯn^{4}; CM khɯɯn^{1}
CN - LP, LM hɤn^{4}; WN khɯn^{4}, hɯn^{4}; LC, PS kɤn^{4}; NM hen^{4}
N - Y hɯn^{4}; Sk ɣɯn^{4}; WM xɯn^{2}; P hɯn^{2}

0142 - measure from the thumb to the fingertip, DL4
SW - S khɯɯp^{3}; W xɯp^{4}; B kɯp^{5}; Sh khɯp^{3}; LNK khɯɯp^{5}; LCH, LMY xɯɯp^{5}; CM khɯɯp^{4}
CN - WN hup^{5}
N - Y hup^{1} (DS4), cip^{3} (DS2); Sk khɯɯp^{5}

0143 - to go up, C1
SW - S khɯn^{3}; W xɯn^{3}; B, Sh khɯn^{3}; LNK khɯn^{4}; LCH, LMY xɯn^{3}; CM khɯn^{5}
CN - LP, LM khɤn^{3}; WN khɯn^{3}; LC khɤn^{3}; PS khin^{3}; NM hen^{3}
N - Y, Sk, WM, P hɯn^{3}

0144 - to crawl, A4, (cf. 0347)
SW - S khlaan^{1}; W, B caan^{4}; Sh, LMY kaan^{4}; CM kaan^{1}
CN - LM laan^{4}; WN caan^{4}; LC, NM kyaan^{4}
N - Y rɯan^{4} (also, caan^{4} 'to limp; crippled'; which is cognate?); Sk luan^{4}

0145 - person, human being, A4, (cf. 0658)
SW - S khon^{1}; W kun^{4}; B, Sh kon^{4}; LNK khon^{6}; LCH, LMY kun^{4}; CM khon^{1}
CN - LP khɤn^{4}; LM kɤn^{4}; WN kɔn^{4}; LC, PS kɤn^{4}; NM ken^{4}
N - Y, Sk hun^{4}; WM xun^{2}; P hɯn^{2}

0146 - to bite, DS1, (cf. 801)
SW - S, W, B khop^{2}; Sh khop^{4}; LNK khop^{1}; LCH, LMY xop^{1}; CM khop^{2}
CN - LP khop^{2}; LM khop^{3}; WN khap^{6}; PS khop^{2}; NM khop^{1} (tone?)
N - Y hap^{1}; Sk ɣap^{6}, khop^{4} (latter said to be < Lao); WM xap^{6}; P hap^{3} (DS4 in N languages)

0147 - crooked, DS4, (cf. 0967)
SW - S khot^{4}; W kot^{4}; B, Sh kot^{5}; LNK khot^{3}; LMY kot^{5}; CM kot^{6}
CN - LP khot^{4}; LM kot^{3} (DS2?); WN, LC kut^{4}; PS kot^{4}
N - Sk khot^{6}; P kut^{2} (DS2)

0148 - neck, A4
SW - S khɔɔ^{1}; W xɔ^{4}; B kɔ^{4}; Sh khɔ^{4}; LNK khɔɔ^{6}; LCH, LMY xɔɔ^{4}; CM khɔɔ^{1}
CN - LP, LM, WN hoo^{4}; LC, PS koo^{4}; NM hoo^{4}
N - Y ho^{4}; Sk ɣɔɔ^{4}; WM xɤ^{2}

0149 - to beg, A1
SW - S khɔɔ^{5}; W chɔ^{1}; B sɔ^{1}; Sh khɔ^{1}; LNK khɔɔ^{1}; LCH, LMY xɔɔ^{1};
CM khɔɔ^{2}
CN - LP, LM, LC, PS hoo^{1}; NM khyoo^{1}
N - Sk thrɔɔ^{2}

0150 - a pen for animals, DL4
SW - S khɔɔk^{3}; W xɔ^{4}; B kɔʔ^{5}; Sh khɔk^{3}; LNK khɔɔk^{5}; CM khɔɔk^{4}
CN - LP, LM hook^{5}; PS kook^{5}
N - Sk ɣɔɔk^{5}; WM klɤk^{5} (DL?)

0151 - hammer, C4
SW - S khɔɔn^{4}; W xɔn^{6} 'hammer; to beat'; B kɔn^{6}; Sh khɔn^{5}; LNK khɔɔn^{5}; LMY
xɔn^{6}; CM khɔɔn^{6}
CN - LP khoon^{3} 'to beat'; LM hoon^{6} 'to beat'; WN hun^{6} thii^{1} 'hammer';
LC koon^{6} 'to beat'
N - Y hon^{6}; Sk ɣɔɔl^{6} (OG), ɣɔɔn^{6} (YG)

0152 - thing: of, A1
SW - S khɔɔŋ^{5}; W xɔŋ^{1}; B, Sh khɔŋ^{1}; LNK khɔɔŋ^{1}; LCH, LMY xɔŋ^{1};
CM khɔɔŋ^{2}
CN - LP khooŋ^{1}
N - Sk hɔɔŋ^{2}

0153 - fish basket, C1
SW - S khɔŋ^{3}; W chɔŋ^{3}; B sɔŋ^{3}; Sh khɔŋ^{3}; LNK khɔɔŋ^{4}; CM khɔɔŋ^{5}
CN - LP ɬooŋ^{3}; LM looŋ^{3}; LC khooŋ^{3} 'kind of basket'
N - WM klɤŋ^{5} (B1)

0154 - gradually, slowly, carefully, B4
SW - S khɔy^{3}; W, B kɔy^{5}; Sh kɔy^{3}; LCH, LMY kɔy^{5}; CM kɔy^{4}
CN - LP khooy^{5}; LM kooy^{5}; WN kɔy^{5}; LC kooy^{5}

0155 - lazy, C4, (cf. 0815)
SW - S khraan^{4}; W, B caan^{6}; Sh khaan^{5}; LNK (khii^{4}) khaan^{5}; LCH, LMY xaan^{6};
CM khaan^{6}
CN - LP kyaan^{3}; LM laan^{6}; WN caan^{6}; LC, PS, NM kyaan^{6}

0156 - to moan, A4
SW - S khraaŋ^{1}; W, B caaŋ^{4}; Sh khaaŋ^{4}; LCH xaŋ^{4}, xaaŋ^{4}; LMY xaŋ^{4};
CM khaaŋ^{1}
CN - LM laaŋ^{4}; NM taaŋ^{4}
N - Sk reeŋ^{1} (A1, probably not cognate)

0157 - who, A?
SW - S khray^{1} (A4); W phaɰ^{5} (B4); B faɰ^{1} (A1); Sh phaɰ^{1} (A1), phaɰ^{2}; LNK, LCH, LMY phay^{1} (A1); CM phay^{2} (A1)
CN - LP caɰ^{4}; LC naɰ^{4} (A4 in CN languages)
N - WM praɰ^{2} (A4)

0158 - lemongrass, A4
SW - S (tă^{2}) khray^{4} (C4); W (hɔm^{1}) caɰ^{4}; B (fak^{2}) caɰ^{4}; LCH (să-) xay^{4}; LMY (că-) xay^{4}; CM (cak^{6}) khay^{1}
N - Sk (că^{6}) thrɤɤ^{4}, (că^{6}) phrɤɤ^{4}

0159 - utensils, tools, equipment, B4
SW - S khrɯaŋ^{3}; W cɤŋ^{5}; B cɯaŋ^{5}; Sh khɤŋ^{3}; LNK khɯaŋ^{3}; LCH, LMY xɤŋ^{5}; CM khɯaŋ^{4}
CN - LM lɯɯŋ^{5}
N - Sk thrɯaŋ^{5}

0160 - mortar, DS4
SW - S khrok^{4}; W cok^{4}; B cok^{5}; Sh khok^{5}; LNK khok^{3}; LCH, LMY xok^{5}; CM khok^{6}
CN - LP chok^{4}; LM lok^{4}; WN cɔk^{4}; LC kyuk^{4}
N - Y cok^{1}

0161 - to scrape, DL1
SW - S khuut^{2}; W xut^{2}; B, Sh khut^{2}; LNK khuut^{2}; LCH, LMY xuut^{2}; CM khuut^{3}
N - Sk hut^{4} (DS1), khuut^{6} (DL1)

0162 - turbid, B1, (cf. 0954)
SW - S, W khun^{2}; B khun^{2} 'dust'; Sh khun^{2}; LNK khun^{3}; LCH, LMY xun^{2}; CM khun^{3}
CN - LP, LM, PS khon^{2} 'fertilizer'; NM hon^{2} 'fertilizer'
N - Sk khun^{2}

0163 - to dig, DS1
SW - S, W, B khut^{2}; Sh khut^{4}; LNK khut^{1}; LCH, LMY xut^{1}; CM khut^{2}
CN - LP hot^{5} (DS4); LM khot^{4} (DS4); WN khut^{6}; LC kut^{4} (DS4); PS kot^{4} (DS4); NM khot^{4}
N - Y hut^{1}, kut^{1}; Sk khut^{6}; P hut^{3} (DS4 in N languages)

0164 - right (hand), A1
SW - S khwaa^{5}; W xwaa^{1}; B, Sh khwaa^{1}; LNK khua^{1}; LCH kwaa^{1}; LMY kwaa^{1} (rare xwaa^{1}); CM khwaa^{2}
CN - LP ɬaa^{1}; LM, WN saa^{1}; LC, PS ɬaa^{1}; NM kwaa^{4} (A4)
N - Y kwa^{4}; Sk khwaa^{4} (OG), khua^{4} (YG); WM kwaa^{2}; P kwaa^{2} (A4 in N languages)

0165 - matter, affair, A4
SW - S khwaam^{1}; W xaam^{4} 'word, language'; B kwaam^{4} 'word, language'; Sh kwaam^{4} 'word, language'; LNK khuam^{6}; LCH, LMY kwaam^{4}, xwaam^{4}; CM khwaam^{1}
CN - LP vaam^{4} 'language'; LM vaam^{4} 'sentence, word, language'; LC vaam^{4} 'sentence'; PS, NM vaam^{4} 'language'

0166 - to throw, B4
SW - S khwaaŋ^{3}; W xwaaŋ^{5}; B kwaaŋ^{5}; LNK khuaŋ^{3}; LCH, LMY xwaaŋ^{5}; CM khwaaŋ^{4}

0167 - water buffalo, A4
SW - S khwaay^{1}; W xwaay^{4}; B, Sh kwaay^{4}; LNK khuay^{6}; LCH kwaay^{4}, xwaay^{4}; LMY kwaay^{4}; CM khwaay^{1}
CN - LP, LM, WN vaay^{4}; BV vaay^{3}; LC, PS, NM vaay^{4}
N - Y, Sk vaay^{4}; WM xwaay^{2}; P vaay^{2}

0168 - to hang up, A1
SW - S khwɛɛn^{5}; W xwɛn^{1}; B khwɛn^{1}; Sh khɛn^{1}; LNK khɛɛn^{1}; LCH kwɛn^{1}; LMY kwɛn^{1}, xwɛn^{1}; CM khwɛɛn^{2}
CN - LM khween^{1}; WN khen^{1}
N - Y ven^{1}; Sk veen^{2}; WM wen^{3} (C?)

0169 - (to lie) face down, C1
SW - S khwam^{3}; W xam^{3}; B khwam^{3}; Sh khwam^{3}, kɔm^{3}; LNK khuam^{4}; LCH, LMY xɔm^{3}; CM khuam^{5}
CN - LP kham^{3}; LM khom^{3}; WN kham^{3}; LC khum^{3} 'upside down'
N - Y ham^{3}; Sk ŋam^{3}; P hɔm^{3}

0170 - smoke, A4
SW - S khwan^{1}; W xwan^{4}, xɔn^{4}; B kwan^{4}; Sh kwaan^{4}, kɔn^{4}, kan^{4}; LNK khuan^{6}; LCH kɔn^{4}, xɔn^{4}; LMY kwan^{4}; CM khwan^{1}
CN - LP, LM, LC, PS, NM van^{4}
N - Sk ɣɔn^{4}; WM xon^{2}; P hɔn^{2}

0171 - whorl in the hair; spirit, A1
SW - S khwan^{5}; W xwan^{1}, xɔn^{1}; B khwan^{1}; Sh khwan^{1}, khɔn^{1}; LNK khuan^{1}; LCH xwan^{1}; LMY kwan^{1}; CM khwan^{2}
CN - LP, LM khwan^{1}; WN khɔn^{1}; LC, PS khwan^{1}
N - Y van^{1}; Sk hɔn^{2}; P hɔn^{1}

0172 - to pull, drag, DL4
SW - S laak^{3}; W laa^{4}; B laaʔ^{5}; Sh laak^{3}; LNK, LCH, LMY laak^{5}; CM laak^{4}
CN - LP, LM, WN laak^{5}; LC laak^{4}; PS, NM laak^{5}
N - Y raak^{5}, laak^{5}; WM raak^{6}; P laak^{6}

0173 - to destroy, C4
SW - S laaŋ^{4}; W, B maaŋ^{6}; LNK maaŋ^{5}; LMY, CM maaŋ^{6}

0174 - stripe, design, mark, A4
SW - S laay^{1}; W, B, Sh laay^{4}; LNK laay^{6}; LCH, LMY laay^{4}; CM laay^{1}
CN - LP, LM, WN, LC laay^{4}
N - Y raay^{4}; Sk laay^{4}; WM raay^{2}; P laay^{2}

0175 - many, much, A1
SW - S laay^{5}; W, B laay^{1}; Sh laay^{1} 'how many?'; LNK, LCH, LMY laay^{1}; CM laay^{2}
CN - LP, LM, WN laay^{1}; BV laay^{2}; LC, PS, NM laay^{1}
N - Y laay^{1}; Sk laay^{2}; WM, P laay^{1}

0176 - to steal, DS4
SW - S, W lak^{4}; B, Sh lak^{5}; LNK lak^{3}; LCH, LMY lak^{5}; CM lak^{6}
CN - LP, LM, WN, LC, PS, NM lak^{4}
N - Y rak^{1}; Sk lak^{6}; P lak^{3}

0177 - to close (the eyes), DS1
SW - S, W, B lap^{2}; Sh lap^{4}; LNK, LCH, LMY lap^{1}; CM lap^{2}
CN - LP lap^{2}; LM lap^{3}; WN lap^{6}; LC, PS lap^{2}; NM lap^{4}
N - Y lap^{3}; WM lap^{5}; P lap^{2}

0178 - liquor, C1
SW - S, W, B, Sh law^{3}; LNK law^{4}; LCH, LMY law^{3}; CM law^{5}
CN - LP, LM, WN, LC, PS, NM law^{3}
N - Y, Sk, WM, P law^{3}

0179 - to chase, B4, (cf. 0121)
SW - S lay^{3}; W, B lay^{5}; LNK lay^{3}; LCH, LMY lay^{5}; CM lay^{4}
CN - LM ley^{5}; WN lay^{5} 'to inspect (water in ditches)' (cognate?); LC lay^{5} 'to put' (cognate?)
N - Y, Sk lay^{5}; P lay^{6}

0180 - to flow, A1
SW - S lay^{5}; W, B, Sh, LNK, LCH, LMY lay^{1}; CM lay^{2}
CN - LP, LM, WN, LC, PS, NM lay^{1}
N - Y lay^{1}

0181 - great-grandchild, A1
SW - S leen^{5}; W lin^{1}; B len^{1}; Sh lin^{1}; LNK leen^{1}; LCH, LMY lin^{1}; CM leen^{2}, len^{2}
CN - LP, LM lin^{3}; WN lan^{3}; PS lin^{3}; NM len^{3} (C1 in CN languages)
N - Sk leen^{1}, leen^{2}; P lan^{3} (C1?)

0182 - liquid, soft, A1
SW - S leew^{5}; W, B lɛw^{1}; Sh lɛw^{1} 'bruised, reduced to particles', lɛw^{3} 'thin, as a liquid'; LNK lɛɛw^{1}; LCH, LMY lɛw^{1}; CM lɛɛw^{2}
CN - LP liiw^{1}; LM niiw^{1}; WN lɛw^{1}; LC liiw^{1} 'thin (liquid)'
N - Sk lɛɛw^{1}

0183 - iron (the metal), DS1, (cf. 0847)
SW - S, W, B lek^{2}; Sh lek^{4}; LNK, LCH, LMY lek^{1}; CM lek^{2}
CN - LP lik^{2}; LM lyak^{3}; WN lɛk^{6}; LC, PS lik^{2}; NM lek^{4} (lɤk^{4}?)
N - P lɛk^{2}

0184 - to play, C1, (cf. 1090)
SW - S len^{3}; W din^{3}; B lin^{3}; Sh len^{3}; LNK len^{4}; LCH din^{3}; LMY lin^{3}; CM len^{5}

0185 - fingernail, toenail, DS4
SW - S, W lep^{4}; B lep^{5}; Sh nep^{5}; LNK lep^{3}; LCH, LMY lep^{5}; CM lep^{6}
CN - LP lip^{4}; LM lyap^{3} (DS1, rare lyap^{4}); WN lɛp^{4}; LC, PS, NM lip^{4}
N - Y rit^{1}; Sk liip^{5} (DL4); WM rip^{6}; P lit^{3}

0186 - evening meal, A4
SW - S lɛɛŋ^{1}; W, B lɛŋ^{4}; LNK lɛɛŋ^{6}; LCH, LMY lɛŋ^{4} 'meal at 2 or 3 P.M.'; CM lɛɛŋ^{1}
CN - LP, LM leeŋ^{4}; WN leŋ^{4}; LC, PS, NM leeŋ^{4} ('meal at noon, lunch' for all six languages)
N - Y riŋ^{4}; Sk lɛɛŋ^{4}; WM riŋ^{2}; P liŋ^{2}

0187 - to raise, feed, C4, (cf. 0955)
SW - S liaŋ^{4}; W leŋ^{6}; B liaŋ^{6}; Sh leŋ^{5}; LNK liaŋ^{5}; LCH, LMY leŋ^{6}; CM liaŋ^{6}
CN - WN liŋ^{5} (B4?)
N - Sk liaŋ^{6}

0188 - to dodge, avoid, DL1
SW - S liik^{2}; W liʔ^{2}; B niʔ^{2}; Sh lik^{2}; LNK liik^{2}; LCH liik^{2}

0189 - tongue, C4
SW - S lin^{4}; W, B lin^{6}; Sh, LNK lin^{5}; LCH, LMY, CM lin^{6}
CN - LP lin^{3}; LM, WN, LC, PS lin^{6}; NM len^{6}
N - Y lin^{6}; Sk liin^{6}; WM, P lin^{4}

0190 - to choose, DL4
SW - S lɯak^{3}; W lɤ^{4}; B lɯaʔ^{5}; Sh lɤk^{3}; LNK lɯak^{5}; LCH, LMY lɤɤk^{5}; CM lɯak^{4}
CN - LP lɤɤk^{5}; LM lɯɯk^{5}; WN lɤk^{5}; LC lɤɤk^{4}; PS lɤɤk^{5}; NM lɯɯk^{5}
N - Y le^{5}

0191 - blood, DL4
SW - S lɯat^{3}; W lɤt^{4}; B lɯat^{5}; Sh lɤt^{3}; LNK lɯat^{5}; LCH, LMY lɤɤt^{5}; CM lɯat^{4}
CN - LP lɤɤt^{5}; LM lɯɯt^{5}; WN lɤt^{5}; LC lɤɤt^{4}; PS lɤɤt^{5}; NM lɯɯt^{5}
N - Y lɯat^{5}; Sk luat^{5}; WM lɯat^{6}; P lɯɯt^{6}

0192 - a saw, to saw, B4, (0940)
SW - S lɯay^{3}; W kɯ^{5}; B kɯa^{5}; Sh lɤ^{3}; LNK lɯay^{3}; LCH, LMY lɤɤ^{5};
CM lɯay^{6} (C4)
N - Sk lɯay^{6} (C4)

0193 - to forget, A4
SW - S lɯɯm^{1}; W, B, Sh lɯm^{4}; LNK lɯɯm^{6}; LCH, LMY lɯm^{4}; CM lɯɯm^{1}
CN - LP, LM lom^{4}; WN lum^{4}; LC lum^{4}
N - Y lum^{4}; WM, P lum^{2}

0194 - to open (the eyes), A4
SW - S lɯɯm^{1}; W, B, Sh mɯn^{4}; LNK mɯɯn^{6}; LCH, LMY mɯn^{4}; CM mɯɯn^{1}
CN - WN men^{4}
N - Sk mlɔɔn^{4}

0195 - slippery, smooth, B4, (cf. 0813)
SW - S lɯɯn^{3}; W, B mɯn^{5}; Sh mɯn^{3}; LNK mɯɯn^{3}; LCH, LMY mɯn^{5};
CM mɯɯn^{4}
CN - LP lɤɤn^{5}; LM lɯɯn^{2} (B?), lɯɯn^{3} (C?), lɤn^{5} 'to slide'; LC, PS lɤɤn^{2} (B?)
N - Sk mlɯɯl^{5} (OG), mlɯɯn^{5} (YG), mlɯl^{5} (OG), mlɯn^{5} (YG)

0196 - deep, DS4
SW - S lɯk^{4}; W lɤk^{4}; B lɯk^{5}, lɤk^{5}; Sh lɯk^{5}; LNK lɤk^{3} (modern lɯk^{3}); LCH,
LMY lɯk^{5}; CM lɤk^{6}
CN - LP dak^{2}; LM nak^{3}; WN dak^{6}; LC, PS dak^{2}; NM lak^{4} (DS3 in CN
languages)
N - Y lak^{1}; Sk, WM lak^{6}

0197 - spool, DL1, (cf. 0896)
SW - S lɔɔt^{2}; W, B lɔt^{2}; Sh lɔt^{2} 'conduit, pipe'; LNK lɔɔt^{2} 'drinking straw';
LCH, LMY lɔɔt^{2}; CM lɔɔt^{3}
CN - LP, LM loot^{2} 'shuttle'; WN lɔt^{2}; LC, PS loot^{2} 'shuttle'
N - Sk luut^{6}; WM lut^{5}

0198 - to float, A4, (cf. 0787)
SW - S lɔɔy^{1}; W, B lɔy^{4} 'to swim'; Sh lɔy^{4} 'to rinse'; LNK lɔɔy^{6} 'to swim';
LMY lɔy^{4} 'to float; to swim'; CM lɔɔy^{1}

0199 - to scald, DL4
SW - S luak^{3}; W lo^{4}; B luaʔ^{5}; LNK luak^{5}; LCH, LMY look^{5}; CM luak^{4}
CN - LP, LM luuk^{5}; LC luuk^{4}; PS, NM luuk^{5}
N - Y luk^{3} (DS1); Sk luak^{5} (but nam^{6} lɔɔk^{5} 'hot water')

0200 - big, A1, (cf. 0396, 0765)
SW - S luaŋ^{5} (also, 'royal'); W loŋ^{1}; B luaŋ^{1}; Sh loŋ^{1}; LNK luaŋ^{1}; LCH, LMY loŋ^{1}; CM luaŋ^{2}
CN - LP looŋ^{1} (luuŋ^{1}?); LM luuŋ^{1}; BV luuŋ^{2}; LC, PS, NM luuŋ^{1}
N - Sk luaŋ^{2}

0201 - (one's) child, DL4, (cf. 0439)
SW - S luuk^{3}; W lu^{4}; B luʔ^{5}; Sh luk^{3}; LNK, LCH, LMY luuk^{5}; CM luuk^{4}
CN - LP, LM lok^{5}; WN luk^{5}; LC luk^{4}; PS lok^{5}; NM laak^{5}
N - Y lɯk^{1}; Sk lɯk^{6}; WM lɯk^{6}; P lɯk^{3} (DS4 in N languages)

0202 - to stroke, DL4
SW - S luup^{3}; W lup^{4}; B lup^{5}; Sh lup^{3}; LNK, LMY luup^{5}; CM luup^{4}
CN - LP, LM lop^{5}; WN lup^{4} (DS4); PS lop^{5}; NM luup^{5}
N - Y rup^{1} (DS4); Sk luup^{5}; P lup^{3} (DS4)

0203 - to come, A4
SW - S maa^{1}; W, B, Sh maa^{4}; LNK maa^{6}; LCH, LMY maa^{4}; CM maa^{1}
CN - LP, LM, WN, LC, PS, NM maa^{4}
N - Y ma^{1}; Sk maa^{2} 'to return'; WM, P maa^{1} (A1 in N languages)

0204 - horse, C4
SW - S maa^{4}; W, B maa^{6}; Sh ma^{5}; LNK maa^{5}; LCH, LMY, CM maa^{6}
CN - LP maa^{3}; LM, WN, LC, PS, NM maa^{6}
N - Y ma^{6}; Sk maa^{6}; WM, P maa^{4}

0205 - dog, A1
SW - S maa^{5}; W, B, Sh, LNK, LCH, LMY maa^{1}; CM maa^{2}
CN - LP, LM, WN maa^{1}; BV maa^{2}; LC, PS, NM maa^{1}
N - Y ma^{1}; Sk maa^{2}; WM, P maa^{1}

0206 - fruit, DL1
SW - S maak^{2} 'areca'; W, B maaʔ^{2}; Sh maak^{2}; LNK, LCH, LMY maak^{2} (but in Lue usually pronounced as a syllabic [m^{2}] in ordinary speech); CM maak^{3} 'areca'
CN - LP, LM, WN, LC, PS, NM maak^{2}
N - Y maak^{2}; Sk maak^{6}; WM maak^{5}

0207 - widowed, C1
SW - S, W, B, Sh maay^{3}; LNK maay^{4}; LCH, LMY maay^{3}; CM maay^{5}
CN - LP, LM, WN, LC, PS, NM maay^{3}
N - Y maay^{2}; Sk maay^{6}; WM maay^{5} (B1 in N languages)

0208 - wood, C4
SW - S maay^{4}; W, B may^{6}; Sh, LNK may^{5}; LCH, LMY, CM may^{6}
CN - LP may^{3}; LM, WN may^{6}; LC may^{6} 'tree'; PS, NM may^{6}
N - Y, Sk may^{6}; WM fay^{4}; P may^{4}

0209 - flea, DS1
SW - S, W, B mat^{2}; Sh mat^{4}; LNK, LCH, LMY mat^{1}; CM mat^{2}
CN - LP mat^{2}; LM mat^{3}; WN mat^{6}; LC, PS mat^{2}; NM mat^{4}
N - Y mat^{3}; Sk mat^{4}; WM mat^{5}; P mat^{2}

0210 - to tie up; a bundle, DS4, (cf. 0659, 0839)
SW - S, W mat^{4}; B, Sh, LCH, LMY mat^{5}; CM mat^{6}
CN - WN mat^{4}

0211 - new, B1
SW - S may^{2}; W, B, Sh maɰ^{2}; LNK may^{3}; LCH, LMY may^{2}; CM may^{3}
CN - LP, LM, WN, LC, PS, NM maɰ^{2}
N - Y mo^{2}; Sk mɔɔ^{6}; WM mɤ^{5}; P moo^{5}

0212 - to burn (intransitive), C1, (cf. 0638)
SW - S, W, B, Sh may^{3}; LNK may^{4}; LCH, LMY may^{3}; CM may^{5}
CN - LP, LM, WN, LC, PS, NM may^{3}

0213 - a seed, grain, DS4, (cf. 0457, 0943)
SW - S met^{4}, mă^{4} let^{4}; W mit^{4}; B mit^{5}; Sh met^{5}; LNK met^{3}; LCH, LMY met^{5}; CM met^{6}
CN - LM, WN mat^{4}
N - Y nat^{1}; Sk mlɛk^{6} (less frequent mlɛt^{6}); WM nat^{6}; P nɛt^{3}

0214 - mother, B4
SW - S mɛɛ^{3}; W, B mɛ^{5}; Sh mɛ^{3}; LNK mɛɛ^{3}; LCH mee^{5}; LMY mɛɛ^{3}; CM mɛɛ^{4}
CN - LP, LM, WN, LC, PS, NM mee^{5}
N - Y me^{5}; Sk mee^{5}; WM me^{5} (B?); P mee^{6}

0215 - insect, A4
SW - S mɛɛŋ^{1}, mă^{4} lɛɛŋ^{1}; W, B, Sh mɛŋ^{4}; LNK mɛɛŋ^{6}; LCH, LMY mɛŋ^{4}; CM mɛɛŋ^{1}
CN - LP, LM meeŋ^{4}; WN meŋ^{4}; LC, PS, NM meeŋ^{4}
N - Y neŋ^{4} 'mosquito'; Sk mɛɛŋ^{4}; WM neŋ^{2}; P neeŋ^{2}

0216 - a bear, A1
SW - S mii^{5}; W, B, Sh mi^{1}; LNK mii^{1}; LCH, LMY mii^{1}, mii^{1} mɤy^{1}; CM mii^{2}
CN - LP mii^{1}; LM mey^{1}; WN mɯy^{1}; BV mii^{2}; LC, PS mii^{1}; NM mey^{1}
N - Y mɯay^{1}; Sk mii^{2} (said to be < Lao or Siamese), mɯay^{2}, mɤɤy^{2}; WM mɯy^{1}

0217 - wife, A4, (cf. 0737, 0876)
SW - S mia^{1}; W me^{4}; B mia^{4}; Sh me^{4}; LNK mia^{6}; LCH, LMY mee^{4}; CM mia^{1}
CN - WN mii^{4}

0218 - knife, DL4
SW - S miit^{3}; W mit^{4}; B mit^{5}; Sh mit^{3}; LNK, LCH, LMY miit^{5}; CM miit^{4}
CN - LM miit^{5}; WN mit^{5} 'razor'
N - Y mit^{1}; WM mit^{6}; P mit^{3} (DS4 in N languages)

0219 - hand, A4
SW - S mɯɯ^{1}; W, B, Sh mɯ^{4}; LNK mɯɯ^{6}; LCH, LMY mɯɯ^{4}; CM mɯɯ^{1}
CN - LP mɤɤ^{4}; LM mɤɰ^{4}; WN mɯŋ^{4}; BV mɯɯ^{3}; LC, PS mɯɯ^{4}; NM maɰ^{4}
N - Y fɯŋ^{4}; Sk mɯɯ^{4}; WM faɰ^{2}, fɯŋ^{2}; P fɯŋ^{2}

0220 - a meal, C4
SW - S mɯɯ^{4}; W, B mɯ^{6} 'day'; Sh mɯ^{5} 'day, not used alone'; LNK mɯɯ^{5} 'day'; LCH, LMY mɯɯ^{6} 'day'; CM mɯɯ^{6} 'a turn'
CN - WN mɯɯ^{6} 'a meal, a time'
N - Y fɯ^{6} 'meal'; Sk mɯɯ^{6} 'day'

0221 - city, a country, A4
SW - S mɯaŋ^{1}; W mɤŋ^{4}; B mɯaŋ^{4}; Sh mɤŋ^{4}; LNK mɯaŋ^{6}; LCH, LMY mɤŋ^{4}; CM mɯaŋ^{1}
CN - WN mɯŋ^{4}
N - Y pɯaŋ^{4} (but mɯaŋ^{4} in place names); Sk phiaŋ^{4}

0222 - stiff and tired, B4
SW - S mɯay^{3}; W mɤy^{5}; B mɯay^{5}; Sh moy^{3}; LNK mɯay^{3}; LMY mɤy^{5}; CM mɯay^{4}
CN - WN mɯy^{5}
N - Y mɯay^{5}

0223 - dark, DL4
SW - S mɯɯt^{3}; W mɯt^{4}; B mɯt^{5}; Sh mɯt^{5}, mɯt^{4} (DS?); LNK, LCH, LMY mɯɯt^{5}; CM mɯɯt^{4}

0224 - ink, DS4
SW - S mɯk^{2} (DS?); W mɯk^{4}; B mɯk^{5}; Sh (nam^{5}) mɯk^{5}; LNK, LMY mɯk^{1} (DS?); CM mɯk^{3} (DL?)
CN - LP, LM mɤk^{4}; WN mak^{4}; LC, PS mɤk^{4}; NM mak^{4}
N - Y mak^{1}; Sk mɯk^{6}; WM mak^{6}

0225 - all, all gone, DS1, (cf. 1020)
SW - S mot^{2}; W, B met^{2}; Sh mot^{4}; LNK mɤt^{1} (modern mot^{1}); LCH, LMY mot^{1}; CM mot^{2}
C - LM mɤt^{4} (DS4)
N - Y mɯat^{5} (DL4, cognate?); Sk mɔt^{4} 'clean'

0226 - ant, DS 4
SW - S, W mot^{4}; B, Sh mot^{5}; LNK mot^{3}; LCH, LMY mot^{5}; CM mot^{6}
CN - LP mot^{4}; LM mɤt^{4}; WN mat^{4}; LC, PS mɤt^{4}; NM met^{4}
N - Y mat^{1}; Sk mɛk^{6}; WM mot^{6}; P mɔt^{3}

0227 - cooking pot, C1, (cf. 1136)
SW - S mɔɔ^{3}; W, B, Sh mɔ^{3}; LNK mɔɔ^{4}; LCH, LMY mɔɔ^{3}; CM mɔɔ^{5}
CN - LP, LM, WN, LC, PS, NM moo^{3}
N - Y mo^{3}; Sk mɔɔ^{3}

0228 - fog, DL1
SW - S mɔɔk^{2}; W, B mɔʔ^{2}; Sh mɔk^{2}; LNK, LCH, LMY mɔɔk^{2}; CM mɔɔk^{3}
CN - LP, LM mook^{2}; WN mɔk^{2} 'cloud'; LC, PS, NM mook^{2}
N - Y mok^{2}; Sk mɔɔk^{6}

0229 - pillow, A1
SW - S mɔɔn^{5}; W, B, Sh mɔn^{1}; LNK mɔɔn^{1}; LCH, LMY mɔn^{1}; CM mɔɔn^{2}
CN - LP, LM moon^{1}; WN mon^{1}; LC, PS, NM moon^{1}

0230 - to roof, A4
SW - S muŋ^{1}; W, B, Sh muŋ^{4}; LNK muŋ^{6}; LCH, LMY muŋ^{4}; CM muŋ^{1}
CN - LP, LM foŋ^{4}; WN muŋ^{4}; LC fuŋ^{4}; PS foŋ^{4}
N - Y foŋ^{4}; SK vɔɔŋ^{1} (A1?)

0231 - rice field, A4
SW - S naa^{1}; W, B, Sh naa^{4}; LNK naa^{6}; LCH, LMY naa^{4}; CM naa^{1}
CN - LP, LM, WN, LC, PS, NM naa^{4}
N - Y na^{4}; Sk naa^{4}; WM, P naa^{2}

0232 - water, C4
SW - S naam^{4}; W, B nam^{6}; Sh nam^{5}; LNK naam^{5}; LCH, LMY, CM nam^{6}
CN - LP nam^{3}; LM, WN, LC, PS, NM nam^{6}
N - Y ram^{6}; Sk nam^{6}; WM ram^{4}; P lam^{4}

0233 - thorn, A1, (cf. 0757)
SW - S naam^{5}; W, B, Sh, LNK, LCH, LMY naam^{1}; CM naam^{2}
CN - LP, LM, WN, LC, PS, NM naam^{1}

0234 - cold, A1
SW - S naaw^{5}; W, B naaw^{1}; Sh naaw^{1} 'fever'; LNK, LCH, LMY naaw^{1}; CM naaw^{2}
CN - LP, LM naaw^{1} 'fever, illness'

0235 - heavy, DS1
SW - S, W, B nak^{2}; Sh nak^{4}; LNK, LCH, LMY nak^{1}; CM nak^{2}
CN - LP nak^{2}; LM nak^{3}; WN nak^{6}; LC, PS nak^{2}; NM nak^{4}
N - Y nak^{3}; Sk nak^{4}; WM nak^{5}; P nak^{2}

0236 - to sit, B4
SW - S naŋ^{3}; W, B naŋ^{5}; Sh, LNK naŋ^{3}; LCH, LMY naŋ^{5}; CM naŋ^{4}
CN - LP, LM, WN, LC, PS, NM naŋ^{5}
N - Y, Sk naŋ^{5}; WM, P naŋ^{6}

0237 - to count, DS4
SW - S, W nap^{4}; B, Sh nap^{5}; LNK nap^{3}; LCH, LMY nap^{5}; CM nap^{6}
CN - WN nap^{4}
N - Sk nap^{6}

0238 - stinger (of a bee), A4
SW - S nay^{1}; W, B lay^{4}; LNK lay^{6}; LCH, LMY may^{4}; CM may^{1}
CN - WN lay^{4}
N - Y, Sk lay^{4}; P lay^{2}

0239 - finger, toe, C4, (cf. 0868)
SW - S niw^{4}; W, B niw^{6}; Sh, LNK niw^{5}; LCH, LMY, CM niw^{6}
CN - LP niiw^{3}; LM niiw^{6}; WN niw^{6}; LC, PS niiw^{6}

0240 - one, B4?, (cf. 0754)
SW - S nɯŋ^{2} (B?); W, B nɯŋ^{5} (B4); Sh, LNK nɯŋ^{3} (B4); LCH, LMY nɯŋ^{5} (B4); CM nɯŋ^{4} (B4), nɯŋ^{3}
CN - LC nɤŋ^{1} used in connected speech, nɤŋ^{5} (B4) used in counting; PS nɯŋ^{1}, nɯŋ^{5} (B4)
N - Sk nɯŋ^{5} (B4)

0241 - to steam, C1
SW - S, W, B, Sh nɯŋ^{3}; LNK nɯŋ^{4}; LCH, LMY nɯŋ^{3}; CM nɯŋ^{5}
CN - LM nɤŋ^{3}; WN nɯŋ^{3}, naŋ^{3}; NM naŋ^{3}
N - Y naŋ^{3}; Sk nɯŋ^{3}; WM naŋ^{3}

0242 - bird, DS4
SW - S, W nok^{4}; B, Sh nok^{5}; LNK nok^{3}; LCH, LMY nok^{5}; CM nok^{6}
CN - LP, LM, WN nok^{4}; LC nuk^{4}; PS, NM nok^{4}
N - Y rok^{1}; Sk nɔk^{6}; WM rok^{6}; P lɔk^{3}

0243 - a sprout, shoot, B1, (cf. 0882)
SW - S nɔɔ^{2}; W, B, Sh nɔ^{2}; LNK nɔɔ^{3}; LCH, LMY nɔɔ^{2}; CM nɔɔ^{3}
CN - LP, LM, LC, PS, NM noo^{2}

0244 - outside, DL4
SW - S nɔɔk^{3}; W nɔ^{4}; B nɔʔ^{5}; Sh nɔk^{3}; LNK, LCH, LMY nɔɔk^{5}; CM nɔɔk^{4}
CN - LP, LM nook^{5}; WN nɔk^{5}; LC nook^{4}; PS, NM nook^{5}
N - Y rok^{5}; Sk lɔɔk^{5}; WM rɤk^{6}; P look^{6}

0245 - to lie down, to sleep, A4
SW - S nɔɔn^{1}; W, B, Sh nɔn^{4}; LNK nɔɔn^{6}; LCH, LMY nɔn^{4}; CM nɔɔn^{1}
CN - LP, LM noon^{4}; WN non^{4}; LC, PS, NM noon^{4}
N -Y nin^{4}; Sk nuun^{4}; WM nin^{2}, nɯn^{2}; P nɯn^{2}

0246 - small, few, C4, (cf. 1119)
SW - S nɔɔy^{4}, nɔy^{2}; W, B nɔy^{6}; Sh nɔy^{5}; LNK nɔɔy^{5} (also, in certain phrases nɔɔy^{3}, nɔɔy^{4}); LCH, LMY nɔy^{6} (both also have nɔy^{2} in certain expressions); CM nɔɔy^{5} (C?)
CN - LP nooy^{3}; LM nooy^{2}, nooy^{6}; WN nɔy^{6}; LC nooy^{3}; PS nooy^{6} 'little in quantity'; NM nooy^{6} 'little'
N - Y noy^{5} (B4); Sk nɔɔy^{5} (B4); WM nɤy^{4}

0247 - beard, DL1, (cf. 0857)
SW - S nuat^{2}; W not^{2}; B nuat^{2}; Sh not^{2}; LNK nuat^{2}; LCH, LMY noot^{2}; CM nuat^{3}

0248 - midday meal, A4
SW - S ŋaay^{1}; W, B ŋaay^{4}; LNK ŋaay^{6} 'breakfast'; LCH, LMY ŋaay^{4} 'morning meal'; CM ŋaay^{1}
CN - LP, LM ŋaay^{4} 'morning meal'; WN, LC ŋaay^{4} 'breakfast'; PS, NM ŋaay^{4} ('morning meal' in PS, NM)
N - Y, Sk ŋaay^{4}; WM, P ŋaay^{2}

0249 - easy, B4
SW - S ŋaay^{3}; W, B ŋaay^{5}; Sh, LNK ŋaay^{3}; LCH, LMY ŋaay^{5}; CM ŋaay^{4}
CN - WN ŋaay^{5}
N - Y, Sk ŋaay^{5}

0250 - silver, money, A4, (cf. 0986)
SW - S ŋɤn^{1}; W ŋɯn^{4}; B ŋɤn^{4}; Sh ŋɯn^{4}; LNK ŋɤn^{6}; LCH, LMY ŋɯn^{4}; CM ŋɤn^{1}
CN - LP, LM ŋɤn^{4}; WN ŋan^{4}; LC, PS ŋɤn^{4}; NM ŋen^{4}
N - Y ŋan^{4}; Sk ɲɛn^{4}; WM ŋan^{2}

0251 - kapok tree, C4, (cf. 0613)
SW - S ηiw^{4}; W, B ηiw^{6}; LNK ηiw^{5}; LCH niw^{6}; LMY ηiw^{6}; CM ηiw^{6} 'kapok'
CN - WN ðɛw^{6}
N - Y rew^{6}; Sk ηiiw^{3} (OG), ηiw^{3} (YG) 'kapok' (C?)

0252 - sweat, B1
SW - S ηɯa^{2}, hɯa^{2}; W hɤ^{2}; B hɯa^{2}; Sh hɤ^{2}; LNK hɯa^{3}; LCH, LMY hɤɤ^{2}; CM hɯa^{3}
CN - LP hɤɤ^{2}; LM thɯɯ^{2}; WN thɯy^{2}; LC, PS hɯɯ^{2}; NM ɬɯɯ^{2}

0253 - the gums, gills, DL1
SW - S ηɯak^{2}; W hɤʔ^{2}; B hɯaʔ^{2}; Sh hɤk^{2}; LNK hɯak^{2}; LCH, LMY ηɤɤk^{2}; CM ηɯak^{3}
CN - LP hɤɤk^{2}; LM hɯɯk^{2}; WN ηɤk^{2}; LC, PS hɤɤk^{2}
N - Y ηɯk^{3} (DS1); P ηɯɯk^{5} 'palate', ηɯk^{2} 'gills'

0254 - grey-haired, DL1
SW - S ηɔɔk^{2}; W, B hɔʔ^{2}; LNK, LCH, LMY ηɔɔk^{2}; CM ηɔɔk^{3}
CN - LM, LC, PS hook^{2}
N - Sk huuk^{6}

0255 - cockscomb, A1
SW - S ηɔɔn^{5}; W, B, Sh hɔn^{1}; LNK hɔɔn^{1}; LCH, LMY hɔn^{1}; CM ηɔɔn^{2}
CN - LP hoon^{1}; LM khoon^{1}; WN mon^{1}; BV hɔɔn^{1}; LC, PS, NM hoon^{1}
N - Sk hɔɔn^{1} (more commonly called khial^{4} [OG], khian^{4} [YG])

0256 - ox, A4, (cf. 1069)
SW - S ηua^{1}, wua^{1}; W ηo^{4}; B ηua^{4}; Sh ηo^{4}, wo^{4}; LNK ηua^{6}; LCH hoo^{4} (colloquial), voo^{4} (literary); LMY ηoo^{4}; CM ηua^{1}

0257 - snake, A4
SW - S ηuu^{1}; W, B, Sh ηu^{4}; LNK ηuu^{6}; LCH, LMY ηuu^{4}; CM ηuu^{1}
CN - LP vuu^{4}; LM ηow^{4}; WN, LC, PS ηuu^{4}; NM lɯɯ^{4}
N - Y ηɯa^{4}; Sk ηua^{4}; WM ηɯ^{2}; P ηɯɯ^{2}

0258 - forest, B2, (cf. 0448, 0900)
SW - S, W, B, Sh paa^{2}; LNK paa^{3}; LCH, LMY paa^{2}; CM paa^{3}
CN - WN paa^{2}
N - Sk paa^{6}

0259 - aunt, older sister of either parent, C2
SW - S, W, B, Sh paa^{3}; LNK paa^{5}; LCH, LMY paa^{3}; CM paa^{5}
CN - LP, LM, WN, LC, PS, NM paa^{3}
N - Y pa^{3}; Sk, WM, P paa^{3}

0260 - to announce, B2
SW - S, W, B, Sh paaw^{2}; LNK paaw^{3}; LCH, LMY paaw^{2}; CM paaw^{3}
N - Y paaw^{2}; Sk paaw^{6}

0261 - to go, A2
SW - S, W, B, Sh pay^{1}; LNK pay^{2}; LCH pay^{1}; LMY pay^{4} (LCH and LMY have pay^{1} 'don't' before verbs; for this, LCH also has yaa^{2} pay^{1}); CM pay^{1} (A2?)
CN - LP pay^{2}; LM pey^{1}; WN, LC, PS, NM pay^{1}
N - Y, Sk pay^{1}; WM poy^{1}; P pay^{1}

0262 - to blow, B2
SW - S, W, B, Sh paw^{2}; LNK paw^{3}; LCH, LMY paw^{2}; CM paw^{3}
CN - LP paw^{5}; LM, WN paw^{2}; PS paw^{2}; NM puu^{2}
N - Y po^{2}; Sk phɔɔ^{6}

0263 - to be, become, A2
SW - S pen^{1}; W pin^{1}; B, Sh pen^{1}; LNK pen^{2}; LCH, LMY pin^{1}; CM pen^{2}
CN - LP phin^{4}; LM pin^{4}; WN pan^{4}; LC, PS pin^{4} ; NM pen^{4} (A4 in CN languages)
N - Y pan^{4}; Sk phal^{4} (OG), phan^{4} (YG); WM, P pan^{2} (A4 in N languages)

0264 - duck, DS2
SW - S, W, B pet^{2}; Sh pet^{4}; LNK, LCH, LMY pet^{1}; CM pet^{2}
CN - LP pit^{2}; LM pyat^{3}; WN pat^{6}; LC, PS pit^{2}; NM pet^{4}
N - Y pit^{3}; Sk pit^{4}; WM pit^{5}

0265 - eight, DL2
SW - S pɛɛt^{2}; W, B, Sh pɛt^{2}; LNK, LCH, LMY pɛɛt^{2}; CM pɛɛt^{3}
CN - LP peet^{5}; LM peet^{2}; WN pɛt^{2}; LC, PS, NM peet^{2}
N - Y pet^{2}; Sk peet^{6}; WM pet^{5}; P peet^{5}

0266 - wing, DL2, (cf. 0784)
SW - S piik^{2}; W, B piʔ^{2}; Sh pik^{2}; LNK, LCH, LMY piik^{2}; CM piik^{3}
CN - LP pik^{2}; LM pik^{3} (DS2); WN pik^{6} (DS2); LC, PS pik^{2}; NM piik^{2}

0267 - tender, decayed, B2
SW - S pɯay^{2}; W pɤy^{2}; B pɯay^{2}; Sh poy^{2}; LNK pɯay^{3}; LCH, LMY pɤy^{2}; CM pɯay^{3}
N - Sk pɯay^{6}

0268 - gun, A2
SW - S pɯɯn^{1}; W, B, Sh pɯn^{1} 'arrow'; LNK pɯɯn^{2}; LCH, LMY pɯn^{1} 'arrow'; CM pɯɯn^{2}

0269 - fish, A2
SW - S plaa^1; W, B, Sh paa^1; LNK paa^2; LCH, LMY paa^1; CM paa^2
CN - LP pyaa^2; LM pyaa^1; WN paa^1; LC, PS, NM pyaa^1
N - Y pya^1; Sk plaa^1 (OG), praa^1 (YG); WM plaa^1; P pyaa^1

0270 - end, tip, A2, (cf. 0746)
SW - S plaay^1; W, B, Sh paay^1; LNK paay^2; LCH, LMY paay^1; CM paay^2
CN - LM pyaay^1; WN paay^1; LC pyaay^1 'summit of the tree'; PS, NM pyaay^1
N - Y pyaay^1; Sk plaay^1 (OG), praay^1 (YG); WM plaay^1; P pyaay^1

0271 - empty, B2
SW - S plaaw^2; W, B, Sh paw^2; LNK paw^3; LCH, LMY paw^2; CM paw^3
CN - LP pyaw^5; LM pyaw^2; WN paw^2; LC, PS pyaw^2
N - Y pyu^2; Sk pluu^6 (OG), pruu^6 (YG); WM plaw^5; P pyuu^5

0272 - to fell (a tree), C2
SW - S plam^3 'to wrestle'; W, B, Sh pam^3; LNK pam^5 'to wrestle, fell a tree'; LCH, LMY pɔm^3; CM pam^5
N - Sk plam^3 (OG), pram^3 (YG)

0273 - flame, A2
SW - S plew^1; W, B pɛw^1; Sh pew^1; LNK peew^2; LCH, LMY pew^1; CM pew^2
CN - LM, PS piiw^1
N - Sk pleew^1 (OG), preew^1 (YG)

0274 - leech, A2
SW - S pliŋ^1; W, B, Sh piŋ^1; LNK piŋ^2; LCH, LMY piŋ^1; CM piŋ^2
CN - LP piŋ^2; LM, WN piŋ^1; LC, PS piŋ^1; NM pɤŋ^1
N - Y piŋ^1; Sk pliŋ^1 (OG), priŋ^1 (YG); WM pliŋ^1; P piŋ^1

0275 - to blow away, A2
SW - S pliw^1; W, B, Sh piw^1; LNK piw^2; LCH, LMY piw^1; CM piw^2
N - Sk pliw^1 (OG), priw^1 (YG)

0276 - to take down, put down, A2
SW - S ploŋ^1; W puŋ^1; B, Sh poŋ^1; LNK poŋ^2; LCH, LMY puŋ^1; CM poŋ^2
CN - WN pɔŋ^1
N - Y pyoŋ^1; Sk plɔŋ^1 (OG), prɔŋ^1 (YG)

0277 - to remove, take down, DS2
SW - S plot^2; W pot^2 (but pɯt^2 in certain expressions); B pot^2; Sh pot^4 'to unloose, loosen; to teach to read'; LNK pot^1; CM pot^2
CN - LM pyot^3
N - Sk plɛt^4 (OG), prɛt^4 (YG)

0278 - to release, B2
SW - S plɔy^{2}; W, B, Sh pɔy^{2}; LNK pɔɔy^{3}; LCH, LMY pɔy^{2}; CM pɔy^{3}
CN - LP pyɤɤy^{5}; LM pyuuy^{2}; WN pɔy^{2}; LC pyuuy^{2}

0279 - white ant, DL2
SW - S pluak^{2}; W poʔ^{2}; B puaʔ^{2}; Sh pok^{2}; LNK puak^{2}; LCH, LMY pook^{2}; CM puak^{3}
CN - LP cuuk^{5}; LM pyuuk^{2}; WN cuk^{2}; PS kuuk^{2}
N - Y suk^{3}; Sk (că^{6}) pluk^{4} (OG), (că^{6}) pruk^{4} (YG) (DS2 in N languages)

0280 - to awaken (someone), DS2, (cf. 0901)
SW - S pluk^{2}; W, B puk^{2}; Sh pok^{4}; LNK puk^{1}; CM puk^{2}
CN - LM pyok^{3}; WN pɔk^{6}; LC pyuk^{2}; PS pyok^{2}
N - Y pyok^{3}; Sk pluk^{4} (OG), pruk^{4} (YG); P pyok^{2}

0281 - to plant, DL2
SW - S pluuk^{2}; W, B puʔ^{2}; Sh phuk^{2}; LNK, LCH, LMY puuk^{2}; CM puuk^{3}
CN - LM pyɯɯk^{2} 'to transplant', pyok^{3} 'to plant seeds' (which is cognate?); WN puk^{6} (DS2); LC pyɤɤk^{2} 'to stop; to transplant to some other place'
N - Sk plɔɔk^{6} (OG), prɔɔk^{6} (YG)

0282 - to cover, DS2, (cf. 0794, 1078)
SW - S, W, B pok^{2}; LNK, LCH, LMY pok^{1}; CM pok^{2}
N - Sk pok^{4}, pɔk^{4}

0283 - to peel, DL2
SW - S pɔɔk^{2}; W, B pɔʔ^{2}; Sh pɔk^{2}; LMY pɔɔk^{2}; CM pɔɔk^{3}
CN - LP pook^{5} 'to skin'; LM pook^{2}; WN pɔk^{2}; LC pook^{2} 'to skin' (Li says < Chinese); PS, NM pook^{2} 'to skin'
N - Y pok^{2}

0284 - to split, B1
SW - S, W phaa^{2}; B faa^{2}; Sh phaa^{2}; LNK phaa^{3}; LCH, LMY phaa^{2}; CM phaa^{3}
CN - LM, WN phaa^{2}
N - Y pa^{2}; Sk phaa^{6}; P paa^{5}

0285 - cloth, C1
SW - S, W phaa^{3}; B faa^{3}; Sh phaa^{3}; LNK phaa^{4}; LCH, LMY phaa^{3}; CM phaa^{5}

0286 - to lay (a cloth) across, DL4
SW - S phaat^{3}; W paat^{4}; B paat^{5}; Sh paat^{3}; LNK phaat^{5}; LCH, LMY paat^{5}; CM paat^{4}
CN - WN paat^{5}
N - Y paat^{5}

0287 - vegetable, DS1
SW - S, W phak^{2}; B fak^{2}; Sh phak^{4}; LNK, LCH, LMY phak^{1}; CM phak^{2}
CN - LP phyak^{2}; LM phyak^{3}; WN phak^{6}; LC, PS phyak^{2}; NM phyak^{4}
N - Y piak^{2} (DL1); Sk phrak^{4}; WM plak^{5}; P pyak^{2}

0288 - to fold, DS4, (cf. 0374, 0422)
SW - S phap^{4}; W pap^{4}; B pap^{5}; LNK phap^{3}; CM phap^{6}
CN - WN pap^{4}
N - Y pap^{1}; Sk thrap^{6}, phap^{6}, phlap^{6}; WM pap^{6}

0289 - daughter-in-law, C4, (cf. 1091)
SW - S (să^{2}) phay^{4}; W, B paɰ^{6}; LNK phay^{5}; LCH, LMY, CM pay^{6}
N - Y paɰ^{6}; SK khwɤɤ^{6}; WM, P paɰ^{4}

0290 - goat, C3
SW - S phɛʔ^{4} (?); W, B bɛ^{3}; Sh pɛ^{5} (C4); LNK bɛɛ^{5}; LCH, LMY bɛɛ^{3}, pɛʔ^{5} (LMY informant thinks these are two different kinds of goats); CM pɛʔ^{6} (C4)
CN - LP bee^{3}; LM mee^{3}; WN bɛɛ^{3}; LC bee^{3} 'sheep'; PS, NM bee^{3}
N - Y be^{6}; Sk bɛɛ^{3}

0291 - raft, A4
SW - S phɛɛ^{1}; W, B, Sh pɛ^{4}; LNK phɛɛ^{6}; LCH, LMY pɛɛ^{4}; CM pɛɛ^{1}
CN - LM pee^{4}; WN pɛɛ^{4}; PS, NM pee^{4}
N - Y pe^{4}; Sk phee^{4}

0292 - to clean, C1
SW - S phɛɛw^{3}; W phɛw^{3} 'to sweep'; B fɛw^{3} 'to sweep'; Sh phew^{3}; LNK phɛɛw^{4}; LCH, LMY phew^{3}; CM phiaw^{5} 'to sweep'
CN - LM pheew^{3} 'to clear (grass)'
N - Y pew^{3} 'to clear out'

0293 - fat, A4
SW - S phii^{1}; W, B, Sh pi^{4}; LNK phii^{6}; LCH, LMY pii^{4}; CM pii^{1}
CN - LP phii^{4}; LM pey^{4}; WN, LC, PS pii^{4}; NM pey^{4}
N - Y pi^{4}; Sk phuuy^{4} (cognate?); WM pi^{2}; P pii^{2}

0294 - older sibling, B4
SW - S phii^{3}; W, B pi^{5}; Sh pi^{3}; LNK phii^{3}; LCH, LMY pii^{5}; CM pii^{4}
CN - LP phii^{5}; LM pey^{5}; WN, LC, PS pii^{5}; NM pey^{5}
N - Y pi^{6} (C4); Sk phii^{5} (B4); WM poy^{4} (C4); P pii^{4} (C4)

0295 - wrong, DS1, (cf. 0988)
SW - S, W phit^{2}; B fit^{2}; Sh phit^{4}; LNK, LCH, LMY phit^{1}; CM phit^{2}
CN - WN phit^{6}
N - Sk phit^{4}

0296 - to whistle, A1
SW - S phiw^{5}; W, B thiw^{1}; Sh, LNK phiw^{1}; LCH, LMY thiw^{1}; CM phiw^{2}
CN - LP khwiiw^{2} (B1); LM viiw^{1}; WN thiw^{1}; PS khwiiw^{2} (B1); NM khwii^{2} (B1)
N - Sk thiw^{2}, phriw^{2}, hiiw^{2} (OG), hiw^{2} (YG)

0297 - bee, beeswax, C1
SW - S, W phɯŋ^{3}; B fɯŋ^{3}; Sh phɯŋ^{3}; LNK phɤŋ^{4}, phɤɤŋ^{4}; LCH, LMY phɯŋ^{3}; CM phɤŋ^{5}
CN - LM phyɤŋ^{3} (usual word is mii^{4} foŋ^{1})

0298 - to turn (something) over, DS4
SW - S phlik^{4}; W pik^{4}; B pik^{5}; CM pik^{6} (in W, B, and CM also 'to turn back, return')

0299 - betel, A4
SW - S phluu^{1}; W, B pu^{4}; Sh pu^{5} (C4); LNK phuu^{6}; LCH, LMY puu^{4}; CM puu^{1}
N - Y pyu^{4}; Sk phluu^{4} (OG), phruu^{4} (YG)

0300 - hair of the head, A1
SW - S phom^{5}; W phum^{1}; B fom^{1}; Sh, LNK phom^{1}; LCH, LMY phum^{1}; CM phom^{2}
CN - LP, LM phyom^{1}; WN pham^{1}; BV phom^{1}; LC phyum^{1}; PS, NM phyom^{1}
N - Y piam^{1}; Sk phram^{2}; WM plom^{1}; P pyɔm^{1}

0301- father, B4
SW - S phɔɔ^{3}; W, B pɔ^{5}; Sh pɔ^{3}; LNK phɔɔ^{3}; LCH, LMY pɔɔ^{5}; CM pɔɔ^{4}
CN - LP phoo^{5}; LM, WN, LC, PS, NM poo^{5}
N - Y po^{5}; Sk phɔɔ^{5}; WM pɤ^{6}; P poo^{6}

0302 - coconut, C4
SW - S (mă^{4}) phraaw^{4}; W, B (maaʔ^{2}) paaw^{6}; LNK (maak^{2}) phaaw^{5}; LCH, LMY (maak^{2}) paaw^{6}; CM (baʔ^{2}) paaw^{6}
CN - LM pyaaw^{5}; WN phaaw^{5} (B4 in CN languages)
N - Y paaw^{5} (B4), piaw^{4} (A4); Sk phlaaw^{6} (OG), phraaw^{6} (YG)

0303 - root, DL4
SW - S raak^{3}; W haa^{4}; B haaʔ^{5}; Sh haak^{3}; LNK haak^{5}; LCH, LMY haak^{5} (literary raak^{5}, laak^{5}); CM haak^{4}
CN - LP, LM, WN laak^{5}; LC laak^{4}; PS, NM laak^{5}
N - Y raak^{5}; Sk raak^{6} (DL?); WM raak^{6}; P laak^{6}

0304 - to love, DS4
SW - S rak^{4}; W hak^{4}; B, Sh hak^{5}; LNK hak^{3}, lak^{3}; LCH hak^{5}; LMY hak^{5} (literary rak^{5}, lak^{5}); CM hak^{6}

0305 - we (you and I, not others), A4
SW - raw^{1}; W, B, Sh haw^{4}; LNK haw^{6}; LCH haw^{4}; LMY haw^{4} (literary raw^{4}); CM haw^{1}
CN - LP ɬaw^{4}; LM law^{4}; WN ðaw^{4}; LC, PS, NM law^{4}
N - Y raw^{4}; Sk roo^{4}; WM raw^{1} (A?); P law^{2}

0306 - dry field, B4
SW - S ray^{3}; W, B hay^{5}; Sh, LNK hay^{3}; LCH, LMY hay^{5}; CM hay^{4}
CN - LP ɬay^{5}; LM lay^{5}; WN ðay^{5}; LC, PS ɬay^{5}
N - Y ri^{5}; Sk rii^{5}; WM roy^{6}; P lii^{6}

0307 - armpit, second syllable C4; first syllable DS4
SW - S (rak^{4}) rɛɛ^{4}; W (hak^{4}) hɛ^{6}, (haaŋ^{1}) hɛ^{6}; B (hak^{5}) hɛ^{6}; LNK (khii^{4}) hɛɛ^{5}; LMY hɛɛ^{6}, lɛɛ^{6}; CM hɛɛ^{6}
CN - LP (ɬak^{4}) ɬee^{3}; LM (lak^{4}) lee^{6}; PS (ɬak^{4}) ɬee^{6}
N - Sk khɛɛ^{5} (B4)

0308 - a snare, C4
SW - S rɛɛw^{4}; W, B hɛw^{6}; Sh hɛw^{5}; LNK hɛɛw^{5}; LCH, LMY hɛw^{6}; CM hɛɛw^{6}
CN - LM heew^{6} 'loop in a snare'; WN ðiw^{6}
N - Sk reew^{6}

0309 - edge, A4, (cf. 1137)
SW - S rim^{1}; W, B, Sh him^{4}; LNK him^{6}; LCH, LMY him^{4}; CM him^{1}
N - Sk rim^{4}

0310 - boat, A4
SW - S rɯa^{1}; W hɤ^{4}; B hɯa^{4}; Sh hɤ^{4}; LNK hɯa^{6} (modern lɯa^{6}); LCH hɤɤ^{4}; LMY hɤɤ^{4} (literary rɤɤ^{4}, lɤɤ^{4}); CM hɯa^{1}
CN - LP lɤɤ^{4}; LM, WN, LC, PS, NM lɯɯ^{4}
N - Y rua^{4}; Sk rua^{1} (A?); WM ru^{2}

0311 - house, A4
SW - S rɯan^{1}; W hɤn^{4}; B hɯan^{4}; Sh hɤn^{4}; LNK hɯan^{6}; LCH hɤn^{4}; LMY hɤn^{4} (rare, literary rɤn^{4}); CM hɯan^{1}
CN - LP ɬɤɤn^{4}; LM lɯɯn^{4}; WN ðɯn^{4}; LC, PS ɬɤɤn^{4}; NM lɯɯn^{4}
N - Y, Sk raan^{4}; WM raan^{2}; P laan^{2}

0312 - day after tomorrow, A4
SW - S (mă^{4}) rɯɯn^{1}; W, B, Sh hɯ^{4}; LNK hɯɯ^{6}; LCH, LMY hɯɯ^{4}; CM hɯɯ^{1}
CN - LP ɬɤɤ^{4}; LM lɤɰ^{4}; WN, LC, PS lɯɯ^{4}; NM laɰ^{4}
N - Y rɯ^{4}; Sk rɯɯ^{1} (A?)

0313 - shade, B4
SW - S rom^{3}; W hum^{5}; B hom^{5}; Sh, LNK hom^{3}; LCH, LMY hum^{5} (literary rum^{5}, lum^{5}); CM hom^{4}
CN - LM lom^{5}; WN ɲum^{5} 'shade', lam^{5} 'shady' (which is cognate?)
N - Y ram^{5}; Sk yum^{1} (A?); WM ram^{6}

0314 - hot, C4, (cf. 1006)
SW - S rɔɔn^{4}; W, B hɔn^{6}; Sh hɔn^{5}; LNK hɔɔn^{5} (modern lɔɔn^{5}); LCH, LMY hɔn^{6} (also, literary rɔn^{6}, lɔn^{6}); CM hɔɔn^{6}
N - Sk ruul^{6} (OG), ruun^{6} (YG)

0315 - hundred, C4, (cf. 0912)
SW - S rɔɔy^{4}; W, B hɔy^{6}; LNK hɔɔy^{5} (also, 'to string'), lɔɔy^{5} 'hundred'; LCH, LMY hɔy^{6} (literary rɔy^{6}, lɔy^{6}; in both Lue dialects the usual word for 'hundred' is paak^{2}); CM lɔɔy^{6}, hɔɔy^{6}
N - Y roy^{6} 'to string'; Sk rɔɔy^{6}; WM rɤy^{4} 'to string'

0316 - to leak, B4
SW - rua^{3}; W ho^{5}; B hua^{5}; Sh ho^{3}; LNK hua^{3}; LCH, LMY hoo^{5}; CM hua^{4}
CN - LP ɬuu^{5}; LM luu^{5}; WN ðuu^{5}; LC, PS ɬuu^{5}; NM low^{5}
N - Y ro^{5}; Sk rɔɔ^{5}; WM rɤ^{6}

0317 - fence, C4
SW - S rua^{4}; W ho^{6}; B hua^{6}; Sh ho^{5}; LNK hua^{5}; LCH, LMY hoo^{6}; CM hua^{6}
CN - LM luu^{6} 'to fence'

0318 - hole, A4, (cf. 0038, 0546)
SW - S ruu^{1}; W, B, Sh hu^{4}; LNK huu^{6}; LCH huu^{4}; LMY huu^{4} (literary ruu^{4}); CM huu^{1}
CN - LP ɬuu^{4}; LM low^{4}; WN ðuu^{4}; LC, PS ɬuu^{4}; NM low^{4}
N - WM ru^{1} (A?)

0319 - to know, C4
SW - S ruu^{4}; W, B hu^{6}; Sh hu^{5}; LNK huu^{5} (modern luu^{5}); LCH huu^{6}; LMY huu^{6} (literary ruu^{6}, luu^{6}); CM huu^{6}
CN - LP ɬuu^{3}; LM low^{6}; WN ðuu^{6}; LC, PS ɬuu^{6}; NM low^{6}
N - Y ro^{6}; Sk rɔɔ^{6}; WM rɤ^{4}; P loo^{4}

0320 - young unmarried woman, A1
SW - S saaw^{5}; W, B saaw^{1}; Sh shaaw^{1}; LNK, LCH, LMY saaw^{1}; CM saaw^{2}
CN - LP ɬaaw^{1}; LM, WN saaw^{1}; BV ɬaaw^{2}; LC, PS, NM ɬaaw^{1}
N - Y θaaw^{1}; Sk saaw^{2}; WM θaaw^{1}; P ɬaaw^{1}

0321 - sand, A4
SW - S saay^{1}; W, B saay^{4}; Sh shaay^{4}; LNK saay^{6}; LCH, LMY saay^{4}; CM saay^{1}
CN - LP ɬaay^{4}; LM, WN saay^{4}; LC, PS, NM ɬaay^{4}
N - Y θɯay^{4}; Sk yooy^{4}, yoy^{4} (fast speech)

0322 - left (hand), C4
SW - S saay^{4}; W, B saay^{6}; Sh shaay^{5}; LNK saay^{5}; LCH, LMY, CM saay^{6}
CN - LP ɬaay^{3}; LM, WN saay^{6}; LC, PS, NM ɬaay^{6}
N - Y θɯay^{6}; WM θɯy^{4}; P ɬɯɯy^{4}

0323 - cord, string, A1, (cf. 1086)
SW - S saay^{5}; W, B saay^{1}; Sh shaay^{1}; LNK, LCH, LMY saay^{1}; CM saay^{2}
CN - LP ɬaay^{1}; LM, WN saay^{1}; BV ɬaay^{2}; LC, PS ɬaay^{1}
N - Y θaay^{1}; Sk saay^{2} 'cord, string' (but saay^{1} 'necklace'); WM θaay^{1}

0324 - late in the morning, A1
SW - S saay^{5}; W, B saay^{1}; LNK suay^{1}; LCH, LMY xwaay^{1}; CM khwaay^{2}
CN - LP ɬaay^{1}; LM, WN saay^{1}; BV ɬaay^{2}; LC, PS ɬaay^{1}
N - Y kwaay^{4}; Sk thlaa^{4} (OG), thraa^{4} (YG) (probably not cognate); P kwaay^{2}
(A4 in N languages)

0325 - to wash (clothes), DS4, (cf. 0552, 1116)
SW - S, W sak^{4}; B sak^{5}; Sh shak^{5}; LNK sak^{3}; LCH, LMY sak^{5}; CM sak^{6}
CN - LP ɬak^{4}; LM, WN sak^{4}; LC, PS ɬak^{4}
N - Y θak^{1}; Sk yak^{6}; WM θak^{6}; P ɬak^{3}

0326 - to repeat, C4
SW - S sam^{4}; W, B sam^{6}; Sh sham^{5}; LNK sam^{5}; LCH, LMY sam^{6} 'all, completely' (cognate?); CM sam^{6}
N - Sk yam^{6}

0327 - animal, DS1
SW - S, W, B sat^{2}; Sh shat^{4}; LNK sat^{1}; LCH sɛt^{1}; LMY sat^{1}; CM sat^{2}
N - Sk sɛt^{4}, sat^{4}

0328 - banyan, A4
SW - S say^{1}; W, B hay^{4}; LNK say^{6}; LCH, LMY hay^{4}; CM hay^{1}
CN - LM hay^{4}; WN ðay^{4}
N - Sk hay^{4}

0329 - to put, B1
SW - S say^{2}; W, B saɰ^{2}; Sh shaɰ^{2}; LNK say^{3}; LCH, LMY say^{2}; CM say^{3}
N - Y so^{2}; Sk cɔɔ^{6}

0330 - intestines, C1
SW - S, W, B say^{3}; Sh shay^{3}; LNK say^{4}; LCH, LMY say^{3}; CM say^{5}
CN - LP ɬay^{3}; LM, WN say^{3}; LC, PS, NM ɬay^{3}
N - Y θay^{3}; Sk say^{3}; WM θay^{3}; P ɬay^{3}

0331 - clear, transparent, A1
SW - S say^{5}; W, B saɰ^{1}; Sh shaɰ^{1}; LCH, LMY say^{1}; CM say^{2}
CN - LP ɬaɰ^{1}; LM, WN saɰ^{1}; BV ɬaɰ^{2}; LC, PS, NM ɬaɰ^{1}
N - Y, WM θaɰ^{1}; P ɬaɰ^{1}

0332 - spade, A1
SW - S siam^{5}; W sem^{1}; B siam^{1}; Sh shem^{1}; LNK siam^{1}; LCH, LMY sem^{1}; CM siam^{2}
CN - LC ɬiim^{1}

0333 - sound, A1
SW - S siaŋ^{5}; W seŋ^{1}; B siaŋ^{1}; Sh sheŋ^{1}; LNK siaŋ^{1}; LCH, LMY seŋ^{1}; CM siaŋ^{2}
CN - LP, LM hiŋ^{1}; WN hɛŋ^{1}; LC heeŋ^{1}; PS heeŋ^{1} 'voice'; NM hɤŋ^{1} 'voice'
N - Y hiŋ^{1}; Sk siaŋ^{2}; WM θiŋ^{1} (Li says < Chinese)

0334 - ten, DS1
SW - S, W, B sip^{2}; Sh ship^{4}; LNK, LCH, LMY sip^{1}; CM sip^{2}
CN - LP ɬip^{2}; LM sip^{3}; WN sip^{6}; LC, PS ɬip^{2}; NM ɬop^{4}
N - Y sip^{1}; Sk sip^{6}; WM šip^{6}; P šip^{3} (DS4 in N languages)

0335 - chisel, B1
SW - S, W, B siw^{2}; Sh shiw^{2}; LNK siw^{3}; LCH, LMY siw^{2}; CM siw^{3}
CN - LM siiw^{2}; WN siw^{2}; LC ɬiiw^{2}
N - Y θiw^{2}, θiaw^{2}; Sk siiw^{6} (OG), siw^{6} (YG); P ɬiw^{5}

0336 - pimple, A1
SW - S siw^{5}; W, B siw^{1}; Sh shiw^{1}; LNK, LCH, LMY siw^{1}; CM siw^{2}
N - Y saw^{4} (A4); Sk siiw^{1} (OG), siw^{1} (YG)

0337 - shirt, C1, (cf. 0880)
SW - S sɯa^{3}; W sɤ^{3}; B sɯa^{3}; Sh shɤ^{3}; LNK sɯa^{4}; LCH, LMY sɤɤ^{3}; CM sɯa^{5}
CN - LP ɬɤɤ^{3}; LM, WN sɯɯ^{3}; LC, PS, NM ɬɯɯ^{3}

0338 - straight, B4
SW - S sɯɯ^{3} 'honest'; W, B sɯ^{5}; Sh shɯ^{3}; LNK sɯɯ^{3}; LCH, LMY sɯɯ^{5}; CM sɯɯ^{4}
CN - LM sɤɰ^{5}; WN sɯɯ^{5}; LC ɬɯɯ^{5}
N - Y θo^{5}; Sk yɔɔ^{5}

0339 - heel, C1
SW - S son^{3}; W sun^{3}; B son^{3}; Sh shon^{3}; LNK son^{4}; LCH, LMY sun^{3}; CM son^{5}
CN - LP ɬɤn^{3}; LM sɤn^{3}; WN san^{3}; LC, PS ɬɤn^{3}; NM ɬen^{3}
N - Y θan^{2} (B1); Sk son^{3}

0340 - elbow, DL1
SW - S sɔɔk^{2}; W, B sɔʔ^{2}; Sh shɔk^{2}; LNK, LCH, LMY sɔɔk^{2}; CM sɔɔk^{3}
'lower arm'
CN - LP ɬook^{2}; LM sook^{2}; WN sɔk^{2}; PS ɬook^{2}
N - Y suak^{5} (DL4); Sk sɔɔk^{6}, suak^{6}

0341 - two, A1, (cf. 0734)
SW - S sɔɔŋ^{5}; W, B sɔŋ^{1}; Sh shɔŋ^{1}; LNK sɔɔŋ^{1}; LCH, LMY sɔŋ^{1}; CM sɔɔŋ^{2}
CN - LP ɬooŋ^{1}; LM sooŋ^{1}; WN soŋ^{1}; BV ɬɔɔŋ^{2}; LC, PS, NM ɬooŋ^{1}
N - Y θoŋ^{1}; Sk sɔɔŋ^{2}; WM θɤŋ^{1}; P ɬooŋ^{1}

0342 - garden A1
SW - S suan^{5}; W son^{1}; B suan^{1}; Sh shon^{1}; LNK suan^{1}; LCH, LMY son^{1};
CM suan^{2}
CN - LP ɬuun^{1}; LM suun^{1}; WN sɯn^{1}; BV ɬuun^{2}; LC, PS, NM ɬuun^{1}
N - Y θɯan^{1}; Sk suan^{2}; WM θuan^{1}; P ɬɯɯn^{1}

0343 - cooked, ripe, DS1
SW - S, W, B suk^{2}; Sh shuk^{4}; LNK, LCH, LMY suk^{1}; CM suk^{2}
CN - LP ɬok^{4} (DS4); LM sok^{3}; WN suk^{6}; LC ɬuk^{2}; PS ɬok^{2}; NM ɬok^{4}
N - Y suk^{1}; Sk suk^{6}; P šuk^{3}, ɬuk^{3} (DS4 in N languages)

0344 - high, tall, A1
SW - S suuŋ^{5}; W, B suŋ^{1}; Sh shuŋ^{1}; LNK suuŋ^{1}; LCH, LMY suŋ^{1}; CM suuŋ^{2}
CN - LP ɬoŋ^{1}; LM soŋ^{1}; WN suŋ^{1}; BV ɬuŋ^{2}; LC ɬuŋ^{1}; PS, NM ɬoŋ^{1}
N - Y θaaŋ^{1}; Sk saaŋ^{2}; WM θaaŋ^{1}; P ɬaaŋ^{1}

0345 - to expose to the sun, DL2
SW - S taak^{2}; W, B taaʔ^{2}; Sh taak^{2}; LNK, LCH, LMY taak^{2}; CM taak^{3}
CN - LP, LM phyaak^{2}; WN thaak^{2}; LC, PS phyaak^{2}; NM thaak^{2}
(DL1 in CN languages)
N - Y taak^{2}; Sk praak^{6}; WM raak^{5}; P taak^{5}

0346 - to die, A2
SW - S, W, B, Sh taay^{1}; LNK taay^{2}; LCH, LMY taay^{1}; CM taay^{2}
CN - LP haay^{1}; LM, WN, BV thaay^{1}; LC, PS haay^{1}; NM thaay^{1}
N - Y taay^{1}; Sk praay^{1}; WM raay^{1}; P taay^{1}

0347 - to crawl, B2, (cf. 0144)
SW - S taay^{2}; W, B tay^{2} (in W and B 'to cross a bridge'); Sh tay^{2}; LNK tay^{3}; LCH, LMY tay^{2}; CM tay^{3}
CN - WN tay^{2} 'to walk'
N - Y raay^{5} (B4); Sk tay^{6}

0348 - below, south, C2
SW - S taay^{3}; W, B, Sh taɯ^{3}; LNK tay^{5}; LCH, LMY tay^{3}; CM tay^{5}
CN - LP, LM, WN, LC, PS, NM taɯ^{3}
N - Sk tɤɤ^{3}

0349 - to dip out, DS2
SW - S, W, B tak^{2}; Sh tak^{4}; LNK, LCH, LMY tak^{1}; CM tak^{2}
CN - LP tak^{2}; LM tak^{3}; WN tak^{6}; LC, PS tak^{2}; NM tak^{4}
N - Y tak^{3}; Sk tak^{4}; WM tak^{5}; P tak^{2}

0350 - low, short (not tall), B2, (cf. 0697)
SW - S, W, B tam^{2}; Sh tam^{2}, tɛm^{2} 'low, lowly'; LNK tam^{3}; LCH, LMY tɛm^{2}; CM tam^{3}
CN - LP tam^{5}; LM, WN, LC, PS, NM tam^{2}
N - Y tam^{2}; Sk tam^{6}; P tam^{5}

0351 - stool, B2
SW - S, W, B, Sh taŋ^{2}; LNK taŋ^{3}; LCH, LMY taŋ^{2}; CM taŋ^{3}
CN - LP taŋ^{5}; LM, WN, LC, PS, NM taŋ^{2}
N - Y taŋ^{2}; Sk taŋ^{6}; WM taŋ^{5} 'bench' (Li says < Chinese)

0352 - liver, DS2
SW - S, W, B tap^{2}; Sh tap^{4}; LNK, LCH, LMY tap^{1}; CM tap^{2}
CN - LP tap^{2}; LM tap^{3}; WN tap^{6}; LC, PS tap^{2}; NM tap^{4}
N - Y tap^{3}; Sk tap^{4}; WM tap^{5}; P tap^{2}

0353 - gizzard, A2
SW - S tay^{1} 'kidney, gland'; W, B taɯ^{1}; Sh taɯ^{1} 'callous caused by friction of the skin'; LNK tay^{2}; LCH, LMY tay^{1}; CM tay^{2}
CN - LP taɯ^{2}; LM taɯ^{1}; WN thaɯ^{1}; PS, NM taɯ^{1}
N - Y taɯ^{1}; Sk tɤɤ^{1}

0354 - full, A2
SW - S tem^{1}; W tim^{1}; B, Sh tem^{1}; LNK tem^{2}; LCH, LMY tim^{1}; CM tem^{2}
CN - LP tim^{2}; LM tim^{1}; WN tam^{1}; LC, PS tim^{1}; NM tom^{1}
N - Y rim^{1}; Sk rim^{2} (A1); WM rim^{1}; P lim^{1}

0355 - to break (intransitive), DL2, (cf. 0073)
SW - S tɛɛk^{2}; W, B, tɛʔ^{2}; Sh tɛk^{2}; LNK, LCH, LMY tɛɛk^{2}; CM tɛɛk^{3}
CN - LP, LM pheek^{2}; WN thɛk^{2}; LC pheek^{2} (DL1 in CN languages)
N - Y tek^{2}; Sk preek^{6}; P teek^{5}

0356 - foot, A2
SW - S tiin^{1}; W, B, Sh tin^{1}; LNK tiin^{2}; LCH, LMY tin^{1}; CM tiin^{2}
CN - LP tin^{2} (usual word is haa^{1}); LM tin^{1} (usual word is khaa^{1}); WN tin^{1}
N - Y tin^{1}; Sk tiin^{1} (usual word is ɣeeŋ^{5}); WM, P tin^{1}

0357 - shallow, C2
SW - S tɯɯn^{3}; W, B, Sh tɯn^{3}; LNK tɯɯn^{5}; LCH, LMY tɯn^{3}; CM tɯɯn^{5}

0358 - to fall, DS2
SW - S, W, B tok^{2}; Sh tok^{4}; LNK, LCH, LMY tok^{1}; CM tok^{2}
CN - LP tok^{2}; LM tok^{3}; WN tɔk^{6}; LC tuk^{2}
N - Y tok^{3}; Sk tɔk^{4}; WM tok^{5}; P tɔk^{2}

0359 - to boil (transitive), C2, (cf. 0447)
SW - tom^{3}; W tum^{3}; B, Sh tom^{3}; LNK tom^{5}; LCH, LMY tum^{3}; CM tom^{5}
CN - LP, LM tom^{3}; LC khaw^{3} tum^{3} 'dumpling of glutinous rice'; PS, NM tom^{3}
N - Y tum^{2}; Sk rɔɔm^{6}; WM tum^{5} (B2 in N languages)

0360 - bamboo strip for tying, DL2
SW - S tɔɔk^{2}; W, B tɔʔ^{2}; Sh tɔk^{2}; LCH, LMY tɔɔk^{2}; CM tɔɔk^{3}
CN - LP, LM phyook^{2}; WN thɔk^{2}; LC, PS, NM phyook^{2} (DL1 in CN languages)
N - Y tuk^{3}; Sk pluk^{4} (OG), pruk^{4} (YG); WM ruk^{5}; P tuk^{2} (DS2 in N languages)

0361 - to nibble, peck, DL2
SW - S tɔɔt^{2}; W, B tɔt^{2}; Sh tɔt^{2} 'to strike, as a snake'; LNK tɔɔt^{2}; LCH, LMY tɔɔt^{2} 'to bite, of a fish or snake'; CM tɔɔt^{3}
CN - LP toot^{5}; WN tɔt^{2}; LC, PS, NM toot^{2}
N - Y tot^{2}; Sk tɔɔt^{6}; WM tɤt^{5}

0362 - classifier for animals, A2
SW - S tua^{1}; W, B, Sh to^{1}; LNK too^{2}, tua^{2}; LCH, LMY too^{1}; CM tua^{2}
CN - LP tuu^{2}; LM, WN, LC, PS, NM tuu^{1}
N - Y tua^{4}; Sk thua^{4}; WM tu^{2}; P tuu^{2} (A4 in N languages)

0363 - land leech, DL4
SW - S thaak^{3}; W taa^{4}; B taaʔ^{5} (also, 'to measure'); Sh taak^{3}; LNK thaak^{5} 'land snail'; LCH, LMY taak^{5}; CM taak^{4}
CN - LM, WN taak^{5}; LC tɤk^{4}; PS tɤk^{4}, taak^{5}
N - Y taak^{2} (DL?, also, tɯk^{3} 'kind of water leech'); Sk thaak^{5} (but thɛɛk^{5} 'to measure'); WM taak^{5}; P taak^{6} 'to measure'

0364 - road, way, A4, (0474, 1101)
SW - S thaaŋ^{1}; W, B, Sh taaŋ^{4}; LNK thaaŋ^{6}; LCH, LMY taaŋ^{4}; CM taaŋ^{1}
CN - WN taaŋ^{4} (only in certain idioms)
N - Sk thaaŋ^{4}

0365 - cave, C1, (cf. 0974)
SW - S, W, B, Sh tham^{3}; LNK tham^{4}; LCH, LMY tham^{3}; CM tham^{5}
CN - LP, LM, PS tham^{3}
N - Sk tham^{3}

0366 - ashes, B4
SW - S thaw^{3}; W, B taw^{5}; Sh taw^{3}; LNK thaw^{3}; LCH, LMY taw^{5}; CM taw^{4}
CN - LP phyaw^{5}; LM pyaw^{5}; WN taw^{5}; LC, PS pyaw^{5}; NM phyaw^{5}
N - Y taw^{5}; Sk thaw^{5}; WM, P taw^{6}

0367 - equal, B4
SW - S thaw^{3}; W, B tɔ^{5}; LNK thɔɔ^{3}; LCH, LMY taw^{5}, tɔɔ^{5}; CM taw^{4}
CN - LP thoo^{5}; LM too^{6} (C4); LC too^{6} 'like, equal to' (C4); PS too^{6} (C4)
N - Y to^{5} 'enough'

0368 - a plow, to plow, A1
SW - S thay^{5}; W, B, Sh, LNK, LCH, LMY thay^{1}; CM thay^{2}
CN - LP, LM thay^{1}; WN thay^{1} (noun only; the verb is thɯɯ^{1}); BV, LC, PS thay^{1}
N - Y say^{1}; Sk thay^{2}; WM, P šay^{1}

0369 - candle, A4
SW - S thian^{1}; W ten^{4}; B tian^{4}; Sh ten^{4}; LNK thian^{6}; LCH, LMY ten^{4};
CM tian^{1}, thian^{1}
N - Sk thian^{4}

0370 - closely spaced, miserly, B1
SW - S thii^{2}; W, B, Sh thi^{2}; LNK thii^{3}; LCH, LMY thii^{2}; CM thii^{3}
CN - LP thii^{2}; LM thay^{2}; WN thii^{2}; LC thii^{2} 'hard, solid'; NM they^{2} (in CN languages always means 'dense, solidly packed', slightly different meaning in SW languages)
N - Y ti^{5}; Sk thii^{5}; WM toy^{6}; P tii^{6} (B4 in N languages)

0371 - place, B4
SW - S thii^{3}; W, B ti^{5}; Sh ti^{3}; LNK thii^{3}; LCH, LMY tii^{5}; CM tii^{4}
CN - LP thii^{5}; LM tey^{5} (believed by LP and LM informants to be < Cantonese); WN tii^{5}; LC, PS tii^{5}; NM they^{5}
N - Y ti^{5}; Sk thii^{6} (B?, only in certain expressions); WM ti^{5}, toy^{6} (Li says both < Chinese)

0372 - to hold, carry, A1, (cf. 0834)
SW - S thɯɯ^{5}; W, B, Sh tɯ^{4} (A4, also, in W, B 'to wear hat, shoes'); LNK thɯɯ^{1}; LCH, LMY tɯɯ^{4} (A4, also in certain expressions thɯɯ^{1} 'to hold or carry'); CM thɯɯ^{2}
CN - LP thɤɤ^{1}; LM thɤɰ^{1}; WN, LC, PS thɯɯ^{1}
N - Y tɯ^{4}; Sk thɯɯ^{4}; WM taɰ^{2}; P tɯɯ^{2} (A4 in N languages)

0373 - to stomp (on), DL4
SW - S (krǎ^{2}) thɯɯp^{3}; W tɯp^{4}; B tɯp^{5}; Sh tɯp^{3}; LNK thɯɯp^{5}; LMY tɯp^{5} (perhaps an error for thɯɯp^{5}?); CM tɯɯp^{4}
N - Sk thɯɯp^{5}

0374 - to fold double, DS4, (cf. 0288, 0422)
SW - S thop^{4}; W top^{4}; B, Sh top^{5}; LNK thop^{3}; LCH, LMY top^{5}; CM top^{6}
N - Sk thop^{6}

0375 - stomach, belly, C4
SW - S thɔɔŋ^{4}; W, B, tɔŋ^{6}; Sh tɔŋ^{5}; LNK thɔɔŋ^{5}; LCH, LMY tɔŋ^{6}; CM tɔɔŋ^{6}
CN - LP thooŋ^{3}; LM tooŋ^{6}; WN toŋ^{6}; LC, PS tooŋ^{6}; NM toŋ^{6}
N - Y tuŋ^{6}; Sk thuŋ^{6}; WM, P tuŋ^{4}

0376 - to remove, DL1
SW - S thɔɔt^{2}; W, B, Sh thɔt^{2}; LNK, LMY thɔɔt^{2}; CM thɔɔt^{3}
CN - LP thuut^{2}, thoot^{2}; LM thoot^{2}; WN thɔt^{2}; LC thut^{2} (Li says < Chinese); PS thoot^{2}; NM thuut^{2}
N - Y tot^{2}; Sk thuut^{6}; WM tuat^{5} (Li says < Chinese)

0377 - bean, B1
SW - S thua^{2}; W tho^{2}; B thua^{2}; Sh tho^{2}; LNK thua^{3}; LCH, LMY thoo^{2}; CM thua^{3}
CN - LP, LM, WN, LC, PS, NM thuu^{2}
N - Y tua^{5}; Sk thua^{5}; WM tu^{6}; P tuu^{6} (B4 in N languages)

0378 - bowl, cup, C1
SW - S thuay^{3}; W thoy^{3}; B thuay^{3}; LNK thuay^{4}; LCH, LMY thoy^{3}; CM thuay^{5}
CN - LP thooy^{3}; LM, LC, PS, NM thuuy^{3}
N - Y tɯay^{6}; Sk thooy^{6}; P tuy^{4} (C4 in N languages)

0379 - armspread (a measure), A4
SW - S waa^{1}; W, B vaa^{4}; Sh waa^{4}; LNK waa^{6}; LCH, LMY vaa^{4}; CM waa^{1}
CN - WN vaa^{4}
N - Sk vaa^{4}

0380 - to say, B4
SW - S waa^{3}; W, B vaa^{5}; Sh waa^{3}; LNK waa^{3}; LCH, LMY vaa^{5}; CM waa^{4}
CN - LP, LM vaa^{5} 'to lie' (said by LP and LM informants to be < Cantonese); WN vaa^{2} (B?); LC vaa^{5} 'sentence; to speak'; PS, NM vaa^{5}
N - Sk ɣaa^{5}

0381 - yesterday, A4
SW - S waan^{1}; W, B ŋwaa^{4}; Sh waa^{4}; LNK waan^{6}; LCH, LMY vaa^{4}; CM waa^{1}, waan^{1}
CN - LP, LM vaa^{4}; WN ŋaa^{4}; LC van^{4} vaa^{4}; PS, NM vaa^{4}

0382 - sweet, A1
SW - S waan^{5}; W vaan^{1}; B vaan^{1}, baan^{1}; Sh waan^{1}; LNK waan^{1}; LCH, LMY vaan^{1}; CM waan^{2}
CN - LP, LM, WN vaan^{1}; BV vaan^{2}; LC, PS, NM vaan^{1}
N - Y vaan^{1}; Sk vaal^{2} (OG), vaan^{1} (YG); WM waan^{1}; P vaan^{1}

0383 - day, A4
SW - S wan^{1}; W vin^{4}; B ven^{4}; Sh wan^{4} 'the sun, a day'; LNK wen^{6}, (also, wan^{6} in names of days of the week); LCH, LMY van^{4}; CM wan^{1}
CN - LP, LM, WN, LC, PS van^{4}; NM ŋan^{4}
N - Y van^{4}; Sk ɲɛn^{4}, (also, van^{4} in names of days of the week); WM ŋon^{2}; P ŋɔn^{2}

0384 - housefly, A4
SW - S (mɛɛŋ^{1}) wan^{1}; W (mɛŋ^{4}) mun^{4}; B (mɛŋ^{4}) ŋwan^{4}; LNK (mɛɛŋ^{6}) wan^{6}; LCH, LMY (mɛŋ^{4}) mun^{4}; CM (mɛɛŋ^{1}) ŋon^{1}
CN - LP (meeŋ^{4}) fɤn^{4}; WN (meŋ^{4}) fan^{4}; LC (meeŋ^{4}) fan^{4}
N - Y ɲan^{1}; Sk ɲɛl^{2} (OG), ɲɛn^{2} (YG) (A1 in N languages)

0385 - a cold, DS1
SW - S wat^{2}; W, B vat^{2}; Sh wat^{4}; LNK wat^{1}; LCH, LMY vat^{1}; CM wat^{2}
N - Sk vat^{4}

0386 - to put away, C4
SW - S way^{4}; W, B vay^{6}; Sh, LNK way^{5}; LCH, LMY vay^{6}; CM way^{6}
CN - LM, WN, LC vay^{6}

0387 - medicine, A3
SW - S, W, B, Sh yaa^{1}; LNK yaa^{2}; LCH yaa^{1}; LMY yaa^{4}; CM yaa^{1}
CN - LP yaa^{2}; LM yaa^{4}; WN, LC, PS, NM yaa^{1}
N - Y yia^{1}; Sk yaa^{1} (only in certain phrases < Lao and Siamese), WM ʔyɯ^{1}; P yii^{6}

0388 - paternal grandmother, B4
SW - S yaa^{3}; W, B yaa^{5}; Sh yaa^{3} ‘an appellation given to elderly females, now nearly obsolete in colloquial language’; LNK ɲaa^{3}; LCH, LMY yaa^{5}; CM ɲaa^{4} ‘old woman’
CN - LP, LM yaa^{5}; WN yaa^{5} ‘wife, woman’; PS yaa^{5}
N - Y ya^{5}; Sk yaa^{5}; WM, P yaa^{6}

0389 - grass, C1, (cf. 0498)
SW - S yaa^{3}; W, B ɲaa^{3}; Sh yaa^{3}, yɤ^{3}; LNK ɲaa^{4}; LCH, LMY yaa^{3}; CM ɲaa^{5}
CN - LP, LM yaa^{3}; WN ɲaa^{3}; LC, PS yaa^{3}; NM ɲaa^{3}
N - Y ɲia^{3}, ɲa^{1} (A?); Sk ɲua^{3}; WM ɲɯ^{3}

0390 - difficult, DL4, (cf. 0968)
SW - S yaak^{3}; W yaa^{4}; B yaaʔ^{5}; Sh yaak^{3}; LNK ɲaak^{5}, yaak^{5}; LCH, LMY yaak^{5}; CM ɲaak^{4}

0391 - coarse; vulgar, DL3
SW - S yaap^{2}; W, B ɲaap^{2}; Sh yaap^{2}; LNK yaap^{2}, ɲaap^{2}; LCH, LMY yaap^{2}; CM ɲaap^{3}
CN - LP yaap^{2} (DL?); LM yaap^{2}; WN ɲaap^{2}; LC yaap^{2}
N - Y ɲaap^{2}; Sk ɲiap^{6}; WM ɲaap^{5}

0392 - to step on, B4, (cf. 1072)
SW - yam^{3}; W, B ɲam^{5}; Sh yam^{3}; LNK ɲam^{3}; LCH, LMY yam^{5}; CM ɲam^{4}
CN - LM yam^{6} (C4); WN ɲam^{5}; LC, PS yam^{5}
N - Y ɲam^{5}

0393 - still, yet, A4
SW - S yaŋ^{1}; W, B ɲaŋ^{4}; Sh yaŋ^{4}, (also, ‘negative, not’); LNK ɲaŋ^{6}; LCH, LMY yaŋ^{4}; CM ɲaŋ^{1}, yaŋ^{1}
CN - LP, LM yaŋ^{4}; WN nɯŋ^{4}, naŋ^{4}; LC naŋ^{4}
N - Y naŋ^{2} (B?)

0394 - to stop, C4
SW - S yaŋ^{4}; W, B yaŋ^{6}; Sh yaŋ^{5}; LCH, LMY yaŋ^{6}; CM ɲaŋ^{6}
CN - LP yaŋ^{3}; LM, LC yaŋ^{6} ‘to lift (the foot)’ (same meaning in LP, LM; also, ‘to lift the arm’)

0395 - spiderweb, fiber, membrane, A4
SW - S yay^{1}; W, B, Sh yaɰ^{4}; LNK ɲay^{6}; LCH, LMY yay^{4}; CM ɲay^{1}

0396 - big, B1, (cf. 0200, 0765)
SW - S yay^{2}; W, B ɲaɰ^{2} ‘to grow bigger’; Sh yaɰ^{2}; LNK ɲay^{3}; LCH, LMY yay^{2}; CM ɲay^{3}
CN - WN ɲaɰ^{2} (< Lao)
N - Sk ɲay^{6}

0397 - to open (the mouth), C3
SW - S, W, B, Sh ʔaa^{3}; LNK ʔaa^{5}; LCH, LMY ʔaa^{3}; CM ʔaa^{5}
CN - LP, LM, WN, LC, PS, NM ʔaa^{3}
N - Y ʔa^{6}; Sk, WM ʔaa^{3}

0398 - saddle, A3
SW - S, W, B, Sh ʔaan^{1}; LNK ʔaan^{2}; LCH ʔaan^{1}; LMY ʔaan^{4}
CN - LP ʔaan^{2}; LM ʔaan^{4}; WN, PS, NM ʔaan^{1}
N - Y, Sk ʔaan^{1}

0399 - tendon, A3
SW - S ʔen^{1}; W ʔin^{1}; B, Sh ʔen^{1}; LNK ʔen^{2}; LCH ʔin^{1}; LMY ʔin^{4}
CN - LP yin^{2}; LM yin^{4}; WN yen^{4} (A4); LC, PS yin^{4} (A4); NM ŋen^{4} (A4)
N - Y ɲin^{4} (A4); Sk ʔin^{1}; WM ɲin^{2} (A4)

0400 - swallow (a bird), B3
SW - S, W, B, Sh ʔɛn^{2}
CH - LP ʔeen^{5}; LM ʔeen^{2}; WN ʔen^{2}; LC, PS, NM ʔeen^{2}
N - Y ʔen^{2}; Sk ʔeen^{6}; P ʔween^{5}

0401 - to bake, DS3
SW - S, B ʔop^{2}; LNK ʔop^{1} 'to steam' (modern synonym of nɯŋ^{4}); LCH, LMY ʔop^{1}; CM ʔop^{2}

0402 - cradle, B3
SW - S ʔuu^{2}; B, Sh ʔu^{2}; LNK ʔuu^{3}; LCH, LMY ʔuu^{2}; CM ʔuu^{3}
N - Sk ʔuu^{6}

0403 - shoulder, B3
SW - S, W, B baa^{2}; Sh maa^{2}; LNK baa^{3}; LCH, LMY baa^{2}; CM baa^{3}
CN - LP baa^{5}; LM maa^{2}; WN, LC, PS, NM baa^{2}
N - Y ba^{2}; Sk vaa^{6}; WM ʔbaa^{5}; P maa^{5}

0404 - village, C3
SW - S baan^{3} (also, 'house'); W, B baan^{3}; Sh maan^{3}; LNK baan^{5}; LCH, LMY baan^{3}; CM baan^{5}
CN - LP baan^{3}; LM maan^{3}; WN, LC, PS, NM baan^{3}
N - Y baan^{6}; Sk baan^{3}; WM ʔbaan^{3}; P maan^{3}

0405 - thin (not thick), A3, (cf. 0645)
SW - S, W, B baaŋ^{1}; Sh maaŋ^{1}; LNK baaŋ^{2}; LCH baaŋ^{1}; LMY baaŋ^{4}; CM baaŋ^{1}
CN - LP baaŋ^{2}; LM maaŋ^{4}; WN, LC, PS, NM baaŋ^{1}
N - Y baaŋ^{1}; Sk vaaŋ^{1}; WM ʔbaaŋ^{1}; P mɛɛŋ^{6}

0406 - flying squirrel, B3, (cf. 0888)
SW - S, W, B baaŋ^{2}; Sh waaŋ^{2}; LNK baaŋ^{3}; LCH baaŋ^{2}
CN - WN baaŋ^{2}
N - Y baaŋ^{2}; Sk paaŋ^{6}

0407 - young unmarried man, B3
SW - S, W, B baaw^{2}; Sh maaw^{2}; LNK baaw^{3}; LCH, LMY baaw^{2}; CM baaw^{3}
CN - LP baaw^{5}; LM maaw^{2}; WN, LC, PS, NM baaw^{2}
N - Y baaw^{2}; Sk baaw^{6}; WM ʔbaaw^{5}; P maaw^{5}

0408 - light (not heavy), A3
SW - S, W, B baw^{1}; Sh maw^{1}; LNK baw^{2}; LCH baw^{1}; LMY baw^{4}
CN - LP baw^{2}; LM maw^{4}; LC, PS, NM baw^{1}
N - Y baw^{1}; Sk vaw^{1}; WM ʔbaw^{1}; P maw^{6}

0409 - to strain, make an effort, B3
SW - S beŋ^{2}; W biŋ^{2}; B beŋ^{2}; Sh meŋ^{2}, weŋ^{2} 'to groan or grunt, as a person in sickness'; LNK beŋ^{3}; LMY biŋ^{2}
CN - LM miŋ^{2}; WN bɛŋ^{2}
N - Sk beŋ^{6}, bɛŋ^{6} (but some say the genuine Sk pronunciation is bliŋ^{6})

0410 - to twist, wring, DS3
SW - S, W, B bit^{2}; Sh mit^{4}; LNK, LCH, LMY bit^{1}; CM bit^{2}
CN - LP bit^{2}; LM mit^{3} ('to pinch, pluck' in both LP and LM); LC bit^{2} 'to pick, to break with fingers (flowers, fruits from the tree)' (or cognate rather with 0440?);
N - Y bit^{3} 'to pinch'; Sk bit^{4}

0411 - bored, B3, (cf. 0598, 1041)
SW - S, B bɯa^{2}; Sh mɤ^{2} 'sickened, poisoned'; LNK bɯa^{3} 'to be poisonous; to be bored' (cf. 1041); LMY bɤɤ^{2} 'bored, poisonous'; CM bɯa^{3}
CN - LP bɤɤ^{5}; LM mɯɯ^{2}; LC bɯɯ^{2} 'bored, disgusted' (same word as 1042, or perhaps the two words have become confused in some languages?); PS, NM bɯɯ^{2}
N - Y bɯa^{2}; WM ʔbɯ^{5}; P mɯɯ^{5}

0412 - side, C3
SW - S bɯaŋ^{3}; W bɤŋ^{3}; B bɯaŋ^{3}
CN - LP bɤɤŋ^{3}; LM mɯɯŋ^{3}; WN bɯŋ^{3}; LC, PS bɤɤŋ^{3}
N - Sk viaŋ^{3}; WM ʔbɯaŋ^{3}

0413 - dry land, DS3
SW - S, W, B bok^{2}; LNK, LCH, LMY bok^{1}
CN - LP bok^{2}; LM mok^{3}; WN bɔk^{6}; LC buk^{2} 'water goes down, dries up'; PS bok^{2} 'water goes down'; NM bok^{4} 'water goes down'
N - Y bok^{3} 'shallow'; Sk bɔk^{4}; WM ʔbok^{5}; P mɔk^{3}

0414 - on, A3, (cf. 0607, 0808)
SW - S bon^{1}; Sh mun^{1}, mon^{1}; LNK bon^{2}; LCH bun^{1}; LMY bun^{4}; CM bon^{1}
N - Y bun^{1}; Sk bɯn^{1}; WM ʔbun^{1}; P mɯn^{6} ('sky' in N languages)

0415 - well, spring, B3
SW - bɔɔ^{2}; W, B bɔ^{2}; Sh mɔ^{2} 'pit or mine in the ground'; LNK bɔɔ^{3}; LCH, LMY bɔɔ^{2}; CM bɔɔ^{3}
CN - LP boo^{5}; LM moo^{2}; WN, LC, PS, NM boo^{2}
N - Y bo^{2}; Sk bɔɔ^{6} 'mine'; WM ʔbɤ^{5}; P moo^{6} (B4)

0416 - blind, DL3, (cf. 1154)
SW - bɔɔt^{2}; W, B bɔt^{2}; Sh mɔt^{2}; LNK, LCH, LMY bɔɔt^{2}
CN - LP boot^{5}; LM moot^{2}; WN bɔt^{2}; LC, PS boot^{2}
N - Y bot^{2}

0417 - cicada (first syllable), DS2, (cf. 0418)
SW - S cak^{4} (DS4) (kă^{2} can^{2}); W, B cak^{2} (can^{2}); Sh sak^{4} (saa^{3}); LNK cak^{1} (can^{3}); LCH cak^{1} kuη^{2} 'kind of edible insect similar to a cricket but larger'; LMY in some other animal names: cak^{1} kin^{3} 'house lizard', cak^{1} khee^{3} 'crocodile'; CM cak^{6} can^{3} (DS4)

0418 - cicada (last syllable), B2, (cf. 0417)
SW - S (cak^{4} kă^{2}) can^{2}; W, B, (cak^{2}) can^{2}; LNK (cak^{1}) can^{3}; LCH cɛn^{2}; LMY can^{2}; CM (cak^{6}) can^{3}

0419 - to catch, DS2
SW - S, W, B cap^{2}; Sh sap^{4}; LNK, LCH, LMY cap^{1}; CM cap^{2}
CN - LP cap^{2} 'to perch'; LM cap^{3} 'to perch'; WN cɛp^{6} (but šɛp^{6}, šap^{6} 'to perch'); LC cap^{2} 'to light on (speaking of a bird)'
N - Sk cap^{4}

0420 - to tend (animals), C4
SW - W cɤη^{6}; Sh sɤη^{5} 'a female attendant upon a princess, a lady-in-waiting'
CN - LP chɤɤη^{3}; LM cɯɯη^{6}; WN ciη^{6}; LC cɤɤη^{6} 'to bring up (a child), to raise'
N - Y siaη^{6}; WM šɯaη^{4}; P šiiη^{4}

0421 - to pick (the teeth), C2
SW - S, W, B cim^{3}; LNK cim^{5}; LCH, LMY cim^{3}
N - Sk cim^{3}, ciim^{6} (B2)

0422 - to pleat, DL2, (cf. 0288, 0374)
SW - S ciip^{2}; W, B cip^{2}; LNK ciip^{2}
CN - LP ciip^{5}; LM cip^{3} (DS2); WN cip^{6} (DS2); LC, PS, NM cip^{2}

0423 - hoe, DL2
SW - S cɔɔp^{2}; W, B cɔp^{2}; LNK cɔɔp^{2}

0424 - peak, summit, A2
SW - S cɔɔm^{1}; W, B cɔm^{1}; Sh sɔm^{1}; LNK cɔɔm^{2}; LCH, LMY cɔm^{1}

0425 - swift (of water), B4, (cf. 0884)
SW - S chiaw^{3}; B tiaw^{5}; Sh sɛw^{3}; LCH ciw^{5}, cew^{5}, cɛw^{5}, xiw^{5}; LMY ciw^{5}, cew^{5}, cɛw^{5}; CM ciaw^{3} (B2?)
N - Sk riiw^{4} (OG), riw^{4} (YG) (perhaps < Siamese rew^{1} 'quick')

0426 - name, B4
SW - S chɯɯ^{3}; W, B cɯ^{5}; Sh sɯ^{3}; LCH, LMY cɯɯ^{5}; CM cɯɯ^{4}
CN - LM cɤɰ^{5} ('school name'; LM uses miŋ^{4} for 'name'); WN cɯɯ^{5}
N - Y so^{5}; Sk sɔɔ^{5}; WM šɤ^{6}; P šɯɯ^{6}

0427 - elephant, C4
SW - S chaaŋ^{4}; W, B caaŋ^{6}; Sh, LNK saaŋ^{5}; LCH, LMY, CM caaŋ^{6}
CN - LP chaaŋ^{3}, chɤɤŋ^{5} (B4), ɬɤɤŋ^{5} (B4); LM caaŋ^{6}, cɯɯŋ^{5} (B4); WN caaŋ^{6}; LC, PS caaŋ^{6}; NM cɯɯŋ^{5} (B4)
N - Y, Sk saaŋ^{6}; WM šɯaŋ^{6} (B4, Li says < Chinese); P šaaŋ^{4}

0428 - to weigh, B4
SW - S, Sh chaŋ^{3}; LNK saŋ^{3}; LCH, LMY caŋ^{5}; CM caŋ^{4}
CN - LP chaŋ^{5}; LM, WN caŋ^{5}; LC caŋ^{5} 'steelyard'; PS, NM caŋ^{5}
N - Y, Sk saŋ^{5}; WM šaŋ^{6} 'scales'; P šaŋ^{6}

0429 - to scold, revile, B3
SW - S, W daa^{2}; B daa^{2}, laa^{2}; Sh laa^{2}; LNK daa^{3}; LCH, LMY daa^{2}; CM daa^{3}
CN - LP daa^{5}; LM naa^{2}; WN, LC, PS, NM daa^{2}
N - Y da^{2}; WM ʔda^{5}; P naa^{5}

0430 - preverbal indicating present progressive time, A3
SW - W, B daaŋ^{1}
CN - LP daaŋ^{2} 'body'; LM naaŋ^{4} 'body'; WN daaŋ^{1} 'body; progressive'; LC daaŋ^{1} 'body'
N - Y daaŋ^{1} 'body'; Sk daaŋ^{1} 'in, during'; WM ʔdaaŋ^{1} 'body'; P naaŋ^{6} 'body'

0431 - spotted or splotched with white, B3
SW - S daaŋ^{2}; W baaŋ^{2}; B naŋ^{1} daaŋ^{2} daaw^{1} 'freckles'; Sh laaŋ^{2} ' a cutaneous disease appearing as white spots on the skin'; LNK daaŋ^{3}; LCH, LMY daaŋ^{2}
CN - LM maaŋ^{2}; WN daaŋ^{2}; PS, NM byaaŋ^{2}
N - Y daaŋ^{2}; Sk daaŋ^{6}

0432 - lye (water), B3
SW - S daaŋ^{2}; W, B daŋ^{2}; Sh laŋ^{2}
CN - LP daŋ^{5}; LM naŋ^{2}; WN daŋ^{2} (also, 'salty'); LC, PS, NM daŋ^{2}
N - Y daŋ^{2}; Sk daŋ^{6}; WM ʔdaŋ^{5}; P naŋ^{5}

0433 - sword, DL3, (cf. 0939)
SW - S, W daap^{2}; B, Sh laap^{2}; LNK, LCH, LMY daap^{2}
N - Sk daap^{6}

0434 - to weed, A3
SW - S daay^{1}; W, B baay^{1}; Sh maay^{1}; LNK daay^{2}; LCH baay^{1}; LMY baay^{4};
CN - LP yaay^{2}; LM myaay^{4}; WN daay^{1} (also, maak^{5} baay^{1} 'hoe'); LC, PS, NM byaay^{1}
N - Y daay^{1}; WM ʔdaay^{1}; P daay^{6}

0435 - nose, A3
SW - W, B daŋ^{1}; LNK daŋ^{2}; LCH daŋ^{1}; LMY daŋ^{4}; CM daŋ^{1}
CN - LP daŋ^{2}; LM naŋ^{4}; WN, LC, PS, NM daŋ^{1}
N - Y, Sk daŋ^{1}; WM ʔdaŋ^{1}; P naŋ^{4} (C4)

0436 - to transplant (young rice plants), A3
SW - S, B dam^{1}; LNK dam^{2}
CN - LP dam^{2}; LM nam^{4}; WN, LC, PS, NM dam^{1}
N - Y dam^{1}; Sk tram^{1}; WM ʔdam^{1}; P nam^{6}

0437 - to extinguish, DS3
SW - S, W dap^{2}; B dap^{2}, lap^{2}; Sh lap^{4} 'to be dark'; LNK, LCH, LMY dap^{1}; CM dap^{2}
CN - LP dap^{2}; LM nap^{3}; WN dap^{6}; LC, PS dap^{2}; NM dap^{4}
N - Y dap^{3}; Sk dap^{4}; P nap^{3}

0438 - which, what, any, A3, (cf. 1037)
SW - S day^{1}; W daɰ^{1}; B daɰ^{1}, laɰ^{1}; Sh laɰ^{1}; LNK day^{1}; LCH day^{1}; LMY day^{4}
CN - LP naɰ^{4} (A4); LM lɤɰ^{4}; WN ðaɰ^{4} (A4); LC naɰ^{4} (A4)
N - Sk dɤɤ^{1} 'who'

0439 - child, DS3, (cf. 0201)
SW - S dek^{2}; W dek^{2} nɔy^{6}, diŋ^{2} nɔy^{6}; B dek^{2}; LNK, LCH, LMY dek^{1}
CN - LP, LC, PS dik^{2}; NM dek^{4}
N - Sk dɛk^{4}

0440 - to pluck, DS3, (cf. 0916)
SW - S, W, B det^{2}; LNK, LCH, LMY det^{1}; CM det^{2}
CN - WN bit^{6} 'to pick (flowers)'; dɛt^{6} 'to pinch between the fingernails'; LC, PS bit^{2}; NM bet^{4} (cf. 0410)
N - Y biat^{3}; Sk rɛk^{4}; P mit^{3}

0441 - red, A3, (cf. 0491)
SW - S dɛɛŋ^{1}; W, B dɛŋ^{1}; Sh lɛŋ^{1}; LNK dɛɛŋ^{2}; LCH dɛŋ^{1}; LMY dɛŋ^{4}; CM dɛɛŋ^{1}
CN - LP deeŋ^{2}; LM neeŋ^{4}; WN deŋ^{1}; LC, PS, NM deeŋ^{1}
N - Y diŋ^{1}; Sk riiŋ^{1}; WM ʔdiŋ^{1}

0442 - good, A3
SW - S dii^{1}; W di^{1}; B di^{1}, li^{1}; Sh li^{1}; LNK dii^{2}; LCH dii^{1}; LMY dii^{4}; CM dii^{1}
CN - LP day^{2}; LM nay^{4}; WN, LC, PS day^{1}; NM dey^{1}
N - Y di^{1}; Sk dii^{1}; WM ʔdoy^{1}; P nii^{6}

0443 - gallbladder, A3
SW - S dii^{1}; W, B bi^{1}; Sh li^{1}; LNK bii^{2}; LCH dii^{1}; LMY dii^{4}
CN - LP dii^{2}; LM ney^{4}; WN, LC, PS dii^{1}
N - Y di^{1}; Sk blii^{1} (OG), bii^{1} (YG); WM ʔboy^{1}; P nii^{6}

0444 - to kick, DL3
SW - S diit^{2}; W, B dit^{2} 'to pounce'; LNK, LCH, LMY diit^{2}; CM diit^{3}
N - Sk bliit^{6} (OG), diit^{6} (YG)

0445 - earth, dirt, A3, (cf. 1004)
SW - S, W, B din^{1}; Sh lin^{1}; LNK din^{2}; LCH din^{1}; LMY din^{4}; CM din^{1}
CN - WN din^{1} 'land, country' (for 'earth' WN uses naam^{5})
N - Y naam^{5} 'earth'

0446 - raw, not ripe, DS3
SW - S, W dip^{2}; B dip^{2}, lip^{2}; Sh lip^{4}; LNK, LCH, LMY dip^{1}; CM dip^{2}
CN - LP dip^{2}; LM nip^{3}; WN dip^{6}; LC, PS dip^{2}; NM dop^{4}
N - Y dip^{3}; Sk rip^{4}; WM ʔdip^{5}; P nip^{3}

0447 - to boil (intransitive), DL3, (cf. 0359)
SW - S dɯat^{2}; Sh lɤt^{2}; LNK dɯat^{2}; LCH, LMY dɤɤt^{2}; CM dɯat^{3} 'angry'
CN - LP dɤɤt^{5} 'very hot'; LM nɯɯt^{2}; WN daat^{2} 'hot'; LC dɤɤt^{2} 'hot, angry' (current in the countryside)
N - Y daat^{2} 'hot'; Sk daat^{6} 'to scorch'; WM ʔdaat^{5} 'hot'; P naat^{5} 'hot'

0448 - forest, A3, (cf. 0258, 0900)
SW - S doŋ^{1}; W duŋ^{1}; B doŋ^{1}; Sh loŋ^{1}; LNK doŋ^{2}; LCH duŋ^{1}; LMY duŋ^{4};
CN - LP doŋ^{2}; LM noŋ^{4}; WN dɔŋ^{1}; LC duŋ^{1}; PS, NM doŋ^{1}
N - Y doŋ^{1}; Sk dɔŋ^{1}; P nɔŋ^{6}

0449 - winnowing basket, C3
SW - S (kă^{2}) doŋ^{3}; W duŋ^{3}; B doŋ^{3}; Sh loŋ^{3}; LNK (kă-) doŋ^{5}; LMY duŋ^{3}
CN - LP doŋ^{3}; LM noŋ^{3}; WN dɔŋ^{3}; LC duŋ^{3}; PS, NM doŋ^{3}
N - P nɔŋ^{3}

0450 - to look, watch over, A3
SW - S duu^{1}; W du^{1}; B du^{1}, lu^{1}; Sh lu^{1}; LNK duu^{2}; LCH duu^{1}; LMY duu^{4}
CN - LP duu^{2}; LC duu^{1} 'to tend to cattle, sheep, etc.'; PS duu^{1}

0451 - with, C3, (cf. 0482)
SW - S duay^{3}; W dɤy^{3}; Sh loy^{3}; LNK duay^{5}; LCH, LMY doy^{3}
CN - LP dooy^{3}; LM nuuy^{3}; LC duuy^{3}
N - Sk duay^{3} (said to be < Lao or Siamese)

0452 - palm, sole, B1
SW - S, W, B faa^{2}; Sh phaa^{2}; LNK faa^{3}; LCH, LMY faa^{2}
CN - LP phaa^{1} (A1); LM, WN, LC, PS, NM phaa^{3} (C1)
N - Y va^{2}; Sk paa^{6}, vaa^{1}; WM paa^{5}

0453 - split bamboo flooring, DL4
SW - S faak^{3}; W faa^{4}; B faaʔ^{5}; Sh phaak^{3}; LNK, LCH, LMY faak^{5}
N - Sk vaak^{5}

0454 - straw, stubble, A4
SW - S faaη^{1}; B fɯaη^{4}; Sh phɤη^{4}; LCH, LMY fɤη^{4}; CM fɯaη^{1}
CN - LP, LM, WN, LC faaη^{4}
N - Y fɯaη^{4}; Sk viaη^{1} (A?); WM fɯaη^{2}; P fɯɯη^{2}

0455 - cotton, C1
SW - S, W, B faay^{3}; LNK faay^{4}; LCH, LMY faay^{3}; CM faay^{5}
CN - LP, LM phaay^{3} 'cloth'; WN phaay^{3}; LC phaay^{3} 'cloth'; PS, NM phaay^{3}
N - Y vaay^{2} (B1); Sk paay^{1} (A?); WM, P faay^{5} (B1)

0456 - tooth, A4, (cf. 0133)
SW - S fan^{1}; W fan^{4} (usual word is xɛw^{3}); B fan^{4} (usual word is khɛw^{3}); LCH, LMY fan^{4} (literary; usual word is xew^{3})
CN - WN, LC fan^{4}
N - Y fan^{4} 'teeth of a saw'; WM fan^{2}

0457 - seed, A4, (cf. 0213, 0943)
SW - W, B fan^{4}; Sh phan^{4}; LCH, LMY fan^{4}
CN - LP, LM, WN, LC, PS fan^{4}
N - Y van^{1}; Sk van^{2}; P fan^{1} (A1 in N languages)

0458 - to dream, A1, (cf. 0460, 0537)
SW - S fan^{5}; W, B fan^{1}; Sh phan^{1}; LNK, LMY fan^{1}; CM fan^{2}
CN - LP, LM, WN phan^{1}; BV phon^{1}; NM phan^{1}
N - Sk van^{4} (A4)

0459 - river bank, B1
SW - S, W, B faŋ^{2}; Sh phaŋ^{2}; LNK faŋ^{3}; LCH, LMY faŋ^{2}; CM faŋ^{3}
CN - LM, WN phaŋ^{2}
N - Sk vaŋ^{6}; WM paŋ^{4} (C4); P faŋ^{5}

0460 - to dream of, B1, (0458, 0537)
SW - S fay^{2}; W, B faɰ^{2}; Sh phaɰ^{2}; LNK fay^{3} 'to desire (e.g., the good)'

0461 - a boil, A1
SW - S fii^{5}; W, B fi^{1}; Sh phi^{1}; LNK, LCH, LMY fii^{1}; CM fii^{2}
N - Y pay^{4} 'a boil not yet broken'; Sk phay^{4} 'impetigo' (A4 in N languages)

0462 - firewood, A4, (cf. 0574)
SW - S fɯɯn^{1}; B fɯn^{4}; Sh phɯn^{4}; LNK fɯɯn^{6}; LCH, LMY fɯn^{4}
CN - LP, LM fɤn^{4}; WN hun^{4}; LC, PS fɤn^{4}
N - Y fun^{4}; Sk vɯl^{1} (OG), vɯn^{1} (YG) (A?); WM fun^{2}; P fɯɯn^{2}

0463 - to grind, sharpen, A1, (cf. 0556, 0560, 1089, 1107)
SW - S fon^{5}; Sh phon^{1}; LNK fon^{1}; LMY fun^{1}; CM fon^{2}
CN - LP, LM phɤn^{1}; WN phan^{1}; LC, PS phɤn^{1}; NM phan^{1}

0464 - (two or more persons) carry, A1
SW - S haam^{5}; W, B, Sh, LNK, LCH, LMY haam^{1}; CM haam^{2}
CN - LP haam^{1}; LM, WN, BV thaam^{1}; LC, PS, NM haam^{1}
N - Y raam^{1}; Sk raam^{2}; WM raam^{1}; P lɛɛm^{1}

0465 - testicles, A1
SW - W, B, Sh, LNK ham^{1}; LCH, LMY ham^{1}, (xă-) lam^{1} (latter form is polite)
CN - LP ham^{1}; LM, WN, BV tham^{1}; PS ham^{1}; NM haam^{1}
N - Y ram^{1}; Sk ram^{2}; WM ram^{1}

0466 - to chop, C1, (cf. 0951)
SW - S, W, B ham^{3}
CN - LP, LM, WN tham^{3}; LC tham^{3} (current in the countryside); PS, NM tham^{3}
N - Y, WM ram^{3}; P lam^{3}

0467 - to close, DS1
SW - S, W, B hap^{2}; Sh hap^{4}; LNK hap^{1} (old-fashioned speech); LCH, LMY hap^{1}; CM hap^{2}
CN - LP hap^{2}; LM hap^{3}; PS hap^{2}; NM hap^{4}
N - Y hap^{3}

0468 - headlouse, A1
SW - S haw^{5}; W, B, Sh, LNK, LCH, LMY haw^{1}
CN - LP haw^{1}; LM, WN, BV thaw^{1}; LC, PS, NM haw^{1}
N - Y raw^{1}; Sk raw^{2}; WM raw^{1}; P law^{1}

0469 - hail, DS1
SW - S hep^{2}; W het^{2}; B hep^{2}; LNK hep^{1}
CN - LM hat^{3}; WN tat^{6}; LC, PS hat^{2}; NM hat^{4}
N - Y rip^{3}

0470 - chasm, A1
SW - S heew^{5}; B hɛw^{1}; LNK heew^{1}; LCH, LMY hew^{1}, hɛw^{1}

0471 - cast-net, A1
SW - S hɛɛ^{5}; W, B hɛ^{1}; Sh khɛ^{1}; LNK, LCH, LMY hɛɛ^{1}; CM hɛɛ^{2}
CN - LP, LM hee^{1}; WN chɛɛ^{1}; BV khee^{1}; LC, PS hee^{1}
N - Y re^{1}; Sk ree^{2} 'a long net'; P lee^{1}

0472 - impetigo, the itch, DS1
SW - S, W, B hit^{2}; Sh hit^{4}; LNK, LCH, LMY hit^{1}; CM hit^{2}
CN - LP khet^{2}, het^{2} (khit^{2}, hit^{2}?); LM lit^{3}; PS het^{2}
N - Sk hit^{4}; P lat^{2} 'measles'

0473 - to carry, as one carries a suitcase, C1
SW - S, W, B, Sh hiw^{3}; LNK hiw^{4}; LCH, LMY tiw^{3} (also, rare hiw^{3}); CM tiw^{5}, hiw^{5}
CN - LP, LM thiiw^{3}; WN thiw^{3}; LC yaw^{3} 'to hold something hanging down'; PS yiiw^{3}; NM thiiw^{3}
N - Y riaw^{3}; Sk riiw^{3} (OG), riw^{3} (YG), hiiw^{5}

0474 - road, A1, (0364, 1101)
SW - S hon^{5}; LNK hon^{1}; LCH, LMY hun^{1}; CM hon^{2}
N - Y ran^{1}; WM hon^{1}; P hɔn^{1}

0475 - to laugh, A1
SW - S hua^{5} (rɔʔ^{4}); B hua^{1}; Sh kho^{1}; LNK hua^{1}; LCH xoo^{1}; LMY xoo^{1}, hoo^{1}; CM hua^{2}
CN - LP vuu^{1}; LM luu^{1}; WN khuu^{1}; LC, PS huu^{1}; NM khuu^{1}
N - Y riaw^{1}; Sk ruaw^{2}; WM riaw^{1}; P liw^{1} (also transcribed as lyuu^{2})

0476 - loop, B1
SW - S huaŋ^{2}; W toŋ^{2}; B tuaŋ^{2}; Sh toŋ^{2}
N - Y kuaŋ^{6} (C?); Sk huaŋ^{6}

0477 - picture, B1
SW - S hun^{2} 'puppet, marionette'; W, B, Sh hun^{2}; LNK hun^{3} 'figure, appearance; robot'; LMY hun^{2}; CM hun^{3}
CN - WN hun^{2} 'image; design'
N - Y hun^{2}; Sk hun^{6}; WM hun^{5} 'track'

0478 - to cook (rice), A1
SW - S huŋ^{5}; W, B, Sh, LNK, LCH, LMY huŋ^{1}; CM huŋ^{2}
CN - WN thuŋ^{1}; LC huŋ^{1} (current in the countryside); NM hoŋ^{1}
N - Y ruŋ^{1}; Sk ruŋ^{2}

0479 - ear, A1
SW - S huu^{5}; W, B, Sh hu^{1}; LNK, LCH, LMY huu^{1}; CM huu^{2}
CN - LP vuu^{1}; LM low^{1}; WN chuu^{1}; BV, LC, PS huu^{1}; NM khyoo^{1}
N - Y rɯa^{4}; Sk rua^{4}; WM rɯ^{2}; P lɯɯ^{2} (A4 in N languages)

0480 - loom for weaving, DL1
SW - S huuk^{2}; W, B huʔ^{2}; Sh huk^{2} 'the warp of cloth'; LNK, LCH, LMY huuk^{2}
CN - LP hok^{2}; LM lok^{3} (DS1); WN thuk^{6} (DS1); LC huk^{2}; PS hok^{2}; NM huuk^{2}
N - Y rok^{2}; Sk huuk^{6}; WM rɤk^{5}; P look^{5}

0481 - a crow, A2
SW - S, W, B, Sh kaa^{1}; LNK kaa^{2}; LCH, LMY kaa^{1}; CM kaa^{2}
CN - LP kaa^{2}; LM kaa^{1}; WN kaa^{1}, ʔaa^{1}; LC, PS, NM kaa^{1}
N - Y ʔa^{1}; Sk kaa^{1}; WM ʔaa^{1}; P ʔaa^{6} (A3)

0482 - with, and, DS2, (cf. 0451)
SW - S, W, B kap^{2}; Sh kap^{4}; LCH, LMY kap^{1}; CM kap^{2}
N - Sk kap^{4}

0483 - old (of things), B2, (cf. 0091, 0712)
SW - S, W, B, Sh kaw^{2}; LNK kaw^{3}; LCH, LMY kaw^{2}; CM kaw^{3}
CN - LP kaw^{5}; LM, WN, LC, PS, NM kaw^{2}
N - Y kaw^{2}; Sk kaw^{6}; WM, P kaw^{5}

0484 - to pick up, DS2
SW - S, W, B kep^{2}; Sh kep^{4}; LNK, LCH, LMY kep^{1}; CM kep^{2}
CN - LP kip^{2}; LM kyap^{3}; WN cɛp^{6}; LC, PS kip^{2}
N - Y cip^{3}; Sk kip^{4}; P cip^{2}

0485 - to undo, untie, C2
SW - S kɛɛ^{3}; W, B, Sh kɛ^{3}; LNK kɛɛ^{5}; LCH, LMY kɛɛ^{3}; CM kɛɛ^{5}
CN - LP, LM kee^{3}; WN cee^{3}; LC, PS, NM kee^{3}
N - Sk kee^{3}; WM ke^{3}; P cee^{3}

0486 - rapids, B2
SW - S kɛŋ^{2}; W, B kɛŋ^{3} (C2?); Sh kɛŋ^{2} nam^{5}; LNK, CM kɛɛŋ^{3}

0487 - to eat, A2
SW - S, W, B, Sh kin^{1}; LNK kin^{2}; LCH, LMY kin^{1}; CM kin^{2}
CN - LP kin^{2}; LM kin^{1}; WN cin^{1}; LC, PS kin^{1}; NM ken^{1}
N - Y kɯn^{1}; Sk kin^{1}; WM, P kɯn^{1}

0488 - branch (of a tree), B2, (cf. 0960)
SW - S, W, B, Sh kiŋ^{2}; LNK kiŋ^{3}; LCH, LMY kiŋ^{2}; CM kiŋ^{3}
CN - LM, LC kiŋ^{2}
N - Sk kiiŋ^{6}, kiŋ^{6} (fast speech), kaaŋ^{6}

0489 - young rice plant, C2
SW - S klaa^{3}; W, B, Sh kaa^{3}; LNK kaa^{5}; LCH, LMY kaa^{3}; CM kaa^{5}
CN - LP caa^{3}; LM kyaa^{3}; WN caa^{3}; LC, PS, NM kyaa^{3}
N - Y ca^{3}; Sk tlaa^{3} (OG), traa^{3} (YG); WM klaa^{3}; P caa^{3}

0490 - hairknot, C2
SW - S klaaw^{3}; W, B, Sh kaw^{3}; LNK kaw^{5} 'to make a hairknot'; LCH, LMY kaw^{3} (both noun and verb); CM kaw^{6}
CN - LP caw^{3}; LM kyaw^{3}; WN caw^{3}; LC kyaw^{3}; PS kyaaw^{3}; NM kyaw^{3}
N - Y caw^{3}; Sk thraw^{3}; WM raw^{3}; P caw^{3} ('head' in all four languages)

0491 - dark (red), B2, (cf. 0441)
SW - S klam^{2}; W, B, Sh kam^{2}; LNK kam^{3}; LCH, LMY kam^{2}
CN - LM kyam^{2}; WN cam^{2} 'kind of leaf used to dye rice red'
N - Y cam^{2}; WM klam^{5} 'plant used as dye'; P cam^{5}

0492 - far, A2
SW - S klay^{1}; B, Sh kay^{1}; LNK kay^{2}; LCH, LMY kay^{1}; CM kay^{2}
CN - LP kway^{2}; LM kway^{1}; WN kay^{1}; LC, PS kway^{1}; NM kyay^{1}
N - Y cay^{1}; Sk tlay^{1} (OG), tray^{1} (YG); WM klay^{1}; P cay^{1}

0493 - drum, A2
SW - S klɔɔŋ^{1}; B, Sh kɔŋ^{1}; LNK kɔɔŋ^{2}; LCH, LMY kɔŋ^{1}; CM kɔɔŋ^{2}
CN - LP cooŋ^{2}; LM kyooŋ^{1}; WN coŋ^{1}; LC, NM kyooŋ^{1}
N - Y coŋ^{1}; Sk tlɔɔŋ^{1} (OG), trɔɔŋ^{1} (YG); WM klɤŋ^{1}; P cooŋ^{1}

0494 - I, A2, (cf. 0533, 1144)
SW - S kuu^{1}; W, B ku^{1}; Sh kaw^{1}; LNK kuu^{2}; LCH kaw^{1}, kuu^{1}; LMY kaw^{1}, kuu^{4}; CM kuu^{1} (A?)
CN - LP kaw^{2}; LM kaw^{1}; WN kuu^{1}, kuu^{6} (latter more frequent); LC, PS kaw^{1}; NM kow^{1}
N - Y ku^{1}; Sk kuu^{1}; WM kaw^{1}; P kuu^{1}

0495 - wicker hat, DS2
SW - W, B kup^{2}; Sh kup^{4}; LNK, LCH, LMY kup^{1}; CM kup^{2}
CN - LP cop^{2}; LM kip^{3} 'cape made of grass'; LC, PS kip^{2}
N - Y cap^{3}; P cop^{2}

0496 - more than, B2
SW - S, B kwaa^{2}; Sh kwaa^{2} 'to go'; LCH, LMY kwaa^{2} (also, 'to go past'); CM kwaa^{3}
CN - LP kwaa^{5}; LM kwaa^{2}; WN kaa^{2} 'away, past'; LC kwaa^{2} 'to pass by'; PS, NM kwaa^{2} 'to pass'
N - Y kwa^{2}; Sk kwaa^{6} (OG), kua^{6} (YG); WM, P kwaa^{5} ('to pass' in Y, WM, and P)

0497 - stuck, A4
SW - S khaa^{1}; W, B kaa^{4}; Sh kaa^{4} 'to escape, as an animal pierced by any weapon, and carrying the weapon in its flesh'; LNK khaa^{6}; LMY kaa^{4}
CN - LP khaa^{4}; LM kaa^{4}; WN kaa^{4}, caa^{4}; PS, NM kaa^{4}
N - Y ka^{4}; Sk khaa^{4}

0498 - thatch grass, A4, (cf. 0389)
SW - S khaa^{1}; W xaa^{4}; B kaa^{4}; Sh khaa^{4}; LNK khaa^{6}; LCH, LMY xaa^{4}; CM khaa^{1}
CN - LP, LM, WN haa^{4}; LC, PS, NM kaa^{4}
N - Y ha^{4}; Sk ɣaa^{4}; WM xaa^{2}; P haa^{2}

0499 - galangal, kind of root, B1
SW - S khaa^{2}; W xaa^{2}; B khaa^{2}; LNK khaa^{3}; LCH, LMY xaa^{2}; CM khaa^{3}
CN - LM haa^{2}; WN khaa^{2}
N - Y ha^{2}; Sk haa^{6}

0500 - price, value, B4, (cf. 0947)
SW - S khaa^{3}; W, B kaa^{5}; Sh kaa^{3}; LCH, LMY kaa^{5}; CM kaa^{4}
CN - LM, WN kaa^{5}
N - Y ka^{5}; Sk khaa^{5}; WM, P kaa^{6}

0501 - leg, A1, (cf. 0131, 1150)
SW - S khaa^{5}; W xaa^{1}; B, Sh, LNK khaa^{1}; LCH, LMY xaa^{1}; CM khaa^{2}
CN - LP khaa^{1}; LM khaa^{1} 'foot'; WN, BV khaa^{1}; LC khaa^{1} 'foot'; PS khaa^{1}; NM haa^{1}
N - Y ka^{1}; Sk kwaa^{1} (OG), kua^{1} (YG); WM haa^{1}; P kaa^{1}

0502 - carrying pole, A4
SW - S khaan^{1}; W, B, Sh kaan^{4}; LNK khaan^{6}; LCH, LMY kaan^{4}; CM kaan^{1}
CN - LP khaan^{4}; LM, WN, LC, PS, NM kaan^{4}
N - Y haan^{4}; Sk ɣaan^{4}; WM xaan^{2}; P haan^{2}

0503 - chin, A4
SW - S khaaŋ^{1}; W, B, Sh kaaŋ^{4}; LNK khaaŋ^{6}; LCH, LMY kaaŋ^{4}; CM kaaŋ^{1}
CN - LP khaaŋ^{4}; LM, WN, LC, NM kaaŋ^{4}
N - Y haaŋ^{4}; Sk ɣaaŋ^{4}; WM xaaŋ^{2}; P haaŋ^{2}

0504 - top for spinning, B1
SW - S khaaŋ^{2}; W (maaʔ^{2}) chaaŋ^{2}; B saaŋ^{2}; LNK (maak^{2}) khaŋ^{3}; LMY xaaŋ^{2}
CN - LP haaŋ^{5} (B4); LM laaŋ^{2}; WN chaaŋ^{2}; LC, PS haaŋ^{2}; NM khyaaŋ^{2}
N - Y caaŋ^{2}; WM raaŋ^{5}; P caaŋ^{5}

0505 - side, ribs, C1
SW - S khaaŋ^{3}; W chaaŋ^{3}; B saaŋ^{3}; Sh khaaŋ^{3}; LNK khaaŋ^{4}; LCH, LMY xaaŋ^{3}
CN - LP haaŋ^{3}; LM laaŋ^{3}; WN chaaŋ^{3}; LC, PS haaŋ^{3}; NM khyaaŋ^{3}

0506 - to hold in the jaws, DL4
SW - S khaap^{3}; W kaap^{4}; B kaap^{5}; Sh kaap^{3}; LNK khaap^{5}; LCH, LMY kaap^{5}
N - Y kaap^{5}; Sk khaap^{5}

0507 - to put out of the mouth, A4
SW - S khaay^{1}; W xaay^{4}; B kaay^{4}; Sh khaay^{4}; LNK khaay^{6}; LCH, LMY xaay^{4}
CN - LM, WN haay^{4}
N - Y haay^{4}; Sk ɣaay^{4}; P haay^{2}

0508 - to sell, A1
SW - S khaay^{5}; W xaay^{1}; B khaay^{1}; Sh khaay^{1}; LNK khaay^{1}; LCH, LMY xaay^{1}; CM khaay^{2}
CN - LP, LM, WN, BV, LC, PS khaay^{1}; NM haay^{1}
N - Y kaay^{1}; Sk kwaay^{1} (OG), kuay^{1} (YG); WM haay^{1}; P kaay^{1}

0509 - white, A1, (cf. 1055)
SW - S khaaw^{5}; W xaaw^{1}; B khaaw^{1} 'silver-colored'; Sh khaaw^{1}; LNK khaaw^{1}; LCH, LMY xaaw^{1}; CM khaaw^{2}
CN - LP, LM, WN khaaw^{1}; LC phɤɤk^{2} khaaw^{1}; PS khaaw^{1}
N - Y haaw^{1}; Sk haaw^{2}; WM haaw^{1}

0510 - dike between rice fields, A4
SW - S khan^{1}; W xan^{4}; B kan^{4}; LNK khan^{6}; CM khan^{1}
CN - LP khan^{4}; LM han^{4}; WN hen^{4} 'edge, side'; LC, PS kan^{4}; NM han^{4}
N - Y han^{4}; Sk ɣal^{4} (OG), ɣan^{4} (YG); WM xan^{2}; P han^{3} (C?)

0511 - to sing, DS1
SW - S khap^{2}; W xap^{2}; B khap^{2}; Sh khap^{4} 'to sing a metrical piece alternately, as a man and woman'; LNK khap^{1}; LCH, LMY xap^{1}
N - Sk hap^{4}

0512 - dry, B1, (cf. 0561)
SW - W xaɰ^{2}; B khaɰ^{2}
CN - LP, LM, WN, LC, PS khaɰ^{2}; NM haɰ^{2}
N - Sk khoo^{2} (A1), hɯɯ^{6} (which is cognate?)

0513 - they, other people, A1
SW - khaw^{5}; W chaw^{1}; B saw^{1}; Sh khaw^{1}; LCH, LMY xaw^{1}
CN - LP haw^{1}; LM law^{1}; WN khaw^{1}, thaw^{1}; LC khyaw^{1}; PS, NM haw^{1}
N - Sk raw^{2}

0514 - dove, A1
SW - S (nok^{4}) khaw^{5}; W chaw^{1}; B saw^{1}; LNK khaw^{1}
CN - LM law^{1}; WN chaw^{1}
N - Y raw^{1}; Sk haw^{2}; WM raw^{1}; P law^{1}

0515 - horn (of an animal), A1
SW - S khaw^{5}; W xaw^{1}; B khaw^{1}; Sh khaw^{1}; LNK khaw^{1}; LCH, LMY xaw^{1}; CM khaw^{2}
CN - WN khaw^{1}
N - Y, Sk, P kaw^{1}

0516 - salty, A4
SW - S khem^{1}; W kim^{4}; B kem^{4}; Sh sem^{4}; LNK khem^{6}; LCH, LMY cim^{4}; CM kem^{1}
CN - LP khim^{4}; LC, PS kim^{4}; NM kyom^{4}
N - Y kem^{4}, cem^{4}; Sk khɛm^{4}

0517 - hard, A1
SW - S khɛŋ^{5}; W, B, Sh khɛŋ^{1}; LCH, LMY xɛŋ^{1}
CN - LP kheeŋ^{1}; LM leeŋ^{1}; BV khɛɛŋ^{1}; LC, NM kheeŋ^{1}
N - Sk thriaŋ^{2}; WM kleŋ^{1}; P ceeŋ^{1}

0518 - son-in-law, A1
SW - S khɤɤy^{5}; W khɤy^{1}; B khɯay^{1}; Sh khoy^{1}; LNK khɤɤy^{1}; LCH, LMY xɤy^{1}
CN - LP khɤɤy^{1}; LM khuuy^{1}; WN khuy^{1}, khɯy^{1}; LC, PS khɤɤy^{1}; NM kuuy^{4} (A4)
N - Y kɯay^{4}; Sk khooy^{4}; WM kɯy^{2}; P kɯɯy^{2} (A4 in N languages)

0519 - accustomed, A4
SW - S khɤɤy^{1}; B khɤy^{4}; LNK khɤɤy^{6}; LCH, LMY kɤy^{4}; CM kɤy^{1}
N - Sk khɤɤy^{4}

0520 - to scratch (as chickens do), B1
SW - S khia^{2}; W khwe^{2}; B khia^{2}; Sh khe^{2}; LNK khia^{3}; LCH, LMY xee^{2}
CN - LP vii^{2}; LM lii^{2}; WN kee^{3} (C2?, probably not cognate)
N - Sk khia^{6}

0521 - tripod, A4
SW - S khiaŋ^{1}, khaa^{5} yaaŋ^{2}; W, Sh keŋ^{4}; LCH, LMY xeŋ^{4}
CN - LP khiiŋ^{4}; LM kiiŋ^{4}; WN ciŋ^{4}; LC kiiŋ^{4}
N - Y ciaŋ^{4}; Sk khiaŋ^{4}; WM kiaŋ^{2}; P ciiŋ^{2}

0522 - excrement, C1
SW - S khii^{3}; W, B, Sh khi^{3}; LNK khii^{4}; LCH, LMY xii^{3}; CM khii^{5}
CN - LP, LM khii^{3}; WN chii^{3}; LC, PS khii^{3}; NM khey^{3}
N - Y hay^{6}; Sk ɣay^{6}; WM xay^{4}; P hay^{4} (C4 in N languages)

0523 - ginger, A1
SW - S khiŋ^{5}; W xiŋ^{1}; B, Sh, LNK khiŋ^{1}; LCH, LMY xiŋ^{1}
CN - LP, LM khiŋ^{1}; WN chiŋ^{1}; BV, LC, PS khiŋ^{1}; NM hɤŋ^{1}
N - Y hiŋ^{1}; Sk hiiŋ^{2}; P hiŋ^{1}

0524 - eggplant, A1
SW - S (mǎ^{4}) khɯa^{5}; W khɤ^{1}; B khɯa^{1}; LNK (maak^{2}) khɯa^{1}; LCH, LMY (maak^{2}) xɤɤ^{1}; CM (baʔ^{2}) khɯa^{2}
CN - LP khɤɤ^{1}; LM khɯɯ^{1}; WN kɯɯ^{4} (A4); PS khɯɯ^{1}
N - Y kɯa^{4} (A4); Sk kee^{3} (but khɯa^{1} khɯa^{4} 'tomato', which syllable is cognate with 0524?); P kɯɯ^{4} (A4)

0525 - to grope, feel, A4
SW - S khlam^{1}; W, B cam^{4} (caa^{4}); Sh kam^{4}
CN - WN cam^{4} 'to pet'

0526 - dried sweat and dirt on the skin, A4
SW - S (khii^{3}) khlay^{1}; B (khi^{3}) kay^{4}; Sh khay^{4}; LNK (khii^{4}) khay^{6}; LCH, LMY (xii^{3}) xay^{4}
CN - LM lay^{4}; WN yay^{4}; PS nay^{4}
N - Y hi^{4}; Sk (ɣay^{6}) ɣii^{4}; WM xoy^{2} 'dirt'; P hii^{2}

0527 - to wobble, not firm or tight, A4
SW - S khlɔɔn^{1}; B kɔn^{4}; Sh khɔn^{4}; LMY xɔn^{4}
CN - LM hoon^{4}; WN hon^{4}

0528 - to lasso, C4
SW - S khlɔɔŋ^{4} (khɔɔ^{1}); B cɔŋ^{6} (kɔ^{4}); Sh kɔŋ^{5}; LNK khɔɔŋ^{5}; LMY kɔŋ^{6}
CN - LM looŋ^{6}; LC kyooŋ^{6} 'a loose knot'; PS, NM kyooŋ^{6}
N - Sk ɣɔɔŋ^{6}, tlɔɔŋ^{6}, thlɔɔŋ^{6} (OG), thrɔɔŋ^{6} (YG); WM klɤŋ^{4}

0529 - thick (of fluids), C1, (cf. 0595)
SW - S khon^{3}; LCH, LMY xun^{3}; CM khon^{5}
CN - WN khɔn^{3}
N - Y hun^{3}

0530 - to search, C4
SW - S khon^{4}; B kon^{6}; LCH, LMY xun^{6} 'to awaken someone'; CM khon^{6}
CN - WN hun^{5} (B4)
N - Y hun^{5} (B4); Sk khon^{3} (C1?)

0531 - body hair, A1
SW - S khon^5; W xun^1; B, Sh, LNK khon^1; LCH, LMY xun^1; CM khon^2
CN - LP, LM khon^1; WN khɔn^1; BV khon^1; LC khun^1; PS khon^1; NM hon^1
N - Y pun^1; Sk pul^1 (OG), pun^1 (YG); WM pun^1; P pɯn^1

0532 - bitter, A1
SW - S khom^5; W khum^1; B, Sh, LNK khom^1; LCH, LMY xum^1; CM khom^2
CN - LP, LM khom^1; WN kham^1; BV khom^1; LC khum^1; PS khom^1; NM hom^1
N - Y ham^4; Sk ɣam^4; WM xam^2; P ham^2 (A4 in N languages)

0533 - slave; I, C1, (cf. 0494, 1144)
SW - W xɔy^3; B khɔy^3; LNK khɔɔy^4; LCH, LMY xɔy^3; CM khɔɔy^5
CN - LP, LM khooy^3; WN khɔy^3; LC khooy^3
N - Y hoy^2; Sk hɔɔy^6; WM hɤy^5 (B1 in N languages)

0534 - indigo, A4, (cf. 0958)
SW - S khraam^1; W, B caam^4; Sh khaam^4 'a tree used for dyeing'; LNK khaam^6; LCH, LMY xaam^4
CN - LP chaam^4; LM laam^4; WN caam^4; LC kyaam^4 (also, laam^4 which Li says < Chinese); PS laam^4; NM kyaam^4
N - Y saam^4; Sk khaam^4; P šaam^2

0535 - discarded snake skin, DL4
SW - S khraap^3; W caap^4; B caap^5; Sh khaap^3; LCH, LMY xaap^5
CN - LM laap^5; PS kyaap^5
N - Sk thraap^5

0536 - sticklac, B4
SW - S khraŋ^3; Sh khaŋ^3; LMY xaŋ^5; CM caŋ^5
CN - WN caŋ^4 (A4)
N - Sk thraŋ^5, thaŋ^5

0537 - to desire, B4, (cf. 0458, 0460)
SW - S khray^3; Sh khay^3, khaɰ^3; LCH, LMY xay^5; CM khay^4
N - WM klay^2 (A4)

0538 - vine, A4, (cf. 0922)
SW - S khrɯa^1; W cɤ^4 (cf. 0037); B cɯa^4 'warp (in weaving)'; Sh khɤ^4; LNK khɯa^6; LCH, LMY xɤɤ^4; CM khɯa^1
CN - LM lɯɯ^4 'lengthwise threads in weaving'
N - Sk thaa^4 (probably not cognate?)

0539 - bunch of bananas, A4
SW - S khrɯa^1; W hɤ^4; B hɯa^4; Sh hɤ^4 'a stock or bunch of fruit or flowers'; LNK khɯa^6; LCH, LMY hɤɤ^4
CN - LM lɯɯ^4; WN lɯɯ^4 'a banana tree bearing fruit'

0540 - half, middle, B4
SW - S khrɯŋ^3; W cɯŋ^5; B cɤŋ^5; Sh khɯŋ^3; LNK khɤŋ^3; LCH, LMY xɯŋ^5
CN - LM liŋ^5 'to divide in half'; WN ciŋ^5
N - Sk thrɯŋ^5, khɤŋ^5; WM klaŋ^6 'to block the road half way'; P caŋ^6

0541 - big (tiger), B4, (cf. 0678, 0822)
SW - S (sɯa^5) khrooŋ^3; W (sɤ^1) cuŋ^5; B (sɯa^1) coŋ^5; LNK (sɯa^1) khooŋ^3;
    LCH, LMY (sɤɤ^1) xuŋ^5

0542 - entire, complete, DS4
SW - S khrop^4; B, Sh kop^5
CN - LM lop^4
N - Sk khop^6

0543 - kitchen, A4
SW - S khrua^1; B cua^4; Sh kho^4 'clothes, goods, property'; LNK khua^6; LCH,
    LMY xoo^4
N - Sk thrua^4 'family'

0544 - bridge, A1, (cf. 0952)
SW - W kho^1; B khua^1; Sh kho^1; LNK khua^1; LCH, LMY xoo^1; CM khua^2
N - Sk khaw^4 (A4, cognate?)

0545 - cycle, year, DL1, (cf. 0626)
SW - S, B khuap^2; Sh khop^2; LNK khuap^2; LCH, LMY xoop^2
CN - LP, LM khuup^2; WN khup^2; LC, PS khuup^2; NM khup^2
N - Sk khuap^6, thruap^6 (hypercorrection for khuap^6); P hoop^5

0546 - hole, pit, A1, (cf. 0038, 0318)
SW - S khum^5; W, B, Sh, LNK khum^1; LCH, LMY xum^1; CM khum^2
CN - LP, LM khom^1; WN, BV, LC khum^1; PS khom^1; NM kom^4 (A4)
N - Y kum^4; Sk khum^4; WM, P kum^2 (A4 in N languages)

0547 - pair, B4
SW - S khuu^3; W ku^5 'comrade'; B ku^5; Sh ku^3; LNK khuu^3; LCH, LMY kuu^5;
    CM kuu^4
CN - LP khuu^5; LM kow^5; WN, LC, PS kuu^5; NM koo^5
N - Y ku^5; P kuu^6

0548 - sharpened stake, DL1, (cf. 0554)
SW - S khwaak^2; W khaaʔ^2; B khwaaʔ^2; Sh khwaak^2; LNK khuak^2; LCH,
    LMY xwaak^2
CN - LP kuuk^5 'hoe' (DL2); LM kuuk^2 'hoe', vaak^2 'sharpened stake'; WN
    khaak^2; LC kuuk^2 'hoe' (Li regards all these as cognates; probably the
    words for 'hoe' are not)
N - Y vaak^2; Sk khwaak^6

0549 - axe, A1
SW - S khwaan^5; W, B khwaan^1; Sh khwaan^1 'a thunderbolt'; LNK khuan^1 (homonymous with 0171); LCH, LMY kwaan^1
CN - LM khwaan^1 (rare); WN khaan^1
N - Y vaan^1; Sk vaan^2; P vaan^1

0550 - nephew, niece; grandchild, A1
SW - S laan^5; W, B, Sh, LNK, LCH, LMY laan^1; CM laan^2
CN - LP, LM, WN laan^1; BV laan^2; LC, PS, NM laan^1
N - Y laan^1; Sk laan^2; WM, P laan^1

0551 - below, B4
SW - S laaη^3; W, B laaη^5 'space beneath an elevated house'; Sh laaη^3 'space beneath an elevated house'; LNK laaη^3; LCH, LMY (tay^3) laaη^5 'underneath a house'
CN - LP, LM laaη^5 'a pen'; WN laaη^2 (B?) 'space below'; LC laaη^5 'space beneath an elevated house'
N - Sk luaη^5

0552 - to rinse, wash, C4, (cf. 0325, 1116)
SW - S laaη^4; W, B laaη^6; Sh, LNK laaη^5; LCH, LMY, CM laaη^6
CN - LP laaη^3; LM, WN, LC, NM laaη^6
N - Y rɯaη^6; Sk laaη^6; WM rɯaη^4; P lɯɯη^4

0553 - saliva, A4
SW - S laay^1; W laay^4; B (să) laay^4; LNK laay^6; LCH, LMY laay^4; CM laay^1
CN - LP laay^4; LM, WN naay^4; LC, PS, NM laay^4
N - Y naay^4; Sk mlaay^4; WM mlaay^2; P naay^2

0554 - a stake, DS1, (cf. 0548)
SW - S, W, B lak^2; Sh lak^4; LNK, LCH, LMY lak^1; CM lak^2
CN - LP lak^2; LM lak^3; WN lak^6; PS lak^3 (tone?); NM lak^4
N - Y lak^3; Sk lak^4

0555 - back, A1
SW - S laη^5; W, B, Sh, LNK, LCH, LMY laη^1; CM laη^2
CN - LP, LM, WN laη^1; BV laη^2; LC, PS, NM laη^1
N - Y laη^1; Sk laη^2; WM, P laη^1

0556 - to sharpen (a knife), DS4, (cf. 0463, 0560, 1089, 1107)
SW - S, W lap^4; B, Sh lap^5; LNK lap^3; LCH, LMY lap^5
N - Sk lap^6

0557 - to tell, B4
SW - S law^3; W, B law^5; Sh, LNK law^3; LCH, LMY, CM law^5
N - Sk loo^5 (cognate?)

0558 - body louse, A4
SW - S len^{1}; B, Sh men^{4}; LNK len^{6}; LCH, LMY min^{4}
CN - LP, LM min^{4}; WN man^{4}; LC, PS min^{4}; NM men^{4}
N - Y nan^{4}; Sk mlɛl^{4} (OG), mlɛn^{4} (YG); WM nan^{2}

0559 - to exchange, DL4
SW - S lɛɛk^{3}; W lɛ^{4}; B lɛʔ^{5}; Sh lɛk^{3}; LNK, LCH, LMY lɛɛk^{5}; CM lɛɛk^{4}
N - Y le^{1} (DS4)

0560 - sharp-pointed, A1, (cf. 0463, 0556, 1089, 1107)
SW - S lɛɛm^{5}; W, B, Sh lɛm^{1}; LNK lɛɛm^{1}; LCH, LMY lɛm^{1}
CN - LP ɬiim^{3}; LM siim^{3}; WN lem^{1}; LC, PS ɬiim^{3}; NM ɬom^{1} (C1 in LP, LM, LC, PS)
N - Y lem^{1}; Sk lɛm^{2} 'to sharpen', lɛɛm^{2} 'sharp-pointed'

0561 - dry (of weather, season), C4, (cf. 0512)
SW - S lɛɛŋ^{4}; W, B lɛŋ^{6}; Sh lɛŋ^{5}; LNK lɛɛŋ^{5}; LCH, LMY lɛŋ^{6}; CM lɛɛŋ^{6}
CN - LP leeŋ^{3}; LM leeŋ^{6}; WN leŋ^{6}; LC, PS, NM leeŋ^{6}
N - Y reŋ^{6}; Sk lɛɛŋ^{6}; WM reŋ^{4}; P leeŋ^{4}

0562 - finished, C4
SW - S lɛɛw^{4}; B lɛw^{6}; LNK lɛɛw^{5}; LCH, LMY lɛw^{6}; CM lɛɛw^{6}
CN - LP leew^{3}; LM leew^{6}; WN lɛw^{6}; PS leew^{3} (C?)
N - Y lew^{6}; Sk lɛɛw^{6}; WM liaw^{4}

0563 - to lick, A4
SW - S lia^{1}; W le^{4}; B lia^{4}; Sh le^{4}; LNK lia^{6}; LCH, LMY lee^{4}; CM lia^{1}
CN - LP lii^{4}; LM ley^{4}; LC, PS, NM lii^{4}
N - Y ria^{4}; Sk lia^{4}; WM ri^{2}; P lii^{2}

0564 - monkey, A4
SW - S liŋ^{1}; W, B, Sh liŋ^{4}; LNK liŋ^{6}; LCH, LMY liŋ^{4}
CN - LP, LM, WN, LC, PS liŋ^{4}; NM lɤŋ^{4}
N - Y liŋ^{4}; Sk liiŋ^{4}

0565 - to be left over, A1
SW - S lɯa^{5}; W lɤ^{1}; B lɯa^{1}; Sh lɤ^{1}; LNK lɯa^{1}; LCH, LMY lɤɤ^{1}; CM lɯa^{2}
CN - LP lɤɤ^{1}; LM, WN lɯɯ^{1}; PS, NM lɯɯ^{2} (B?)
N - Y lɯa^{1}; Sk lua^{2}; WM lɯ^{1}; P lɯɯ^{1}

0566 - python, A1
SW - S (ŋuu^{1}) lɯam^{5}; W (ŋu^{4}) lɤm^{1}; B (to^{1}) lɯam^{1}; Sh lɤm^{1}; LNK (ŋuu^{6}) lɯam^{1}; LCH, LMY (ŋuu^{4}) lɤm^{1}
CN - WN num^{1}
N - Y (tua^{4}) nuam^{1}

0567 - yellow, A1
SW - S lɯaŋ^{5}; W lɤŋ^{1}; B lɯaŋ^{1}; Sh lɤŋ^{1}; LNK lɯaŋ^{1}; LCH, LMY lɤŋ^{1}; CM lɯaŋ^{2}
CN - LP lɤɤŋ^{1}; WN lɯŋ^{1} (usual word is hen^{3}); LC, PS lɤɤŋ^{1}; NM lɯɯŋ^{1}
N - Sk vaaŋ^{4} (A4, cognate?)

0568 - gadfly, DL1
SW - S lɯap^{2}; W lɤʔ^{2}; B lɯaʔ^{2}; Sh lɤk^{2}; LNK lɯap^{2}; LCH, LMY lɤɤk^{2}
CN - LM nɯɯk^{2}; WN lɤt^{2}
N - Y lɯak^{2}; Sk lɯap^{6}

0569 - the wind, A4
SW - S lom^{1}; W lum^{4}; B, Sh lom^{4}; LNK lom^{6}; LCH, LMY lum^{4}; CM lom^{1}
CN - LP, LM lom^{4}; WN lam^{4}; LC lum^{4}; PS, NM lom^{4}
N - Y rum^{4}; Sk lum^{4}; WM rum^{2}; P lum^{2}

0570 - to sink into mud, B1
SW - S lom^{2} 'mud'; W lum^{2}; B lom^{2} 'low place'; Sh lom^{2}; LNK lom^{3} 'muddy place in a road'; LCH, LMY lum^{2} 'to step into (mud, a hole, etc.)'; CM lom^{3}
CN - LM lom^{2}; WN lam^{2} 'to step into (mud, a hole)'
N - Y lam^{2} 'to sink'; WM lom^{5}, lom^{1}; P lɔm^{5}

0571 - to go down, A4
SW - S loŋ^{1}; W luŋ^{4}; B, Sh loŋ^{4}; LNK loŋ^{6}; LCH, LMY luŋ^{4}; CM loŋ^{1}
CN - LP noŋ^{4}; LM loŋ^{4}; WN lɔŋ^{4}; LC nuŋ^{4}; PS, NM noŋ^{4}
N - Y roŋ^{4}; Sk lɔŋ^{4}; WM roŋ^{2}; P lɔŋ^{2}

0572 - to cast (metal), B1
SW - S lɔɔ^{2}; W, B, Sh lɔ^{2}; LNK lɔɔ^{3}; LCH, LMY lɔɔ^{2}
CN - WN loo^{2} 'to pour'

0573 - wheel, C4
SW - S lɔɔ^{4}; W lɔ^{6} 'spool'; Sh lɔ^{5} 'cart'; LNK lɔɔ^{5} 'cart, wheel'; LCH, LMY lɔɔ^{6} 'cart; wheel'; CM lɔɔ^{6} 'oxcart'
N - Sk lɔɔ^{3} 'oxcart' (C?, probably < Lao); P luu^{4} 'to roll'

0574 - firewood, A1, (cf. 0462)
SW - W lo^{1}; B lua^{1}; Sh lo^{1}; LNK lua^{1} 'bamboo used for firewood'; LCH, LMY loo^{1}; CM lua^{2}
CN - WN luu^{1} 'small pieces of bamboo for firewood'
N - Sk lua^{2} 'bamboo firewood'

0575 - loose-fitting, A1
SW - S luam^{5}; W lom^{1}; B luam^{1}; Sh lom^{1}; LNK lom^{1} (modern luam^{1}); LCH, LMY lum^{1}
N - Y lom^{1}; WM lɤm^{1}

0576 - uncle, older brother of either parent, A4
SW - S luŋ^{1}; W, B, Sh luŋ^{4}; LNK luŋ^{6}; LCH, LMY luŋ^{4}; CM luŋ^{1}
CN - LP, LM loŋ^{4}; WN, LC luŋ^{4}; PS, NM loŋ^{4}
N - Sk luŋ^{4}; WM, P luŋ^{2}

0577 - to soak, B1, (cf. 0770)
SW - S, W, B maa^{2}; Sh maa^{2} 'to soak in liquor'; LNK maa^{3}; LCH, LMY maa^{2}; CM maa^{3}
CN - LP, LM, WN, PS, NM maa^{2}
N - Y ma^{2}; Sk maa^{6}; P maa^{2} (A4)

0578 - to increase, C1
SW - W maa^{3}; B maa^{3} 'interest, profit'
CN - LP, LM maa^{3}; WN maa^{3} 'to rise, of water'; LC, PS maa^{3}
N - Y ma^{3}; P maa^{3}

0579 - classifier for tools, DL4
SW - W maa^{4}, maʔ^{2}, maaʔ^{4}; B maaʔ^{5}; Sh maak^{3}
CN - LP, LM, WN maak^{5}; LC maak^{4}; PS, NM maak^{5}
N - Y faak^{5}; Sk maak^{5}, maak^{6}; WM faak^{6}

0580 - to mark; to intend, aim, A1
SW - S maay^{5}; W, B, Sh, LNK, LCH, LMY maay^{1}; CM maay^{2}
CN - LM, WN maay^{1}
N - Y maay^{1}; Sk maay^{2}; P maay^{1}

0581 - to like, DS4
SW - S mak^{4} 'to be inclined to'; W mak^{4}; B, Sh mak^{5}; LNK mak^{3}; LMY mak^{5}; CM mak^{6}
N - Sk mak^{6}

0582 - he, it, A4
SW - S man^{1}; W, B, Sh man^{4}; LNK man^{6}; LCH, LMY man^{4}; CM man^{1}
CN - LP min^{4}; WN man^{4}; LC mɤn^{4}; PS min^{4}; NM men^{1}
N - Sk man^{4}

0583 - potato, A4
SW - S man^{1}; W, B man^{4}; Sh man^{4} 'sweet potato'; LNK man^{6}; LCH, LMY man^{4}; CM man^{1}
CN - LP, LM, WN, LC, PS man^{4}
N - Y, Sk man^{4}; P man^{2}

0584 - oil, A4, (cf. 1076)
SW - S man^{1}; B, Sh man^{4}; LNK man^{6}; LCH, LMY man^{4}; CM man^{1}
N - Sk man^{4}

0585 - porcupine, C1
SW - S men^{3}; W min^{3}; B, Sh men^{3}; LNK men^{4}; LCH, LMY min^{3}; CM men^{5}
CN - LP, LM min^{3}; WN man^{3}; LC min^{3}; PS min^{6} (C4); NM men^{3}
N - Sk man^{3}, men^{3}

0586 - to have, A4
SW - S mii^{1}; W, B, Sh mi^{4}; LNK mii^{6}; LCH, LMY mii^{4}; CM mii^{1}
CN - LP mii^{4}; LM mey^{4}; WN, LC, PS mii^{4}; NM mey^{4}
N - Y mi^{4}; Sk mii^{4}; WM mi^{2}; P mii^{2}

0587 - ditch, A1
SW - S mɯaŋ^{5} 'a mine'; W mɤŋ^{1}; B mɯaŋ^{1}; Sh mɤŋ^{1} 'a dam'; LNK mɯaŋ^{1} 'a mine'; LCH, LMY mɤŋ^{1}; CM mɯaŋ^{2}
CN - LP mɤɤŋ^{1}; LM mɯɯŋ^{1}; WN mɯŋ^{1}; LC mɤɤŋ^{1} (current in the countryside); PS mɤɤŋ^{1}
N - Sk mɯaŋ^{1}; WM mɯaŋ^{1}

0588 - you, A4
SW - S mɯŋ^{1}; W, B mɯŋ^{4}; Sh maɰ^{4}; LNK mɯŋ^{6}; LCH, LMY mɯŋ^{4}; CM mɯŋ^{1}
CN - LP, LM, WN, LC, PS maɰ^{4}; NM maŋ^{1}
N - Y, Sk mɯŋ^{4}; P mɯŋ^{2}

0589 - mango, B4
SW - S muaŋ^{3}; W moŋ^{5}; B muaŋ^{5}; LNK muaŋ^{3}; LCH, LMY moŋ^{5}; CM muaŋ^{4} (in each language preceded by the word for 'fruit')
CN - WN mɔŋ^{5}
N - Y moŋ^{5}; Sk miaŋ^{5}

0590 - pig, A1
SW - S muu^{5}; W, B, Sh mu^{1}; LNK, LCH, LMY muu^{1}; CM muu^{2}
CN - LP muu^{1}; LM mow^{1}; WN muu^{1}; BV muu^{2}; LC, PS muu^{1}; NM now^{1}
N - Y mu^{1}; Sk muu^{2}; WM maw^{1}; P muu^{1}

0591 - mucus of the nose, DL4
SW - S muuk^{3}; W muʔ^{4}; B muʔ^{5}; LNK, LCH, LMY muuk^{5}
CN - LP mok^{5}; LM mook^{5}; WN muk^{5}; LC muk^{4}; PS mok^{4} (DS4); NM muuk^{5}
N - Y muk^{1} (DS4); Sk muuk^{5}; WM muk^{5} (DL?); P muk^{3} (DS4)

0592 - face, C1
SW - S, W, B, Sh naa^{3}; LNK naa^{4}; LCH, LMY naa^{3}; CM naa^{5}
CN - LP, LM, WN, LC, PS, NM naa^{3}
N - Y na^{3}; Sk, WM, P naa^{3}

0593 - crossbow, C1
SW - S, W, B naa^{3}; LNK naa^{4}; LMY naa^{3}
CN - WN naa^{3}
N - Y nɯa^{3}; Sk nua^{3}

0594 - mother's younger sibling, C4
SW - S naa^{4}; W, B naa^{6}; Sh na^{5}; LNK naa^{5}; LCH, LMY, CM naa^{6}
CN - LP, LM, WN, LC, PS naa^{5} (B4 in CN languages)
N - Y na^{6}; Sk naa^{6} (C4 in N languages)

0595 - thick, A1, (cf. 0529)
SW - S naa^{5}; W, B, Sh, LNK, LCH, LMY naa^{1}; CM naa^{2}
CN - LP, LM, WN naa^{1}; BV naa^{2}; LC, PS, NM naa^{1}
N - Y na^{1}; Sk naa^{2}; WM, P naa^{1}

0596 - otter, DL4
SW - S naak^{3}; W naa^{4}; B naaʔ^{5}
CN - LP, LM, WN, PS, NM naak^{5}
N - Y naak^{5}; Sk naak^{5}; WM naak^{6}

0597 - long (of time), A4, (cf. 0975, 1058, 1155)
SW - S naan^{1}; W, B, Sh naan^{4}; LNK naan^{6}; LCH, LMY naan^{4}
CN - LM, WN naan^{4}
N - Y naan^{4}; WM naan^{2}; P naan^{2}

0598 - bored, B1, (cf. 0411, 1041)
SW - S, W, B naay^{2}; LNK naay^{3}; LCH, LMY naay^{2}; CM naay^{3}
CN - LP, LM, LC naay^{2} 'tired'
N - Y naay^{2}; Sk naay^{6}; WM nwaay^{5}; P naay^{5} ('tired' in all four languages)

0599 - to soften over a fire, B4
SW - S naay^{3}; B nay^{5}; Sh nay^{3}; LCH, LMY nay^{5}; CM nay^{4}

0600 - skin, A1
SW - S naŋ^{5}; W, B, Sh, LNK, LCH, LMY naŋ^{1}; CM naŋ^{2}
CN - LP, LM, WN naŋ^{1}; BV naŋ^{2}; LC, PS, NM naŋ^{1}
N - Y naŋ^{1}; Sk naŋ^{2}; WM, P naŋ^{1}

0601 - in, inside, A4
SW - S nay^{1}; W, B naɰ^{4} 'yonder'; Sh naɰ^{4}; LNK nay^{6}; LCH, LMY nay^{4}; CM nay^{1}
CN - LP daɰ^{2} (A3); LM naɰ^{4}; WN, LC, PS, NM daɰ^{1} (A3)
N - Y daɰ^{1}; Sk rɤɤ^{1}; WM ʔdaɰ^{1}; P naɰ^{6} (A3 in N languages)

0602 - rotten, B4
SW - S naw^{3}; W, B naw^{5}; Sh, LNK naw^{3}; LCH, LMY naw^{5}; CM naw^{4}
CN - LP, LM, WN, PS, NM naw^{5}
N - Y, Sk naw^{5}; WM, P naw^{6}

0603 - tough, sticky, A1, (cf. 1030)
SW - S niaw^{5}; W new^{1}; B niaw^{1}; Sh new^{1}; LNK niaw^{1}; LCH, LMY new^{1}
CN - LM neew^{1}
N - Y niaw^{1}; Sk niaw^{2}

0604 - to pinch or hold in claws, under the arm, DL1, (cf. 0139)
SW - S niip^{2}; W, B nip^{2}; Sh nip^{3} (DL4); LNK, LMY niip^{2}
CN - LP nip^{2} 'to pick up with chopsticks'; LC nip^{2} 'to pinch, to take with chopsticks'
N - Y nip^{3} (DS1); Sk niip^{6} (said to be < Lao)

0605 - pangolin, B4
SW - S nim^{3}; W, B lin^{5}; Sh, LNK lin^{3}; LCH, LMY lin^{5}
CN - LP, LM, WN lin^{5}; NM len^{5}
N - Y lin^{5}; Sk lil^{5} (OG), lin^{5} (YG); WM lin^{6}

0606 - meat, flesh, C4
SW - S nɯa^{4}; Sh nɤ^{5}; LNK nɯa^{5}; LCH, LMY nɤɤ^{6} (also called cin^{6})
CN - LP nɤɤ^{3}; LM, WN nɯɯ^{6}; LC, PS, NM nɯɯ^{6}
N - Y no^{5}; Sk mlɔɔ^{5}; WM nɤ^{6}; P noo^{6} (B4 in N languages)

0607 - above, north, A1, (cf. 0414, 0808)
SW - S nɯa^{5}; W nɤ^{1}; B nɯa^{1}; Sh nɤ^{1}; LNK nɯa^{1}; LCH, LMY nɤɤ^{1}; CM nɯa^{2}
CN - LP nɤɤ^{1}; LM, WN nɯɯ^{1}; BV nɯɯ^{2}; LC, PS, NM nɯɯ^{1}

0608 - tired, B1
SW - S nɯay^{2}; W nɤy^{2}; B nɯay^{2}; Sh noy^{2}; LNK nɯay^{3}; LCH, LMY nɤy^{2}
CN - WN nɯy^{2}

0609 - worm, A1
SW - S nɔɔn^{5}; W, B nɔn^{1}; Sh nɔn^{1} 'maggot'; LNK nɔɔn^{1}; LMY nɔn^{1}; CM nɔɔn^{2}
CN - LP, LM noon^{1}; WN non^{1}; LC, PS, NM noon^{1}
N - Y non^{1}; Sk nɔɔl^{2} (OG), nɔɔn^{2} (YG); WM nɤn^{1}; P noon^{1}

0610 - younger sibling, C4
SW - S nɔɔη^{4}; W, B nɔη^{6}; Sh nɔη^{5}; LNK nɔɔη^{5}; LCH, LMY nɔη^{6}; CM nɔɔη^{6}
CN - LP nooη^{3}; LM nooη^{6}; WN noη^{6}; LC, PS, NM nooη^{6}
N - Y, Sk nuaη^{6}; WM nuaη^{4}; P nuuη^{4}

0611 - deaf, DL1
SW - S nuak^{2}; W noʔ^{2}; B nuaʔ^{2}; Sh nok^{2}; LNK nuak^{2}; LCH, LMY nook^{2}
CN - LP, LM nuuk^{2}; WN nuk^{2}; LC, PS, NM nuuk^{2}
N - Y nuk^{3} (DS1); Sk nuuk^{6}; WM nuk^{5}; P nuk^{2} (DS1)

0612 - young, B1
SW - S num^{2} (only of men); W, B num^{2}, nɔm^{2}; Sh num^{2}; LNK num^{3}; LCH, LMY num^{2}; CM num^{3}
N - Sk num^{6} (said to be < Lao)

0613 - kapok, B4, (cf. 0215)
SW - S nun^{3}; W, B nun^{5}; Sh, LNK nun^{3}; LMY nun^{5}
N - Y nun^{5}; Sk nun^{6} (C4, said to be < Lao)

0614 - to support, as with a pillow, A1
SW - S nun^{5}; W, B, Sh mun^{1}; LNK nun^{1}, muun^{1}; LCH, LMY nun^{1}, mun^{1}
N - Sk muun^{2}

0615 - rat, mouse, A1
SW - S nuu^{5}; W, B, Sh nu^{1}; LNK, LCH, LMY nuu^{1}; CM nuu^{2}
CN - LP nuu^{1}; LM now^{1}; WN nuu^{1}; BV nuu^{2}; LC, PS nuu^{1}; NM now^{1}
N - Y nu^{1}; Sk nuu^{2}; WM naw^{1}; P nuu^{1}

0616 - elephant's tusk, ivory, A4
SW - S ηaa^{1}; W, B, Sh ηaa^{4}; LNK ηaa^{6}; LCH, LMY ηaa^{4}; CM ηaa^{1}
CN - LP yaa^{4}; LM ηaa^{4}, yaa^{4}; WN ηaa^{4}; PS yaa^{4}
N - Y ηa^{4}; Sk ηaa^{4}

0617 - sesame, A4
SW - S ηaa^{1}; W, B, Sh ηaa^{4}; LNK ηaa^{6}; LCH, LMY ηaa^{4}
CN - LP, LM, WN, LC, PS ηaa^{4}; NM haa^{4}
N - Y ηa^{4}, ra^{4}; WM raa^{2}; P ηaa^{2}

0618 - (to lie) face up, A1
SW - S ηaay^{5}; W, B haay^{1}; Sh ηaay^{1}, haay^{1} 'to turn back or over'; LNK, LCH, LMY ηaay^{1}
CN - LM haay^{1}; WN ηaay^{1}
N - Y haay^{1}; Sk ηaay^{2}

0619 - central root, C1
SW - S ŋaw^{3}; W, B haw^{3}; Sh ŋaw^{3} 'bottom, foundation, origin'; LNK ŋaw^{4}; LCH, LMY ŋaw^{3}
CN - WN ŋaw^{3} 'stem (of fruit)'

0620 - to tilt the head back, A1
SW - S ŋɛɛn^{5}; W, B hɛn^{1}; Sh ŋɛn^{1} 'to look up to, depend upon', hɛn^{1} 'to turn up the face, to look up'; LNK hɛɛn^{1} (modern ŋɛɛn^{1}); LMY ŋɛn^{1}

0621 - mythical water creature, DL4
SW - S ŋɯak^{3}; W ŋɤ^{4}; B ŋɯaʔ^{5}; Sh ŋɤk^{3} 'an alligator, crocodile'; LNK ŋɯak^{5}; LCH, LMY ŋɤɤk^{5}
CN - LP hɤɤk^{5}; LM ŋɯɯk^{5}; WN ŋɤk^{5}; LC ŋɤɤk^{4}; PS ŋɤɤk^{5}
N - Y ŋɯak^{5}; Sk ŋuak^{5}; P ŋɯɯk^{6}

0622 - crippled, B4
SW - S ŋɔy^{3}; W, B ŋɔy^{5}; LNK ŋɔɔy^{3} 'lame'; LCH ŋoy^{5}; LMY ŋɔy^{5} 'paralyzed'

0623 - mouth, DL2, (cf. 1158)
SW - S paak^{2}; W, B paaʔ^{2} 'to speak'; Sh paak^{2} 'to speak; mouth'; LNK paak^{2}; LCH, LMY paak^{2} 'to speak' but 'mouth' in certain contexts; usual word is sop^{1}; CM paak^{3} 'to speak, mouth'
CN - LP paak^{5}; LM, WN, LC, PS paak^{2}; NM paak^{2}, paaʔ^{2}
N - Y paak^{2}; Sk paak^{6}; WM, P paak^{5}

0624 - kind of small frog, DL2
SW - S (tă^{2}) paat^{2}; W (kop^{2}) paat^{2}; B paat^{2}; LNK (tă-) paat^{2}; LMY (xeet^{2}) paat^{2}
CN - LP paat^{5}; LM, PS paat^{2}; NM paaʔ^{2}
N - Y paat^{2}

0625 - to revolve, spin, B2
SW - S, W, B, Sh pan^{2}; LNK pan^{3}; LCH, LMY pan^{2}; CM pan^{3}
CN - LP pan^{5}; LM, WN pan^{2}; LC, PS, NM pan^{2}
N - Y pan^{2}; Sk pin^{6}; pan^{1}, pal^{6} (OG), pan^{6} (YG) 'to spin (cotton)'; P pan^{5}

0626 - year, A2, (cf. 0545)
SW - S pii^{1}; W, B, Sh pi^{1}; LNK pii^{2}; LCH, LMY pii^{1}; CM pii^{2}
CN - LP pii^{2}; LM pey^{1}; WN pii^{1}; BV pii^{2}; LC, PS pii^{1}; NM pey^{1}
N - Y pi^{1}; Sk pii^{1}; WM pi^{1}; P pii^{1}

0627 - banana blossom, A2
SW - S plii^{1}; W, B, Sh pi^{1}; LNK pii^{2}; LCH, LMY pii^{1}; CM pii^{2}
CN - LP pii^{2}; LM pey^{1}; LC, PS pii^{1}; NM pey^{1}
N - Sk plii^{1} (OG), prii^{1} (YG); P pii^{1}

0628 - bark, shell, DL2
SW - S plɯak^{2}; W pɤʔ^{2}; B pɯaʔ^{2}; Sh pɤk^{2}; LNK pɯak^{2}; LCH, LMY pɤɤk^{2}; CM pɯak^{3}
CN - LP pɤɤk^{5}; LM pɯɯk^{2}; WN pik^{2}; LC, PS pɤɤk^{2}; NM pɯɯk^{2}
N - Sk plaak^{6} (OG), praak^{6} (YG); WM plɯk^{5} (pluk^{5}?)

0629 - naked, A2
SW - S plɯay^{1}; B pɯay^{1}; Sh poy^{1}; LNK pɯay^{2}; LCH pɤy^{1}; LMY pɤy^{1}, poy^{1}; CM pɯay^{2}
N - Sk pɯay^{1}

0630 - lung, DL2
SW - S pɔɔt^{2}; W, B, Sh pɔt^{2}; LNK, LCH, LMY pɔɔt^{2}
CN - LP pɤt^{5}; LM pɤt^{3} (DS2); WN pɔt^{2}; LC, PS pɤt^{2}; NM poot^{2}
N - Y put^{3}; WM put^{5}; P pɯt^{2} (DS2 in N languages)

0631 - to be graciously pleased, DL2
SW - S proot^{2}; LNK poot^{2}; LCH, LMY phoot^{2}; CM phoot^{3}
N - Sk phoot^{6}

0632 - crab, A2
SW - S puu^{1}; W, B, Sh pu^{1}; LNK puu^{2}; LCH, LMY puu^{1}; CM puu^{2}
CN - LP puu^{2}; LM pow^{1}; WN, LC, PS puu^{1}; NM pow^{1}
N - Y, Sk paw^{1}

0633 - cliff, rock, A1
SW - S phaa^{5}; W phaa^{1}; B faa^{1}; LNK, LCH, LMY phaa^{1}; CM phaa^{2}
CN - LP, LM phyaa^{1}; WN phaa^{1}; LC, PS, NM phyaa^{1}
N - Sk phraa^{2}; WM plaa^{1}; P pyaa^{1}

0634 - forehead, DL1
SW - S phaak^{2}; LNK, LCH, LMY phaak^{2}
CN - LP, LM phyaak^{2}; WN phaak^{2}; LC, PS, NM phyaak^{2}
N - Y pyaak^{2}; Sk phraak^{6}; WM plaak^{5}; P pyaak^{5}

0635 - to walk, C1
SW - S phaay^{3} (usual word is dɤɤn^{1}); W phaay^{3}; Sh phaay^{3} 'to go'; LCH, LMY phaay^{3} 'to pass'
CN - LP, LM, LC, PS, NM phyaay^{3}
N - Y pyaay^{3}; WM plaay^{3}; P pyaay^{3}

0636 - to rest, DS4
SW - S phak^{4}; LMY phak^{5}; CM phak^{6}
CN - LP phak^{5}; LM pak^{4}; LC pak^{4} 'tired, fatigue'

0637 - to collapse, A4
SW - S phaŋ^{1}; B, Sh paŋ^{4}; LNK phaŋ^{6}; LCH, LMY paŋ^{4}
CN - LM paŋ^{4}

0638 - to burn (transitive), A1, (cf. 0212)
SW - S phaw^{5}; W phaw^{1}; B faw^{1}; Sh, LNK, LCH, LMY phaw^{1}
CN - LM phyaw^{1}; WN phaw^{1}
N - Y piaw^{1}; Sk phraw^{2}; WM plaw^{1}; P pyaw^{1}

0639 - spicy hot, DS1, (cf. 0890, 1065)
SW - S, W phet^{2}; B fet^{2}; Sh phet^{4}; LNK, LCH, LMY phet^{1}; CM phet^{2}
CN - LP phit^{2}; LM phyat^{3}; WN phat^{6}; LC phit^{2}; PS phet^{2}
N - Sk phet^{4} (said to be < Siamese)

0640 - expensive, A4
SW - S phɛɛŋ^{1}; W, B pɛŋ^{4}; Sh pɛŋ^{4} 'to put away'; LNK phɛɛŋ^{6}; LCH, LMY pɛŋ^{4}; CM pɛɛŋ^{1}
CN - LP pheeŋ^{4}; LM peeŋ^{4}; WN peŋ^{4}; LC, NM peeŋ^{4}
N - Y peŋ^{4}; Sk phɛɛŋ^{4}; P peeŋ^{2}

0641 - ghost, A1, (cf. 0849)
SW - S phii^{5}; W phi^{1}; B fi^{1}; Sh phi^{1}; LNK, LCH, LMY phii^{1}; CM phii^{2}
CN - LP phii^{1}; LM phey^{1}; WN, LC, PS phii^{1}; NM phey^{1}
N - Sk phii^{1} (in certain phrases; usual word is maaŋ^{4})

0642 - taro, DL1
SW - S phɯak^{2}; B fɯaʔ^{2}; Sh phɤk^{2}; LNK phɯak^{2}; LCH, LMY phɤɤk^{2}; CM phɯak^{3}
CN - LP phɤɤk^{2}; LM phyɯɯk^{2}; WN phik^{2}; LC phɤɤk^{2} 'kind of potato'; PS phɤɤk^{2}; NM phyɯɯk^{2}
N - Y pɯak^{2}; WM plɯak^{5}; P piik^{5}

0643 - to slip and fall, DL4
SW - S phlaat^{3}; W phaat^{4}; B pă^{2}laat^{5}; Sh phaat^{3} 'to go by, pass by'
CN - LM pyaat^{5}; LC pyaat^{4}
N - Y pyaat^{5}; Sk thlɤɤt^{5} (OG), thrɤɤt^{5} (YG); P pyaat^{6}

0644 - enough, A4, (cf. 1000)
SW - S phɔɔ^{1}; W, B, Sh pɔ^{4}; LNK phɔɔ^{6}; LCH, LMY pɔɔ^{4}; CM pɔɔ^{1}
N - Sk phɔɔ^{4}

0645 - thin (not fat), A1, (cf. 0405)
SW - S phɔɔm^{5}; W phɔm^{1}; B fɔm^{1}; Sh yɔm^{1}; LNK phɔɔm^{1}; LCH, LMY yɔm^{1} (both places also have phɔm^{1} in certain expressions); CM phɔɔm^{2}
CN - LM yoom^{1}; WN phom^{1}; LC phyoom^{1}
N - Y pyom^{1}; Sk phrɔɔm^{2}; WM plɤm^{1}; P pyoom^{1}

0646 - big knife, machete, C4
SW - S phraa^{4}; W, B paa^{6}; Sh pha^{5}; LNK phaa^{5}; LCH, LMY phaa^{6} (general term for knife)
CN - LP phyaa^{3}; LM pyaa^{6}; WN paa^{6}; LC, PS, NM pyaa^{6}
N - Y sa^{6}; Sk thaa^{6}; WM, P šaa^{4}

0647 - to separate, DL4
SW - S phraak^{3}; W paaʔ^{4}; B paaʔ^{5}; Sh phaak^{3}; LNK, LCH, LMY phaak^{5}; CM phaak^{4}
CN - LP phyaak^{5}; LM pyaak^{5}; LC pyaak^{4}; PS pyaak^{5}
N - Y pyaak^{5}; WM plaak^{6}; P pyaak^{6}

0648 - to deceive, A4
SW - S phraaŋ^{1}; Sh phaaŋ^{4} 'unsubstantial, empty, void; unable to see' (last meaning cognate with S faaŋ^{1}, 1154); LNK phaaŋ^{6} 'to conceal'; LCH, LMY phaaŋ^{4}
CN - LM pyaaŋ^{4}; LC pyaaŋ^{4} (current in the countryside)
N - P pyaaŋ^{2}

0649 - common people, B4
SW - S phray^{3}; W, B pay^{5}; LCH, LMY phay^{5}
CN - LM pyay^{5}

0650 - late meal, A4
SW - S phraw^{1} (obsolete); LCH, LMY phaw^{4}
CN - LP phyaw^{4}; LM pyaw^{4}; WN paw^{4}; LC, PS, NM pyaw^{4}
N - Y saw^{4}; WM, P šaw^{2}

0651 - silk cloth, A4
SW - S phrɛɛ^{1}; W, B pɛ^{4}; Sh phɛ^{4} 'satin'; LNK phɛɛ^{6}; LCH, LMY phɛɛ^{4}, hɛɛ^{4}

0652 - pepper, DS4
SW - S phrik^{4}; LNK phik^{3}; LCH, LMY phik^{5}; CM phik^{6}

0653 - altogether, C4
SW - S phrɔɔm^{4}; W, B pɔm^{6}; Sh phɔm^{5}; LNK phɔɔm^{5}; LCH, LMY phɔm^{6}; CM phɔɔm^{6}
N - Sk phrɔɔm^{6}; P šom^{4}

0654 - half gone, partly empty, B4
SW - S phrɔŋ^{3}; LNK phɔɔŋ^{3}; CM phɔŋ^{4} 'some'
CN - LP phyooŋ^{5}; LM pyooŋ^{5}; WN poŋ^{5} 'half'; LC pyooŋ^{5} 'half'; PS pyooŋ^{5}
N - Y pyoŋ^{5} 'half full'; Sk phrɔɔŋ^{5}, phrɔŋ^{5} (fast speech); P pyooŋ^{6}

0655 - tomorrow, DL4 (?)
SW - S phruŋ^3 (nii^4) (?); B puʔ^5; Sh phuk^3; LCH, LMY phuk^5
CN - LP phyok^5, chok^5; LM cok^5; WN pɤk^5; LC pyuk^4; PS pyok^5; NM tuuk^5
N - Y sok^5; Sk thɔɔk^5; WM šɤk^6; P šook^6

0656 - husband, A1
SW - S phua^5; W pho^1; B fua^1; Sh pho^1; LNK phua^1; LCH, LMY phoo^1; CM phua^2
CN - WN phuu^1

0657 - mountain, A4, (cf. 0778, 1002)
SW - S phuu^1; W, B pu^4; LNK phuu^6; LCH, LMY puu^4

0658 - person, C1, (cf. 0145)
SW - S phuu^3; W phu^3; B fu^3; Sh phu^3; LNK, LCH, LMY phuu^3; CM phuu^5
CN - LP phuu^3; LM phow^3; WN phuu^3; LC puu^3; PS phuu^3; NM phow^3
N - Y pu^6; Sk phuu^6; WM paw^4 (C4 in N languages)

0659 - to tie, DL1, (cf. 0210, 0839)
SW - S phuuk^2; W phuʔ^2; B fuʔ^2; Sh phuk^2; LNK phuuk^2
CN - LP phok^2; LM phyok^3; WN phuk^6; LC phuk^2 (DS1 in LP, LM, WN, LC); PS phok^2; NM suuk^2
N - Y suk^1 (DS4)

0660 - to vomit, DL4
SW - S raak^3; W haa^4; B haaʔ^5; Sh haak^3; LNK, LCH, LMY haak^5; CM haak^4
CN - LP ɬaak^5; LM laak^5; LC ɬaak^4; PS, NM ɬaak^5
N - Y, Sk ruak^5; WM ruak^6

0661 - bran, A4, (cf. 1118)
SW - S ram^1; W, B, Sh ham^4; LNK ham^6; LCH ham^4 (literary lam^4); LMY ham^4
CN - LP ɬam^4; LM lam^4; WN ðam^4; LC ɬam^4 'pig feed', ɬam^5 'bran'; PS, NM ɬam^4
N - Y, Sk ram^4; WM ram^2; P lam^2

0662 - chicken louse, A4
SW - S ray^1; B hay^4; LNK hay^6; LCH, LMY hay^4
CN - LP ɬay^4; LM lay^4; WN ðay^4; LC, PS ɬay^4; NM ley^4
N - Y ri^4; Sk rii^4; WM roy^2; P lii^2

0663 - first, DL4
SW - S rɛɛk^3; B hɛʔ^5; LNK, LMY hɛɛk^5; CM hɛɛk^3

0664 - rhinoceros, DL4
SW - S rεεt^{3}; W hεt^{4}; B hεt^{5}; Sh hεt^{3}; LNK hεεt^{5} (modern lεεt^{5}); LCH, LMY hεεt^{5}
N - Y ret^{5}; Sk rεεt^{5}

0665 - long, A4, (cf. 0729)
SW - S rii^{1} (usual word is yaaw^{1}); W, B, Sh hi^{4}; LNK hii^{6} 'oval'
CN - LP ɬii^{4}; LM ley^{4}; WN ðii^{4}; LC, PS ɬii^{4}; NM ley^{4}
N - Y, Sk ray^{4}; WM ray^{2}; P lay^{2}

0666 - track, footprint, A4
SW - S rɔɔy^{1}; W, B, Sh hɔy^{4}; LNK hɔɔy^{6}; LCH, LMY hɔy^{4} (literary lɔy^{4}); CM hɔɔy^{1}
CN - LP ɬooy^{4}; LM looy^{4}; WN ðɔy^{4}; PS ɬooy^{4}
N - Y ri^{4}; Sk rii^{4}; P lii^{2}, lwii^{2}

0667 - ear of rice, A4
SW - S ruaŋ^{1}; W hoŋ^{4}; B huaŋ^{4}; Sh hoŋ^{4}; LCH hoŋ^{4}
CN - LM luuŋ^{4}; WN ðuŋ^{4}; LC, PS ɬuuŋ^{4}
N - Sk ruaŋ^{4}; WM rɯaŋ^{2}; P lɯɯŋ^{1} (A1?)

0668 - rainbow, A4?
SW - S ruŋ^{4} (C4); W (phi^{1}) huŋ^{4} (A4); B (to^{1}) huŋ^{4} (A4); Sh hoŋ^{4} (A4); LNK huŋ^{5}, luŋ^{5} (C4); LCH huŋ^{6} (C4, literary luŋ^{4}); LMY huŋ^{6} (C4, literary ruŋ^{6});
CN - WN ðuŋ^{4} (A4)
N - Sk rɔɔŋ^{4} (A4)

0669 - pestle, DL1
SW - S saak^{2}; W, B saaʔ^{2}; Sh shaak^{2}; LNK, LCH, LMY saak^{2}; CM saak^{3}
CN - LP ɬaak^{2}; LM, WN saak^{2}; LC, PS, NM ɬaak^{2}
N - Y θaak^{2}; Sk saak^{6}; WM θaak^{5}; P laak^{5} 'to pound'

0670 - carcass, DL4
SW - S saak^{3}; W saaʔ^{4}; B saaʔ^{5}; Sh shaak^{3} 'to remain, be left'; LNK saak^{5}; LCH, LMY saak^{5} 'remains of food'
CN - WN saak^{5}

0671 - three, A1
SW - S saam^{5}; W, B saam^{1}; Sh shaam^{1}; LNK, LCH, LMY saam^{1}; CM saam^{2}
CN - LP ɬaam^{1}; LM, WN saam^{1}; BV ɬaam^{2}; LC, PS, NM ɬaam^{1}
N - Y θaam^{1}; Sk saam^{2}; WM θaam^{1}; P ɬaam^{1}

0672 - to weave (baskets, mats), A1, (cf. 0691)
SW - S saan^{5}; W, B saan^{1}; Sh shaan^{1}; LCH, LMY saan^{1}; CM saan^{2}
CN - LP ɬaan^{1}; LM, WN saan^{1}; LC, PS, NM ɬaan^{1}
N - Y θaan^{1}; Sk saan^{2}; WM θaan^{1}; P ɬaan^{1}

0673 - to tattoo, DS1
SW - S, W, B sak^{2}; Sh shak^{4} 'to strike repeatedly, with a short quick motion'; LCH, LMY sak^{1}
N - Sk sak^{4}

0674 - to blow the nose, B1
SW - S, W, B saη^{2}; Sh shaη^{2} 'to instruct'; LNK saη^{4} (C1); LCH, LMY saη^{2}
CN - LP ɬaη^{2}; LM, WN saη^{2}; LC ɬaη^{5} 'to bid, to order'; NM ɬaη^{1} (A?)
N - Y θaη^{2}; Sk saη^{6}; WM θaη^{5}; P ɬaη^{5}

0675 - pillar, A1, (cf. 1108)
SW - S saw^{5}; W, B saw^{1}; Sh shaw^{1}; LNK, LCH, LMY saw^{1}; CM saw^{2}
CN - WN saw^{1}; LC ɬaw^{1}, ɬiiw^{1}; NM ɬaw^{1}
N - Y θaw^{1}; WM šaɰ^{4} (C4, Li says < Chinese); P ɬaw^{1}

0676 - light, A1, (cf. 1081)
SW - S sεεη^{5}; W sεη^{1} 'jewel'; B sεη^{1} 'light, jewel'; Sh shεη^{1} 'a precious stone'; LNK sεεη^{1}; LCH, LMY sεη^{1} 'jewel'
N - Sk sεεη^{2}

0677 - four, B1
SW - S sii^{2}; W, B si^{2}; Sh shi^{2}; LNK sii^{3}; LCH, LMY sii^{2}; CM sii^{3}
CN - LP ɬii^{2}; LM sey^{2}; WN sii^{2}; LC, PS ɬii^{2}; NM ɬey^{2}
N - Y θi^{2}; Sk sii^{6}; P ɬii^{5}

0678 - tiger, A1, (0541, 0822)
SW - S sɯa^{5}; W sɤ^{1}; B sɯa^{1}; Sh shɤ^{1}; LNK sɯa^{1}; LCH, LMY sɤɤ^{1}; CM sɯa^{2}
CN - LP ɬɤɤ^{1}; LM sɯɯ^{1}; BV ɬɯɯ^{2}; LC, PS, NM ɬɯɯ^{1}

0679 - enemy, war, DS1
SW - S sɯk^{2}; W, B sɤk^{2}; Sh shɯk^{4}; LNK sɤk^{1}; LCH sɯk^{1}; LMY sɤk^{1}, sɯk^{2}
CN - WN sɤk^{6}, sak^{6}
N - Y sak^{1} (DS4)

0680 - to buy, C4
SW - S sɯɯ^{4}; W, B sɯ^{6}; Sh shɯ^{5}; LNK sɯɯ^{5}; LCH, LMY, CM sɯɯ^{6}
CN - LP ɬɤɤ^{3}; LM sɤɰ^{6}; WN sɯɯ^{6}; LC, PS ɬɯɯ^{6}; NM saɰ^{6}
N - Y sɯ^{6}; Sk sɯɯ^{6}; WM šaɰ^{4}; P šɯɯ^{4}

0681 - writing, book, A1
SW - S (naŋ^{5}) sɯɯ^{5}; W, B sɯ^{1}; LNK, LCH, LMY (naŋ^{1}) sɯɯ^{1};
CM (naŋ^{2}) sɯɯ^{2}
CN - LP ɬɤɤ^{1}; LM sɤɰ^{1}; WN sɯɯ^{1}; BV ɬɯɯ^{2}; LC, PS ɬɯɯ^{1}; NM ɬaɰ^{1}
N - Y θɯ^{1}; Sk sɯɯ^{2}

0682 - sour, C1
SW - S som^{3} 'orange'; W sum^{3}; B som^{3}; Sh shom^{3}; LNK som^{4}; LCH, LMY sum^{3}
'sour; name of various fruits'; CM som^{5}
CN - LP ɬom^{3}; LM som^{3}; WN sam^{3}; LC ɬum^{3}; PS, NM lom^{3}
N - Y θam^{3}; Sk sam^{3}; WM θom^{3}

0683 - toilet, C1, (cf. 0889)
SW - S suam^{3}; B suam^{3} 'enclosed room'; LNK suam^{4} 'bridal bedchamber';
LCH, LMY som^{3} 'bedroom'
CN - LP ɬoom^{3}; LM suum^{3} 'bedroom'; LC ɬuum^{3} 'room'; PS ɬuum^{3} 'bedroom'

0684 - eye, A2
SW - S, W, B, Sh taa^{1}; LNK taa^{2}; LCH, LMY taa^{1}; CM taa^{2}
CN - LP haa^{1} (A1); LM, WN thaa^{1}; BV thaa^{1} (A1); LC, PS haa^{1}; NM thaa^{1}
N - Y ta^{1}; Sk praa^{1}; WM raa^{1}; P taa^{1}

0685 - maternal grandfather, A2
SW - S, W, B taa^{1}; LNK taa^{2}; LMY taa^{1}
CN - LP taa^{5} (B2); LM, WN taa^{2} (B2); LC, PS, NM taa^{1}
N - Y ta^{1}; Sk, WM, P taa^{1}

0686 - to differ, B2
SW - S, B taaŋ^{2}; Sh taaŋ^{2} 'other'; LNK taaŋ^{3}; LCH, LMY taaŋ^{2}
CN - WN taaŋ^{2}; LC taaŋ^{2} 'other, another; each'
N - Y taaŋ^{2}; Sk taaŋ^{6}; P taaŋ^{5}

0687 - window, B2
SW - S (naa^{3}) taaŋ^{2}; W, B taaŋ^{2}
CN - LP taaŋ^{5}; WN taaŋ^{2}; LC, PS, NM taaŋ^{2}

0688 - to light (a lamp), C2, (cf. 1005)
SW - S taay^{3} 'a torch'; W, B, Sh tay^{3}; LNK tay^{5}; LCH, LMY tay^{3}
CN - LP tay^{3}; LC tay^{3} 'torch'

0689 - grasshopper, DS2
SW - S tak^{4} (tɛɛn^{1}); W tak^{2} (tin^{2}) 'a kind of bee'; B tak^{2} (tɛn^{1}); Sh tak^{4} (tɛn^{1});
LNK tak^{1} (tɛɛn^{2}); LMY tak^{1} (tɛn^{1}); CM tak^{2} (tɛɛn^{2})
CN - LM tak^{3}, thak^{3}; WN tak^{6}
N - Y tak^{3}; WM rak^{5}; P tak^{2}

0690 - to pound, A2, (cf. 0696, 0702, 0718)
SW - S, W, B, Sh tam^{1}; LNK tam^{2}; LCH, LMY tam^{1}; CM tam^{2}
CN - LP tam^{2}; LM, WN, PS, NM tam^{1}
N - Y, Sk, WM tam^{1}

0691 - to weave, B2, (cf. 0672)
SW - S, W, B, Sh tam^{2}; LNK tam^{3}; LCH, LMY tam^{2}
CN - LP tam^{5}; LM, WN tam^{2}; LC, PS, NM tam^{2}
N - Y, Sk, WM, P tam^{3} (C2 in N languages)

0692 - to cut, DS2, (cf. 0959)
SW - S, W, B tat^{2}; Sh tat^{4} 'to head off, put a stop to'; LNK tat^{1}; LCH, LMY tɛt^{1}, tat^{1}; CM tat^{2}
CN - LP, LM tat^{2} 'to cut with scissors'; WN tat^{6}; LC tat^{2} 'to cut with scissors'; PS tat^{2}
N - Y tat^{3}; Sk tɛk^{4}; P tat^{2}

0693 - wasp, A2
SW - S tɛɛn^{1}; W, B tɛn^{1}; Sh tɛn^{1} 'a small hornet'; LNK tɛɛn^{2}; LCH, LMY tɛn^{1}; CM tɛɛn^{2}
CN - LP pheeŋ^{1} (A1); LM pheeŋ^{1}; WN theŋ^{1}; LC, PS pheen^{1}
N - Y tin^{4}; Sk thiil^{4} (OG), thiin^{4} (YG); WM, P tin^{2} (A4 in N languages)

0694 - cucumber, A2
SW - S tɛɛŋ^{1}; W, B, Sh tɛŋ^{1}; LNK tɛɛŋ^{2}; LCH, LMY tɛŋ^{1}; CM tɛɛŋ^{2}
CN - LP pheeŋ^{1} (A1); LM pheeŋ^{1}; WN theŋ^{1}; PS pheeŋ^{1}; NM theeŋ^{1}
N - Y tiaŋ^{1}; Sk priaŋ^{1}; P tiiŋ^{1}

0695 - to add, A2
SW - S tɤɤm^{1}; B tɤm^{1}; LNK tɯɯm^{3} (B2), tɤɤm^{2}; CM tɯam^{3}, tɤɤm^{2} (B2)
CN - LC tim^{1}
N - Y tim^{4} (A4); Sk tɯɯm^{6} (B2)

0696 - to beat, A2, (cf. 0690, 0702, 0718)
SW - S tii^{1}; W, B, Sh ti^{1}; LNK tii^{2}; LCH, LMY tii^{1}; CM tii^{2}
CN - WN thii^{1}
N - Y ti^{4} (A4)

0697 - short, C2, (cf. 0350)
SW - W, B tin^{3}
CN - LP, LM tin^{3}; WN tan^{3}; LC, PS tin^{3}; NM ten^{3}
N - Y, Sk, WM, P tin^{3}

0698 - to break wind, DS2
SW - S, W, B tot^2; Sh tot^4; LNK, LCH, LMY tot^1
CN - LP tɤt^2; LM tɤt^3; WN tat^6; PS tɤt^2; NM thet^4
N - Y rat^3; Sk rɛt^4; P lɔt^2

0699 - to slap, DS2
SW - S, W, B top^2; Sh top^4; LNK, LCH, LMY top^1; CM top^2
CN - LC tup^2 'to beat, to clap (hands)' (cognate with 0718?)
N - Sk tap^4; P tɔp^2

0700 - stump, A2, (cf. 0824)
SW - S tɔɔ^1; W, B, Sh tɔ^1; LNK tɔɔ^2; LCH, LMY tɔɔ^1; CM tɔɔ^2
CN - WN tɔɔ^1

0701 - to join, B2
SW - S tɔɔ^2; W, B, Sh tɔ^2; LNK tɔɔ^3; LCH, LMY tɔɔ^2; CM tɔɔ^3
CN - WN too^2 'toward, to'
N - Y to^2; Sk tɔɔ^6

0702 - to pound, DL2, (cf. 0690, 0696, 0718)
SW - S tɔɔk^2; W, B tɔʔ^2; Sh tɔk^2; LNK, LCH, LMY tɔɔk^2
CN - LP took^5; LM took^2; WN tɔk^2
N - Y tok^2; Sk tɔɔk^6

0703 - big leaf, especially a banana leaf, A2
SW - S tɔɔη^1; W, B, Sh tɔη^1; LNK tɔɔη^2; LCH, LMY tɔη^1; CM tɔɔη^2
CN - LP tooη^2; LM tooη^1; WN toη^1; LC, PS, NM tooη^1
N - Y roη^1; Sk rɔɔη^2 (A1); WM rɤη^1; P looη^1

0704 - door, A2
SW - S (prǎ^2) tuu^1; W, B, Sh tu^1; LNK (phak^1) tuu^2; LCH, LMY (pa-) tuu^1;
CM (paʔ^2) tuu^2
CN - LP tuu^2; LM tow^1; WN, LC, PS tuu^1; NM tow^1
N - Y tu^1; Sk pak^4 tuu^1; WM taw^1; P tuu^1

0705 - cupboard, C2, (cf. 0971)
SW - S tuu^3; B tu^5; LNK tuu^5 'iron chest, safe'; LCH, LMY tuu^3; CM tuu^5
CN - WN tuu^2 (B2)
N - Y tu^2 (B2); Sk tuu^3

0706 - to wait, C1
SW - S, W, B, Sh thaa^3; LNK thaa^4; LCH, LMY thaa^3; CM thaa^5
CN - LM, WN thaa^3
N - Y sa^3; Sk thaa^3; P šaa^3

0707 - landing, B4
SW - S thaa^{3}; W, B taa^{5}; Sh taa^{3}; LNK thaa^{3}; LCH, LMY taa^{5}; CM taa^{4} 'river crossing'
CN - LP thaa^{5}; LM, WN, LC, PS, NM taa^{5} ('river' in CN languages)
N - Y ta^{5} 'river'; Sk thaa^{5}; WM, P taa^{6} 'river'

0708 - to challenge, C4
SW - S thaa^{4}; B taa^{6}; Sh ta^{5}; LNK thaa^{5}; LCH, LMY taa^{6}
CN - WN taa^{6}
N - P taa^{6}

0709 - to ask, A1
SW - S thaam^{5}; W, B, Sh, LNK, LCH, LMY thaam^{1}; CM thaam^{2}
CN - LP, LM thaam^{1}; WN chaam^{1}; LC thaam^{1}
N - Y saam^{1}; Sk thaam^{2}; WM, P šaam^{1}

0710 - charcoal, B1
SW - S, W, B thaan^{2}; Sh thaan^{2}, than^{2}; LNK thaan^{3}; LCH, LMY thaan^{2}; CM thaan^{3}
CN - LP, LM, WN, LC, PS, NM thaan^{2}
N - Y thaan^{2}; Sk thaan^{6}; WM, P taan^{5}

0711 - to change (e.g., clothes), B1, (cf. 0872)
SW - S thaay^{2}; W, B thay^{2}; Sh thay^{2} 'to redeem, ransom'; LCH, LMY thay^{2}, thaay^{2}; CM thaay^{3}
CN - LM thay^{2} 'to ransom'; WN thay^{2} 'to ransom, redeem'; LC thay^{2} 'to take the place of; for, instead' (Li says < Chinese)
N - Sk thay^{6} 'to redeem, ransom'

0712 - old, C1, (cf. 0091, 0483)
SW - S, W, B, Sh thaw^{3}; LNK thaw^{4}; LCH, LMY thaw^{3}; CM thaw^{5}
CN - LP thaw^{3} (in kinship terms only); LC thaw^{3} 'a word added to kinship terms to denote a man's senior relatives'; PS, NM thaw^{3} (in kinship terms)
N - Sk thaw^{3}

0713 - Thai, Tai, A4
SW - S thay^{1}; W, B tay^{4}; Sh tay^{4} 'a Shan or Tai', thay^{4} 'a Siamese'; LNK thay^{6}; LCH, LMY tay^{4} (but thay^{4} refers to the people of Thailand)
CN - LM, WN, LC tay^{4}
N - Y tay^{4}; Sk thay^{4}

0714 - genuine, real, really, C4
SW - S thɛɛ^{4}; W, B tɛ^{6}; Sh tɛ^{5} 'very, exceedingly'; LNK thɛɛ^{5}; LCH tee^{6}; LMY tɛɛ^{6}; CM tɛɛ^{6}
N - Sk thɛɛ^{3} (C?, said to be from < Lao)

0715 - young male animal, DS1
SW - S thɯk^{2}; W, B thɤk^{2}; Sh thɯk^{4}; 'a male buffalo'; LNK thɤk^{1}, thɯk^{1}; LCH, LMY thɯk^{1}
CN - LP thɤk^{4} (DS4); LM tɤk^{3}; WN thak^{6}; LC, PS tɤk^{4} (DS4); NM tak^{4} (DS4)
N - Y tak^{1}; Sk thak^{6}; WM tak^{6}; P tak^{3} (DS4 in N languages)

0716 - to arrive, reach, A1
SW - S thɯŋ^{5}; W thɯŋ^{1}; B thɤŋ^{1}; LNK thɤŋ^{1} (less frequent thɯŋ^{1}); LCH, LMY thɯŋ^{1}; CM thɤɤŋ^{2}, thɯŋ^{2}
CN - LP, LM, BV thɤŋ^{1}; WN thaŋ^{1}; LC, PS thɤŋ^{1}; NM thaŋ^{1}
N - Y taŋ^{4}; Sk thaŋ^{4}; WM, P taŋ^{2} (A4 in N languages)

0717 - bag, A1, (cf. 1023)
SW - S thuŋ^{5}; W thuŋ^{1} 'pocket'; B thoŋ^{1}; Sh thoŋ^{1}; LNK thoŋ^{1} (modern thuŋ^{1}); LCH, LMY thuŋ^{1}; CM thoŋ^{2}
CN - LC thuŋ^{1}
N - Sk thɔŋ^{2}

0718 - to beat, pound, DS4, (cf. 0690, 0696, 0702)
SW - S thup^{4}; W tup^{4}; Sh thup^{5}; LNK thup^{3}; LMY tup^{5}; CM tup^{6}
CN - LP thop^{5}; LM top^{4}; WN tup^{4}; PS top^{4}; NM tuup^{5} (DL4, cf. 0699)
N - Y tup^{1}; Sk thap^{6}; WM tup^{6}; P tup^{3}

0719 - cheap, DL1
SW - S thuuk^{2}; W, B thuʔ^{2}; Sh thuk^{2} 'suitable, in accord'; LNK thɯɯk^{2}, thuuk^{2} 'correct, right, cheap'; LCH, LMY thuuk^{2}; CM thuuk^{3}
CN - LM thok^{3}; WN thuk^{6}; LC thuk^{2} (DS1 in CN languages)
N - Y tɯk^{1}; Sk thɯk^{6} (DS4 in N languages)

0720 - to sow, scatter, B1
SW - S waan^{2}; W vaan^{2}; B vaan^{2}, baan^{2}; Sh waan^{2}; LNK waan^{3}; LCH, LMY vaan^{2}
CN - LP, LM, LC, PS, NM vaan^{2}
N - Sk vaal^{6} (OG), vaan^{6} (YG); WM waan^{5}

0721 - to make a gesture of salutation, C1
SW - S waay^{3}; B vay^{3} 'to go to see royalty'; Sh way^{3}; LNK waay^{4}; LCH, LMY vay^{3}; CM way^{5}
N - Sk vay^{6} (C4, said to be < Lao or Siamese)

0722 - work (noun), DL4, (cf. 0941)
SW - W ve^{4}; B viaʔ^{5}; LNK wiak^{5}; LCH, LMY veek^{5}
CN - WN vik^{5} 'festival'
N - Y, Sk viak^{5}

0723 - a ring, A1
SW - S wɛɛn^{5}; W, B vɛn^{1}; Sh wɛn^{1} 'an anklet or bracelet, a bangle'; LNK wɛɛn^{1}; LCH, LMY vɛn^{1} 'bracelet'; CM wɛɛn^{2}
CN - WN ven^{1} 'earring'
N - Sk vɛɛn^{2}

0724 - a comb, to comb, A1
SW - S wii^{5}; W vi^{1}; B vi^{1}, bi^{1}; Sh wi^{1}; LNK wii^{1}; LCH, LMY vii^{1}; CM wii^{2}
CN - LP vii^{1}; LM vey^{1}; WN vii^{1}; BV vii^{2}; LC, PS vii^{1}; NM vey^{1}
N - Sk roy^{1}; Sk hɔɔy^{2}, hɔy^{2} (fast speech); WM rɤy^{1}

0725 - don't, B3, (cf. 0726)
SW - S yaa^{2}; W, B ɲaa^{4}; Sh yaa^{2}; LNK yaa^{3}; LCH, LMY yaa^{2}
CN - LP yaa^{5} 'finished, already'; LM yaa^{2} 'finished, already'; WN yaa^{2} 'finished'; LC yaa^{2}; PS, NM yaa^{2} 'finished'
N - Y yia^{2}, ya^{2}; Sk yaa^{6}; P yii^{5} ('finished' in all three languages)

0726 - to divorce, B3, (cf. 0725)
SW - S yaa^{2}; W yaa^{2} 'finished'; LNK yaa^{3} (said to be a modern expression); LCH, LMY yaa^{2}

0727 - hungry, DL3, (cf. 0009)
SW - S yaak^{2} 'to want'; W yaaʔ^{2}; B yaaʔ^{2} 'to starve'; Sh yaak^{2}; LNK yaak^{2} 'to want'; LCH, LMY yaak^{2}; CM yaak^{3}
CN - LP yaak^{5}; LM, WN, LC, PS, NM yaak^{2}
N - Y yiak^{2}; Sk yuak^{6}; WM ʔyɯak^{5}; P yiik^{5}

0728 - to fear, C3, (cf. 0840, 0918)
SW - W, B, Sh yaan^{3}; LNK yaan^{5}; LCH, LMY yaan^{3}; CM yaan^{5}
CN - LC yaan^{1} (A?)

0729 - long, A4, (cf. 0665)
SW - S yaaw^{1}; B ɲaaw^{4} (for bamboo tubes only); Sh yaaw^{4}; LNK ɲaaw^{6}; LCH, LMY yaaw^{4}; CM ɲaaw^{1}
CN - LM yaaw^{4}; WN yaaw^{4} 'long, only of bamboo joints'
N - Y yaaw^{6} (C4, only of bamboo joints)

0730 - home, C3
SW - S yaaw^{3} (rɯan^{1}); W yaaw^{3} (hɤn^{4}); B yaaw^{3} (hɯan^{4}); LNK yaw^{5}, yaw^{5} hɯan^{6} 'household'; LCH, LMY yaaw^{3} (hɤn^{4}) (literary)
CN - WN yaaw^{3} 'granary'
N - Y yiaw^{6}; Sk yiaw^{3} ('granary' in both languages)

0731 - maternal grandmother, A4
SW - S yaay^{1}; W, B, Sh naay^{4}; LNK ɲaay^{6} (modern yaay^{6}); LCH yaay^{4}, naay^{4}; LMY yaay^{4}
CN - LP taay^{5} (B2); LM, WN taay^{2} (B2); LC, PS, NM taay^{1} (A2)
N - Y taay^{2} (B2); Sk ʔaay^{4}; WM taay^{1} (A2); P taay^{5} (B2)

0732 - to sew, DS4
SW - S yep^{4}; W ŋip^{4} (Minot has ɲip^{4}); B ɲip^{5}; Sh yep^{5}; LNK ɲip^{1} (DS?); LCH yep^{1}; LMY yip^{1}; CM ɲip^{2}
CN - LP, LM yap^{4}; WN ɲip^{4}, ɲɛp^{4}, thap^{6}; LC, PS yap^{4}; NM ɲop^{4}
N - Y ɲip^{1}; Sk ɲip^{6}; WM ɲip^{6}; P yip^{3}

0733 - to urinate, B4
SW - S yiaw^{3}; W, B nɛw^{5}; Sh yew^{3}; LNK ɲiaw^{3}, ŋiaw^{3}; LCH, LMY yew^{5}; CM ɲiaw^{4}
CN - LP, LM neew^{5}; WN ɲiw^{5}; LC, PS, NM neew^{4} (A4)
N - Y ɲu^{5}; Sk ɲuu^{5}; WM ɲaw^{6}

0734 - two, B4, (cf. 0341)
SW - S yii^{3}; B ɲi^{5}; Sh yi^{3} 'appellation of a second son'; LNK yii^{3}, yii^{5}, ɲii^{3}; LCH, LMY yii^{5}
CN - LP yii^{5}; LM yey^{5}; WN ŋii^{5}, ɲii^{5}; LC, PS, NM yii^{5}
N - Y ŋi^{5}; Sk ɲii^{6} (C4); P ŋii^{6}

0735 - to hear, A4, (cf. 0869, 1012)
SW - S yin^{1}; W, B ŋin^{4}; Sh ŋin^{4}, yin^{4}; LNK ɲin^{6}; LCH, LMY yin^{4}; CM ŋin^{1}, ɲin^{1}
CN - LP, LM yin^{4}; WN ŋin^{4}, ɲin^{4}; LC, PS hin^{1} (A1?); NM ŋen^{1} (A?)

0736 - to shoot, A4
SW - S yiŋ^{1}; B ɲiŋ^{4} 'to take aim'; Sh yeŋ^{4}, yɤŋ^{4}; LNK ɲiŋ^{6}; LCH yɯɯ^{4}; LMY yiŋ^{4}, yɯŋ^{4}; CM ɲiŋ^{1}
CN - LP, LM yaŋ^{4}; WN niŋ^{4} 'to take aim', yiŋ^{4}; LC yaŋ^{4}; NM ɲaɰ^{4}
N - Y ŋiŋ^{4} 'to aim'; Sk ɲiiŋ^{4}, ɲiŋ^{4} (fast speech); WM ɲiŋ^{2}; P ŋiŋ^{2} 'to aim'

0737 - woman, A4, (cf. 0217, 0876)
SW - S yiŋ^{5} (A1); W, B ɲiŋ^{4}; Sh yiŋ^{4}; LNK ɲiŋ^{6} (modern yiŋ^{1}); LCH, LMY yiŋ^{4}; CM ɲiŋ^{1}
CN - LP niŋ^{4}; LM niŋ^{4}, yiŋ^{4}; WN ɲiŋ^{4}; LC niŋ^{1}, niŋ^{4}

0738 - to pick up with the fingers, DS3
SW - S, W, B yip^{2}; Sh yip^{4}; LNK yip^{1}; LCH, LMY yip^{1}; CM yip^{2}, yip^{6}
CN - LP ʔip^{2}; LM ʔip^{3}; WN ʔip^{6}; LC nip^{2}, ʔip^{2}; PS ʔep^{2}; NM ʔop^{4}
N - Y ɲap^{1} (DS4); Sk yip^{4}, yup^{4}; WM ɲap^{6} (DS4)

0739 - bait, B1
SW - S yɯa^{2}; W ɲɤ^{2}; B ɲɯa^{2} (in W, B 'meat, flesh'); Sh yɤ^{2} 'food'; LNK ɲɯa^{3}; LCH, LMY yɤɤ^{2}; CM ɲɯa^{3}
CN - LM nɯɯ^{6} 'meat' (C4)
N - Sk ɲɯa^{6} (C4) (ɲɯa^{2} said to be < Lao or Siamese)

0740 - to borrow, A3
SW - S yɯɯm^{1}; B yɯm^{1}; Sh yim^{1} 'to rent, hire', yɯm^{1}; LNK yɯɯm^{2}; LCH yɯm^{1}; LMY yɯm^{4}; CM ɲɯɯm^{1}
CN - LP yom^{4} (A4); LM yom^{4}; LC, PS yim^{1}; NM yom^{1}

0741 - to stand, A3
SW - S yɯɯn^{1}; W, B yɯn^{1}; LNK yɯɯn^{2}; LMY yɯn^{4} (literary only); CM ɲɯɯn^{1}
CN - LP yin^{2}; LM yin^{4}; WN ʔin^{1}; PS yin^{1}; NM yen^{1}
N - Y dɯn^{1}; WM ʔdun^{1}

0742 - to stretch, DL4, (cf. 1071)
SW - S yɯɯt^{3}; W yɯt^{4}; B yɯt^{5}; Sh yɯt^{3}; LNK yɯɯt^{5}, ɲɯɯt^{5}; LCH, LMY yɯɯt^{2} (DL?); CM yɯɯt^{3} (DL?)
CN - LC yiit^{2} (DL?)
N - Y ɲiat^{5}

0743 - to raise, lift, DS4, (cf. 0744)
SW - S yok^{4}; W ɲok^{4}; B ɲok^{5}; Sh yuk^{5}; LNK ɲok^{3} (modern yok^{3}); LCH, LMY yok^{5}; CM ɲok^{6}
CN - WN yak^{4}
N - Y yak^{1}; Sk ɲuk^{6} (only in certain expressions, < Lao)

0744 - to lift in both hands, A4, (cf. 0743)
SW - S yɔɔ^{1} 'to praise, flatter'; W, B ɲɔ^{4}; Sh yɔ^{4}; LNK ɲɔɔ^{6} 'to praise, flatter'; LCH, LMY yɔɔ^{4} (also, 'to praise, flatter')
CN - WN yoo^{1} (A?)
N - Y yo^{1} (A?)

0745 - to dye, C4
SW - S yɔɔm^{4}; W, B ɲɔm^{6}; Sh yɔm^{5}; LNK ɲɔɔm^{5}; LCH, LMY yɔm^{6}; CM ɲɔɔm^{6}
CN - LP yoom^{3}; LM yoom^{6}; WN ɲom^{6}; LC, PS yoom^{6}; NM ɲoom^{6}
N - Y, Sk ɲum^{6}; WM ɲiam^{4} (Li says < Chinese); P yum^{4}

0746 - highest point, tip, DL4, (cf. 0270)
SW - S yɔɔt^{3}; W ɲɔt^{4}; B ɲɔt^{5}; Sh yɔt^{3} 'to sprout out'; LNK ɲɔɔt^{5} (modern yɔɔt^{5}); LCH, LMY yɔɔt^{5}; CM ɲɔɔt^{4}
CN - LP yoot^{5}; LM yoot^{5} 'young shoot'; WN ɲɔt^{5}; PS yoot^{5}; NM ɲoot^{5}
N - Sk ɲuut^{5}; WM ɲɤt^{6}

0747 - banana stem, DL3
SW - S yuak^{2}; B yuaʔ^{2}; Sh yok^{2}; LNK yuak^{2}; LCH, LMY yook^{2}
CN - LP yuuk^{5}; LM, PS yuuk^{2}

0748 - broom, A4
SW - W, B ɲu^{4}; Sh yu^{4} 'marsh date palm from which brooms are made'; LCH, LMY yuu^{4}; CM ɲuu^{1}
CN - WN ɲiw^{4} (this dialect changes [uu] to [iw] after palatals); LC yuu^{4}
N - Y ɲu^{4}; WM ɲaw^{2} 'rice stubble'

0749 - to be in a place, B3
SW - S yuu^{2}; W, B, Sh yu^{2}; LNK yuu^{3}; LCH, LMY yuu^{2}; CM yuu^{3}
CN - LP yuu^{5}; LM yow^{2}; WN, LC, PS yuu^{2}; NM yow^{2}
N - Y yu^{2}; Sk yuu^{6}; WM ʔyaw^{5}; P yuu^{5}

0750 - mosquito, A4
SW - S yuŋ^{1}; W, B ɲuŋ^{4}; Sh yuŋ^{4}; LNK ɲuŋ^{6}; LCH, LMY yuŋ^{4}; CM ɲuŋ^{1}
CN - LP, LM yoŋ^{4}; WN ɲuŋ^{4}; LC yuŋ^{4}; PS yoŋ^{4}; NM ɲoŋ^{4}
N - Y ɲuŋ^{4}; Sk ɲuŋ^{4}; WM ɲuŋ^{2}

0751 - confused, C1
SW - S yuŋ^{3}; W, B ɲuŋ^{3}; Sh yuŋ^{3}; LNK ɲuŋ^{4}; LCH, LMY yuŋ^{3}; CM ɲuŋ^{5}
CN - LM yoŋ^{3}; WN ɲuŋ^{3}; LC yuŋ^{3}
N - Y ɲuk^{3} (DS?), ɲuŋ^{2} (B?); Sk ɲuŋ^{6} (C4)

0752 - father's younger sibling, A3, (cf. 0935)
SW - S, W, B, Sh ʔaa^{1}; LNK ʔaa^{2}; LCH ʔaa^{1}; LMY ʔaa^{4}
CN - LP ʔaa^{2}; LM ʔaa^{4}; WN, LC, PS ʔaa^{1}
N - Y ʔaaw^{1}; Sk ʔaaw^{5} (B4); WM ʔaaw^{1}

0753 - part of yoke under the neck, C3
SW - B ʔɔŋ^{3}; LNK ʔɔɔŋ^{5}
CN - WN ʔɔŋ^{3}
N - Y ʔoŋ^{6}; Sk ʔɔŋ^{3}; WM ʔɤŋ^{3}

0754 - one (in eleven), DS3, (cf. 0240)
SW - S, W, B ʔet^{2}; Sh ʔet^{4}; LNK, LCH, LMY ʔet^{1}
CN - LP ʔet^{2} (ʔit^{2}?); LM ʔat^{3}; WN ʔat^{6}; LC ʔit^{2}; PS ʔet^{2}; NM ʔet^{4}
N - Y ʔit^{3}; Sk ʔɛt^{4}; WM ʔit^{5}

0755 - to lean back, A3, (cf. 0934)
SW - S, W, B, Sh ʔiŋ^{1}; LNK ʔiŋ^{2}; LCH ʔiŋ^{1}; LMY ʔiŋ^{4}
CN - LM ʔiŋ^{4}; WN ʔiŋ^{1}
N - Y ʔiŋ^{1}; Sk ʔiŋ^{1} (regarded as < Lao or Siamese), biŋ^{1}; WM ʔiŋ^{1}

0756 - other, B3
SW - S ʔɯɯn^{2}; W, B, Sh ʔɯn^{2}; LNK ʔɯɯn^{3}
CN - LP ʔɤn^{5}; LM, LC, PS ʔɤn^{2}; NM ʔen^{2}
N - Sk ʔɯɯn^{6}; WM ʔɯn^{5}

0757 - thorn, A3, (cf. 0233)
Not in SW languages
N - Y ʔwan^{1}; Sk ʔɔn^{1}; WM ʔon^{1}

0758 - brains, DL3
SW - W, B ʔɛʔ^{2}; Sh ʔɔk^{2}; LCH, LMY ʔɛɛk^{2}
CN - LP ʔeek^{5}; LM ʔeek^{2}; WN ʔɔk^{2}, ʔek^{2}; PS ʔeek^{2}
N - Y ʔuk^{3} (DS3); Sk ʔuuk^{6}

0759 - to wound, DL3
SW - S, W baat^{2}; B vaat^{2}; Sh maat^{2}, waat^{2}; LNK, LCH, LMY baat^{2}
CN - LP baat^{5}; LM maat^{2}; WN, LC baat^{2}; PS, NM baat^{2} 'sore, ulcer'
N - Y baat^{2} 'a sore'; Sk baat^{6}; WM ʔbaat^{5} 'a sore'

0760 - bamboo tube, C3
SW - W, B baŋ^{3}; LNK baŋ^{5}; LCH, LMY baŋ^{3}
CN - LP, WN baŋ^{3}
N - Y baŋ^{2}; Sk baŋ^{6} (B3 in N languages)

0761 - to divide, share, B3, (cf. 1052)
SW - S, B bɛŋ^{2}; Sh mɛŋ^{2}, wɛŋ^{2}; LNK bɛɛŋ^{3}; LCH, LMY bɛŋ^{2}
N - Sk beeŋ^{6}

0762 - chipped, nicked, B3
SW - S, W, B bin^{2}; Sh min^{3} (C3?); LNK bin^{3}
CN - LM min^{2}
N - Y baan^{2}; Sk baal^{6} (OG), baan^{6} (YG); WM ʔbaan^{5}

0763 - grass mat, C3, (cf. 1126)
Not in SW languages
N - Y bin^{6}; Sk biin^{3}; WM ʔbin^{3}

0764 - girl, DS3
Not in SW languages
N - Y bɯk^{3}; Sk bɯk^{4}; WM ʔbɯk^{5}; P mɯk^{3}

0765 - big, DS3, (cf. 0200, 0396)
Not in SW languages
N - Y bɯk^{3}; Sk bɯk^{4}

0766 - caterpillar, C3
SW - S, W buŋ^{3}; B boŋ^{3}; Sh moŋ^{3}; LNK boŋ^{5}; LCH, LMY buŋ^{3}
CN - LM moŋ^{3}
N - Sk vɔŋ^{6} (B3)

0767 - to sink, A2
SW - S com^{1}; W cum^{1}; B com^{1}; Sh som^{1}; LNK com^{2}; LCH, LMY cum^{1}
CN - WN cam^{1}
N - Y sam^{1}; Sk cam^{1}, cɔm^{1}; WM šam^{1}

0768 - eaves, A4
SW - S chaay^{1}; B caay^{4}; Sh saay^{4}; LCH, LMY caay^{4}
CN - LM caay^{4}
N - Y θaay^{4}; Sk yaay^{4}

0769 - bruised, C4, (cf. 0785, 0966)
SW - S cham^{4}; B cam^{6}; Sh, LNK sam^{5}; LCH, LMY cam^{6}
N - Y cam^{6}; Sk sam^{6}

0770 - to soak, B4, (cf. 0577)
SW - S chɛɛ^{3}; W, B cɛ^{5}; Sh sɛ^{3}; LNK sɛɛ^{3}; LCH, LMY cɛɛ^{5}
CN - LP chee^{5}; LM cee^{5}; WN cii^{5}; PS cee^{5}
N - Y se^{5}; Sk see^{5}

0771 - to believe, B4
SW - S chɯa^{3}; B cɯa^{5}; Sh sɤ^{3} 'to buy on credit; to delay in acting or doing'; LCH cɤɤ^{5}; LMY cɤɤ^{2} (B?)
N - Sk sɯa^{5}; WM šɯ^{6}

0772 - lover, C4
SW - S chuu^{4}; W, B cu^{6}; Sh su^{5}; LNK suu^{5}; LCH, LMY cuu^{6}
CN - LM cow^{6}
N - Y yu^{6}; Sk yuu^{6}

0773 - thread, C3, (cf. 0851)
SW - S daay^{3}; W daay^{3} 'raw silk'; B daay^{3} 'silk thread'; Sh laay^{3} 'silk'; LNK daay^{5}; LCH, LMY daay^{3} 'silk'
CN - WN daay^{3}
N - Y daay^{6} 'ramie'; Sk daay^{3} 'thread', raay^{3} 'ramie'; WM ʔdaay^{3} 'ramie'

0774 - to trap, DS3, (cf. 1140)
SW - S dak^{2}
N - Y dak^{3}

0775 - asleep, DS3
Not in SW languages
CN - LP dak^{2}; LM nak^{3}; LC noon^{4} dak^{2}; PS dak^{2}; NM dak^{4}
N - Y dak^{3}; Sk dak^{4}

0776 - loud, A3
SW - S, W, B daŋ^{1}; Sh laŋ^{1}; LNK daŋ^{2}; LCH daŋ^{1}; LMY daŋ^{4}
N - Y daŋ^{1}

0777 - to get married (in certain idiomatic phrases), A3
SW - S dɔɔŋ^{1}; W dɔŋ^{1}; Sh lɔŋ^{1} 'appellation given to the father and mother of one's son-in-law or daughter-in-law'; LNK dɔɔŋ^{2}; LCH dɔŋ^{1}; LMY dɔŋ^{4}
CN - LM nooŋ^{4}; WN doŋ^{1}
N - Y doŋ^{1}; Sk trɔɔŋ^{1}

0778 - hill, mountain, A3, (cf. 0657, 1002)
SW - S dɔɔy^{1}; Sh lɔy^{1}; LNK dɔɔy^{2} 'mountain ridge'; LCH dɔy^{1}; LMY dɔy^{4}
CN - LM nooy^{4} 'path up a mountain'
N - Y doy^{1} 'path up a mountain'; Sk rɔɔy^{1}; WM ʔdɤy^{1}

0779 - catfish, DS3
SW - S, B duk^{2}; LNK, LCH, LMY duk^{1}
CN - LP dok^{2}; LM nok^{3}; WN duk^{6}
N - Y duk^{3}; Sk rɔk^{4}

0780 - coconut grub, C3
SW - S duaŋ^{3}; W doŋ^{3}; B duaŋ^{3}; LNK duaŋ^{5}; LCH, LMY doŋ^{3}
CN - LM nuuŋ^{3}; WN duŋ^{3}
N - Y duŋ^{6}; Sk duaŋ^{3}

0781 - to send (a present), DL1
SW - S faak^{2}; W, B faaʔ^{2}; Sh phaak^{2}; LNK, LCH, LMY faak^{2}
CN - LP, LM, WN phaak^{2}; LC, PS, NM phaak^{2}
N - Sk kwaak^{6} (OG), kuak^{6} (YG); WM faak^{5}

0782 - antelope, A4, (cf. 0109, 1034)
SW - S faan^{1}; W, B faan^{4}; Sh phaan^{4} 'barking deer'; LNK faan^{6}; LCH, LMY faan^{4}
N - Y faan^{4}; Sk vaal^{4} (OG), vaan^{4} (YG); P faan^{2}

0783 - to slash, A4
SW - S fan^{1}; W, B fan^{4}; Sh phan^{4}; LNK fan^{6}; LCH fan^{4}
N - Y fan^{4}; Sk val^{1} (OG), van^{1} (YG) (A?)

0784 - wing, DL4, (cf. 0266)
Not in SW languages
N - Y fɯat^{5}; Sk viat^{5}; WM fɯat^{6}; P fɯt^{3} (DS4)

0785 - bruised, swollen, DS4, (cf. 0769, 0966)
SW - S fok^{4}; LNK fok^{3}; LCH, LMY fok^{5}
CN - WN fɔk^{4}
N - Y fok^{1}; Sk vɔk^{5} (DL?)

0786 - bubble, foam, A4
SW - S fɔɔŋ^{1}; W fɔŋ^{4} 'a wave'; B fɔŋ^{4}; Sh phɔŋ^{4} 'expanse or body of water'; LNK fɔɔŋ^{6}; LCH, LMY fɔŋ^{4}
N - Sk phɔɔŋ^{4}

0787 - to float, A4, (cf. 0198)
SW - S fuu^{1} 'to foam up'; W, B fu^{4}; Sh phu^{4}; LNK fuu^{6}; LCH, LMY fuu^{4}
CN - LP fuu^{4}; LM fow^{4}; WN, LC, PS fuu^{4}; NM fow^{4}
N -Y fu^{4}; Sk vuu^{1} (A?)

0788 - dust, B1
SW - S fun^{2}; W fɯn^{2} 'powder'; B khun^{2}; Sh phun^{2}; LNK fun^{3}; LCH, LMY fun^{2}
CN - WN phɯn^{2} 'manure used for fertilizer'
N - Y pun^{5} (B4); Sk phun^{5} (B4); WM fon^{5}

0789 - beach, sandbar, DL1
SW - S, W, B, Sh, LNK, LCH, LMY haat^{2}
CN - LM haat^{2}; LC haat^{2} 'rapids'; PS haat^{2}
N - Sk haat^{6}

0790 - to disappear, A1
SW - S haay^{5}; B, Sh, LNK, LCH, LMY haay^{1}
CN - LP haay^{1} 'to die'
N - Y rɯay^{1}; Sk rɤɤy^{1}

0791 - vessel for steaming rice, A1
SW - S hay^{5} 'jug'; W, B, Sh hay^{1}; LNK hay^{1} 'small-mouthed jug'; LCH, LMY hay^{1}
CN - LM lay^{1}; WN chay^{1}
N - Y ray^{1}; Sk hay^{2}

0792 - a tick, DS1
SW - S, W, B hep^{2}; LNK hep^{1}; LCH hip^{1}, hep^{1}; LMY hep^{1}
CN - LM ʔip^{3}; WN thɛp^{6}
N - Sk rip^{4}

0793 - waist, DL1, (cf. 0005)
Not in SW languages
N - Y hɯat^{2}; Sk vuat^{6}; WM hɯat^{5}

0794 - to cover (with a blanket), B1, (cf. 0282, 1078)
SW - S hom^{2}; W hum^{2}; B, Sh hom^{2}; LNK hom^{3}; LCH, LMY hum^{2}
CN - LP, LM hom^{2}; WN ham^{2}; LC hum^{2}
N - Sk hum^{6}, ham^{6}

0795 - to shrink, DS1
SW - S, W, B hot^{2}; Sh hot^{4}; LNK, LCH, LMY hot^{1}
CN - LP hot^{2}; LM hot^{3}; WN hɔt^{6}; PS hot^{4} (DS4); NM hot^{4}
N - Y rut^{3}; Sk hot^{4}

0796 - a wart, DL1
SW - S huut^{2}; W, B hut^{2}; Sh hut^{4} (DS1); LCH, LMY sut^{1} (DS1)
CN - WN sɔt^{2}
N - Sk truut^{6}

0797 - stem, C2
SW - S kaan^{3}; W kaan^{3} 'classifier for long, slender objects'; B, Sh kaan^{3}; LNK kaan^{5}; LCH, LMY kaan^{3}
CN - WN kaan^{3}
N - Y, Sk, WM kaan^{3}

0798 - to speak, C2
Not in SW languages
CN - LP kyaaŋ^{3}; LM kaaŋ^{3}; LC kyaaŋ^{3} (Li says < Chinese); PS, NM kyaaŋ^{3}
N - Y, WM, P kaaŋ^{3}

0799 - husk, DL2
SW - S, W, B, Sh, LCH, LMY kaap^{2}
CN - WN kaap^{2}
N - Y kaap^{2}; Sk kaap^{6}

0800 - to hold in the closed hand, A2
SW - S, W, B, Sh kam^{1}; LNK kam^{2}; LCH, LMY kam^{1}
CN - LP kam^{2}; LM, WN, LC, PS, NM kam^{1}
N - Y, Sk, WM kam^{1}

0801 - to take a bite, DS2, (cf. 0146)
SW - S, W, B kat^{2}; Sh kat^{4}; LNK kat^{1}
CN - LP kat^{2}; LM kat^{3}; WN kat^{6}; LC, PS kat^{2}; NM kat^{4}
N - Y kat^{3}; Sk kat^{4}; WM kat^{5}

0802 - to scratch, A2, (cf. 0140)
SW - S, W kaw^{1}; LNK kaw^{2}; LCH, LMY kaw^{1}
CN - WN kaw^{1}; LC, PS kaw^{4} (A4?); NM kaw^{1}
N - Y, Sk kaw^{1}

0803 - curry, soup, A2
SW - S kɛɛŋ^{1}; W, B, Sh kɛŋ^{1} 'to cook, applied to preparing curries'; LNK kɛɛŋ^{2}; LCH, LMY kɛŋ^{1} 'to cook'
N - Sk keeŋ^{1}

0804 - Vietnamese, A2
SW - S kɛɛw^{1}; W, B kɛw^{1}; LNK kɛɛw^{2}; LCH, LMY kɛw^{1}
CN - LP keew^{2}; LM keew^{1}; WN ciw^{1}; LC, PS, NM keew^{1}
N - Y cew^{1}; Sk keew^{1}

0805 - glass, crystal, C2
SW - S kɛɛw^{3}; B kɛw^{3} 'jewel'; LNK kɛɛw^{5}; LCH, LMY kɛw^{3}
N - Sk kɛɛw^{3}

0806 - to hide, C4, (cf. 0991, 1001)
Not in SW languages
CN - WN kɯɯ^{6} (C4)
N - Y kɯ^{3} (C2), kɯ^{6} (C4); Sk kɯɯ^{3} 'to put away' (C2); P kɯɯ^{4} (C4)

0807 - to carry on the shoulder, DL4
Not in SW languages
N - Y kɯat^{5}; Sk khuat^{5}; WM kɯat^{6}; P kɯɯt^{6}

0808 - on, above, A4, (cf. 0414, 0607)
Not in SW languages
N - Y kɯn^{4}; Sk khɯn^{4}; WM, P kɯn^{2}

0809 - ringworm, DL2
SW - S klaak^{2}; W, B kaaʔ^{2}; LNK kaak^{2}; LCH, LMY (xii^{3}) xaak^{2}
CN - WN caak^{2}
N - Y caak^{2}; Sk laak^{6}

0810 - last (year), A2
SW - S klaay^{1}; W kaay^{1}; B kaay^{1} 'to pass'; LNK kaay^{2}; LCH, LMY kaay^{1} '(year) before last' ('last year' is pii^{1} lɛw^{6})
CN - LP caay^{2}; LM kyaay^{1}; WN caay^{1}; LC pii^{1} kyaay^{1}; PS, NM kyaay^{1} ('[year] before last' in CN languages)
N - Sk tlaay^{1} (OG), traay^{1} (YG); WM klaay^{1} '(year) before last'

0811 - matchbox, DS2
SW - S klak^{2}
N - Sk plɛk^{4} (OG), prɛk^{4} (YG), plak^{4} (OG), prak^{4} (YG)

0812 - to hold the breath, C2
SW - S klan^{3}; Sh kan^{3}
N - Y can^{3} 'to go without'; Sk kan^{3}

0813 - smooth, C2, (cf. 0195)
SW - S kliaη^{3}; W (maa^{2}) keη^{3} 'orange'; B kiaη^{3} 'smooth kind of orange'; Sh keη^{3} 'to be clear, clean'; LNK kiaη^{5}; LCH, LMY keη^{3}
N - Sk tliaη^{3} (OG), triaη^{3} (YG)

0814 - strand (of rope), A2
SW - S kliaw^{1}; Sh kiw^{1}; LCH kiw^{1}; LMY kiw^{1}, kew^{1}
N - Y cew^{1}; Sk tlɛɛw^{1} (OG), trɛɛw^{1} (YG)

0815 - lazy, DS2?, (cf. 0155)
Not in SW languages
N - Y cik^{3} (DS2); Sk tliik^{6} (OG), triik^{6} (YG) (DL2); WM klik^{5} (DS2); P cik^{2} (DS2)

0816 - to swallow, A2, (cf. 1014)
SW - S klɯɯn^{1}; W, B kɯn^{1}; Sh ʔɯn^{1}; LNK kɯɯn^{2}; LCH, LMY kɯn^{1}
CN - WN kɯn^{6} (C4)
N - Sk tlɯɯn^{1} (OG), trɯɯn^{1} (YG); WM klwaη^{1}

0817 - round, A2, (cf. 1066)
SW - S klom^{1}; W kum^{1}; B, Sh kom^{1}; LNK kom^{2}; LCH, LMY kum^{1}
N - Sk plum^{1} (OG), prum^{1} (YG)

0818 - to build, B2, (cf. 0997)
SW - S kɔɔ^{2}; W kɔ^{2} 'to begin'; B kɔ^{2}; Sh kɔ^{2} 'to pile'; LNK kɔɔ^{3}; LCH, LMY kɔɔ^{2}
CN - LP koo^{5}; LM, WN, PS koo^{2} ('to build a fire' in CN languages)
N - Y ko^{2}; Sk kɔɔ^{6}

0819 - wild olive, DL2
SW - S kɔɔk^{2}; W kɔʔ^{2}
CN - LM kook^{2}; WN kɔk^{2}; NM kuuk^{2}
N - Y kok^{2}; Sk kɔɔk^{6}

0820 - to heap up, A2
SW - S kɔɔη^{1}; W, B, Sh kɔη^{1}; LNK kɔɔη^{2}; LCH, LMY kɔη^{1}
CN - WN koη^{1}
N - Y koη^{1}; Sk kɔɔη^{1}

0821 - to hug, embrace, DL2
SW - S kɔɔt^{2}; W, B, Sh kɔt^{2}; LNK, LCH, LMY kɔɔt^{2}
CN - LP koot^{5}; LM koot^{2}; WN kɔt^{2}; LC, PS, NM koot^{2}
N - Y kot^{2}, kot^{3} (DS2), ko^{3} (C2); Sk kɔɔt^{6}

0822 - tiger, DL2, (cf. 0541, 0678)
Not in SW languages
N - Y kuk^{3} (DS2); Sk kuuk^{6}; WM kuk^{5}; P kuk^{2} (DS2)

0823 - to do, make, DL4, (cf. 1134)
Not in SW languages
N - Y kua^{5}, kuak^{5}; WM kuak^{6}, ku^{5}; P kuk^{3} (DS4)

0824 - stump, B2, (cf. 0700)
Not in SW languages
N - Y kwan^{2}; Sk kɔl^{6} (OG), kɔn^{6} (YG)

0825 - tamarind, orange, A1
SW - S khaam^{5} 'tamarind'; W khaam^{1}; B khaam^{1} 'tamarind'; Sh khaam^{1} 'white jujube'; LNK khaam^{1} 'tamarind'; LCH, LMY xaam^{1} 'tamarind'
CN - LP kaam^{2}; LM, WN, PS, NM kaam^{1} ('orange' and A2 in CN languages)
N - Y, Sk, WM kaam^{1} ('orange' and A2 in N languages)

0826 - to answer a call, A1
SW - S khaan^{5}; W xaan^{1}; B khaan^{1}; Sh khaan^{1} 'to speak, tell'; LCH, LMY xaan^{1}
N - Y haan^{1}; Sk ŋaan^{2}; WM haan^{1}

0827 - fishy smell, A4
SW - S khaaw^{1}; W xaaw^{4}; B kaaw^{4}; Sh khɛw^{4}; LNK khaaw^{6}; LCH xaaw^{4}; LMY xɛw^{4}
CN - LM, WN caaw^{4}; PS ɬaaw^{4}
N - Y haaw^{4}; Sk ɣaaw^{4}; P haaw^{2}

0828 - to itch, A4 (cf. 0835)
SW - S khan^{1}; W xan^{4}; B kan^{4}; Sh khan^{4} 'pungent to the taste or smell, sharp in temper, full of lascivious desire (vulgar)'; LNK khan^{6}; LCH, LMY xan^{4}
CN - LM, WN, NM han^{4}
N - Sk (ɣum^{4}) ɣal^{4} (OG), (ɣum^{4}) ɣan^{4} (YG)

0829 - handle, rod, A4
SW - S khan^{1}; W, B, Sh, LCH, LMY kan^{4}
N - Y kan^{4}; Sk khal^{4} (OG), khan^{4} (YG); WM kan^{2}

0830 - acacia, A4
SW - S khɛɛ^{1}; W, B kɛ^{4}; LNK khɛɛ^{6}; LMY kɛɛ^{4}
CN - LM kee^{4}; WN kɛɛ^{4}
N - Y ke^{4}

0831 - guest, DL1
SW - S khɛɛk^{2}; W, B khɛʔ^{2}; Sh khɛk^{2}; LNK khɛɛk^{2}; LCH, LMY xɛɛk^{2}
CN - LP, LM kheek^{2}; WN chɛk^{2}; LC, PS, NM kheek^{2}
N - Y hek^{2}; Sk heek^{6}

0832 - chopping board, A1
SW - S khiaŋ^{5}; B khiaŋ^{1}; Sh kheŋ^{1}; LNK khiaŋ^{1}; LCH, LMY xeŋ^{1}
CN - LP, LM khiiŋ^{1}; WN chiŋ^{1}; LC, PS khiiŋ^{1}; NM hiiŋ^{1}
N - Y, WM heŋ^{1}

0833 - sharp, sharp edge, A4
SW - S khom^{1}; W xum^{4}; B kom^{4}; Sh khom^{4} 'the edge of a cutting instrument'; LNK khom^{6}; LCH, LMY xum^{4} 'the sharp edge of a blade'
CN - LP khom^{4}; LM hom^{4}; LC kum^{4}; PS, kom^{4}; NM hom^{4}
N - Sk ɣam^{4}

0834 - to carry, transport, A1, (cf. 0372)
SW - S khon^{5}; B khon^{1}; LCH, LMY xun^{1}
N - Sk khun^{2}

0835 - to itch, A4 (cf. 0828)
SW - Sh khom^{4}; LCH, LMY xum^{4}
N - Y hum^{4}; Sk ɣum^{4}; WM xum^{2}

0836 - tame, familiar, C4
SW - S khun^{4}; B kun^{6}; LCH kun^{6}, xun^{6}; LMY kun^{6}
CN - WN kun^{6}
N - Y kun^{6}; Sk khun^{6}

0837 - a litter (of young), DL4
SW - S khrɔɔk^{3}
CN - LM look^{5}; WN cɔk^{5}; LC kyook^{4} ('family' in CN languages)
N - Y cok^{5}; Sk rɔɔk^{5}

0838 - to lie athwart, A1
SW - S khwaaŋ^{5}; W, B, Sh khwaaŋ^{1}; LNK khuaŋ^{1}; LMY xwaaŋ^{1}
CN - LM khwaaŋ^{1}; WN khaaŋ^{1}; LC khwaaŋ^{1} 'unreasonable; perverse, violent'
N - Y vaaŋ^{1}; Sk vaaŋ^{2}

0839 - to tie up, B4, (cf. 0210, 0659)
SW - S laam^{3}; B laam^{5}; Sh laam^{3}; LNK laam^{3}; LCH, LMY laam^{5}
CN - LP, LM, WN, LC, PS laam^{5}
N - Sk laam^{5}; WM, P laam^{6}

0840 - to fear, A1 (cf. 0728, 0918)
Not in SW languages
CN - LP, LM, WN, LC, PS, NM laaw^{1}
N - Y laaw^{1}; Sk laaw^{2}; WM laaw^{1}

0841 - alive, C4
Not in SW languages
N - Y li^{6}; Sk hă^{6} lii^{6} 'still, yet'; WM li^{4}

0842 - water pipe, A4
SW - W, Sh lin^{4}; LNK lin^{6}; LCH, LMY lin^{4}
CN - LM, WN lin^{4}
N - Y, Sk lin^{4}; WM, P lin^{2}

0843 - to fall over, C4
SW - S lom^{4}; W lum^{6}; B lom^{6}; Sh, LNK lom^{5}; LCH, LMY lum^{6}
CN - LP lom^{3}; LM lom^{6}; WN lam^{6}; PS, NM lom^{6}
N - Y, Sk lam^{6}; WM lam^{4}

0844 - to fall (of a leaf, etc.), B1
SW - S lon^{2}; W lun^{2}; B, Sh lon^{2}; LNK lon^{3}; LCH, LMY lun^{2}
CN - LP, LM lɤn^{2}; WN lan^{2}; LC lin^{2} 'to drop quickly'; PS lɤn^{2}; NM len^{2}
N - Y lan^{2}; Sk lɔn^{6}

0845 - to lose one's way, A1
SW - S loŋ^{5}; W luŋ^{1} 'mistaken'; B, Sh loŋ^{1} 'to forget'; LNK loŋ^{1}; LCH, LMY luŋ^{1}
CN - LM loŋ^{1}; WN lɔŋ^{1}; LC luŋ^{2} (B?)
N - Y loŋ^{1} 'wrong'; Sk lɔŋ^{2} 'to forget'; WM loŋ^{1}

0846 - to erase, DS4
SW - S lop^{4}; LNK lɯp^{3}, lop^{3}; LMY lop^{5}
N - Y lup^{1}; Sk lɯp^{6}

0847 - iron (the metal), A4, (cf. 0183)
Not in SW languages
N - Y fa^{4}; Sk maa^{4}

0848 - spleen, C4
SW - S maam^{4}; W, B maam^{6}; Sh, LNK maam^{5}; LCH, LMY mɛm^{6}
CN - LM, WN maam^{6}
N - Y maam^{6}; Sk maam^{3}, maam^{6} (C?, genuine Saek word is said to be paaŋ^{3}); WM maam^{4}

0849 - ghost, A4, (cf. 0641)
Not in SW languages
N - Y faaŋ^{4}; Sk maaŋ^{4}; WM faaŋ^{2}

0850 - sterile, A1
SW - S man^{5}; W, B, Sh, LNK, LMY man^{1}
CN - LP, LM man^{1}
N - Y, Sk man^{1}

0851 - thread, A1, (cf. 0773)
SW - S may^{5} 'silk'; W may^{1}; B may^{1} 'cotton cloth'; Sh may^{1}; LNK may^{1} 'silk, silk thread'; LCH, LMY may^{1}
CN - LP, LM, WN, LC, PS, NM may^{1}
N - Y may^{1}; Sk mii^{2}; WM, P may^{1}

0852 - cat, A4
SW - S mɛɛw^{1}; W, B, Sh mɛw^{4}; LNK mɛɛw^{6}; LCH, LMY mɛw^{4}
CN - LP, LM meew^{4}; WN mɛw^{3}; LC, PS, NM meew^{2} (B?)
N - Y mew^{3} (C?); Sk mɛɛw^{4}

0853 - soot, C1
SW - W mi^{3}; LCH, LMY mii^{3}
CN - LP mii^{3}; LM mey^{3}; LC, PS mii^{3}
N - Y mi^{3}; Sk mii^{3} in plɔɔ^{6} mii^{3} 'coals in fire'

0854 - doctor, shaman, A1
SW - S mɔɔ^{5}; W, B, Sh mɔ^{1}; LNK, LCH, LMY mɔɔ^{1}
CN - LP, LM, WN, LC, PS moo^{1}
N - Y mo^{1}; Sk mɔɔ^{2}

0855 - termite, DL4
SW - S mɔɔt^{3}; W mɔt^{4}; B mɔt^{5}; Sh mɔt^{3}; LNK, LCH, LMY mɔɔt^{5}
CN - LP, LM moot^{5}; WN mɔt^{5}; PS, NM moot^{5}
N - Y mot^{5}; Sk mɔɔt^{5}

0856 - pubic hair, A1
SW - S mɔy^{5}; W, B, Sh mɔy^{1}; LNK mɔɔy^{1}; LCH, LMY mɔy^{1}
CN - PS mooy^{1}
N - Y, WM mi^{1}

0857 - beard, B4, (cf. 0247)
Not in SW languages
CN - LP, LM mom^5; WN, LC mum^5; PS, NM mom^5
N - Y mum^5; WM, P mum^6

0858 - arrow of crossbow, B1
Not in SW languages
N - Y na^2; Sk naa^6; WM naa^5

0859 - jackal, A4
SW - S nay^1; B, Sh nay^4; LNK nay^6; LCH, LMY nay^4
CN - WN nay^4
N - Y, Sk nay^4

0860 - pubic mound, B1
SW - S, B, W naw^2; Sh naw^2 'the lower part of the abdomen'; LCH, LMY naw^2
CN - WN ŋaw^2
N - Y naw^2; Sk naw^6

0861 - debt, C1
SW - S nii^3; Sh ni^3; LNK nii^4; LCH, LMY nii^3
CN - LM ney^3; WN, PS nii^3
N - Y ni^3

0862 - here, this, C1
SW - S nii^3, nii^4; W, B ni^3, ni^6; Sh nay^3, nay^5; LNK nii^4, nii^5; LCH, LMY nii^3, nii^6
CN - LP, LM nay^3; WN nii^5, nay^5 (B4); LC nay^2 (also, nay^6 in certain phrases); PS nay^3
N - Y ni^6 (C?); Sk nii^3, nii^6, rii^6; WM nay^4; P nii^3

0863 - kidney stones, C1
SW - S, B niw^3; LNK niw^4; LCH niw^3; LMY niw^3, new^3
CN - LM niiw^6 (C4); WN ɲiw^3
N - Y niw^3, niaw^3; Sk diiw^3 (OG), diw^3 (YG) (also, niiw^3 [OG], niw^3 [YG], both said to be < Siamese)

0864 - hump of an ox, DL1
SW - S nɔɔk^2; B nɔʔ^2; Sh nɔk^2; LNK, LCH, LMY nɔɔk^2
CN - LP, LM nook^2; WN ŋɔk^2, nɔk^2; PS nook^2
N - Y nok^2; Sk nɔɔk^6

0865 - pus; lake, A1
SW - S nɔɔŋ^5; W, B, Sh nɔŋ^1; LNK nɔɔŋ^1; LCH, LMY nɔŋ^1
CN - LP, LM nooŋ^1; WN noŋ^1; LC, PS, NM nooŋ^1
N - Y noŋ^1; Sk nɔɔŋ^2; WM nɤŋ^1

0866 - shadow, reflection, A4
SW - S ŋaw^{1}; W, B, Sh ŋaw^{4}; LNK ŋaw^{6}; LCH, LMY ŋaw^{4}
CN - LM, WN, LC, PS, NM ŋaw^{4}
N - Y, Sk ŋaw^{4}

0867 - to smell bad, A1, (cf. 0910)
Not in SW languages
N - Y haw^{1}; Sk ŋaw^{2}; WM haw^{1}

0868 - finger, toe, B4, (0239)
Not in SW languages
N - Y ɲiaŋ^{5}; Sk ŋiaŋ^{5}

0869 - to hear, listen, A1, (0735, 1012)
Not in SW languages
N - Y ɲia^{1}; Sk ɲia^{2}

0870 - to dust off, DS2
SW - S pat^{2}; Sh pat^{4} 'to sweep'; LNK pat^{1} 'to sweep'; LCH, LMY pat^{1}
CN - LP pat^{2}; LM pat^{3}; WN pat^{6}; LC pat^{2} ('to sweep' in CN languages)
N - Y pat^{3} 'to sweep'; Sk pɛk^{4}; WM pat^{5}

0871 - to climb, A2
SW - S piin^{1}; W, B pin^{1}; LNK piin^{2}
CN - LM, WN pin^{1}
N - Y pin^{1}; Sk piin^{1}; WM plen^{2} (A4); P pin^{1}, peen^{2}

0872 - to change, B2, (cf. 0711)
SW - S plian^{2}; W phen^{2}; B pian^{2}; Sh pin^{2}, pen^{2}; LNK pian^{3}; LCH, LMY pen^{2}
CN - LP piin^{5}; LM piin^{2}; WN pin^{2}; LC piin^{2} (Li says < Chinese); PS piin^{2}
N - Y pian^{2}; Sk pian^{6}

0873 - to turn upside down or inside out, C2
SW - S plin^{3}; W, B, Sh pin^{3}; LNK pin^{5}; LCH, LMY pin^{3}
CN - LP, WN pin^{3}
N - Y pin^{3}; Sk pliin^{3} (OG), priin^{3} (YG)

0874 - to rob, C2
SW - S plon^{3}; LNK pun^{5}, pon^{5}
CN - LM pyɤn^{3}
N - Sk pun^{3}

0875 - a brush, A2
SW - S prɛɛŋ^{1}
N - Sk prɛɛŋ^{1}

0876 - woman, wife, A4, (cf. 0217, 0737)
Not in SW languages
N - Y pa^{4}; Sk phaa^{4}; WM, P paa^{2}

0877 - crazy, DL4, (cf. 0015)
Not in SW languages
CN - WN paak^{5}
N - Y paak^{5}; P paak^{6}

0878 - thunder, C3, (cf. 1103)
Not in SW languages
N - Y pya^{3}; Sk phraa^{3}; WM plaa^{3}

0879 - to defeat, be defeated, C4
SW - S phɛɛ^{4}; W, B pɛ^{6}; Sh pɛ^{5}; LNK phɛɛ^{5}; LCH, LMY pɛɛ^{6}
N - Y pe^{5} (B4), pe^{6}; Sk phɛɛ^{5} (B4)

0880 - shirt, B4, (cf. 0337)
Not in SW languages
N - Y pɯa^{5}; Sk phia^{5}; WM pu^{6}; P pɯɯ^{6}

0881 - blistered, A4
SW - S phɔɔŋ^{1}; W, B, Sh, LCH, LMY pɔŋ^{4}
CN - WN poŋ^{4}
N - Y poŋ^{4} 'to puff out'; Sk phooŋ^{4}, phɔɔŋ^{4} (latter said to be < Lao or Siamese)

0882 - young bamboo shoot, A4, (cf. 0243)
Not in SW languages
CN - WN ðaaŋ^{4}
N - Y raaŋ^{4}; Sk naaŋ^{4}; WM raaŋ^{2}

0883 - bad, C4
SW - S raay^{4}; W, B haay^{6}; Sh haay^{5}; LNK haay^{5}, laay^{5}; LCH, LMY haay^{6}
CN - LM laay^{6}; WN ðaay^{6}; LC, PS ɬaay^{6}
N - Y rɯay^{6}; Sk raay^{6}

0884 - quick, A4, (cf. 0425)
SW - S rew^{1}; Sh sew^{4}; LNK liw^{6}, leew^{6}; LCH lew^{4}; LMY lew^{4}, rew^{4}
N - Y riaw^{4}; Sk riiw^{4} (OG), riw^{4} (YG) (< Siamese rew^{1} 'quick'?)

0885 - strength, strong, A4
SW - S rɛɛŋ^{1}; W, B, Sh hɛŋ^{4}; LNK hɛɛŋ^{6}; LCH, LMY hɛŋ^{4}
CN - LP ɬeeŋ^{4}; LM leeŋ^{4}; WN ðeŋ^{4}; LC ɬeeŋ^{4}; NM leeŋ^{4}
N - Y reŋ^{4}; Sk reeŋ^{4}; WM reŋ^{2}

0886 - bedbug, DL4
SW - S rɯat^{3}; W hɤt^{4}; B hɯat^{5}; Sh hɤt^{3}; LNK hɯat^{5}
CN - LP lɤɤt^{5}; LM lɯɯt^{5}; WN lɤt^{5}; LC lɤɤt^{4}; PS lɤɤt^{5}; NM lɯɯt^{5}
N - Y rɯat^{5}; Sk ruat^{6} (DL?); WM rɯat^{6}

0887 - to water (plants), DL4?, (cf. 1099)
SW - S rot^{4}; Sh hot^{4} (DS1); LCH, LMY hot^{1} (DS1, 'to shrink')
CN - WN ðɤt^{5} (DL4)
N - Y rɯat^{5} (DL4); Sk rɛk^{6}, hot^{4} (latter said to be < Lao); WM ruak^{6} (DL4)

0888 - squirrel, DL4, (cf. 0406)
SW - S (kă^{2}) rɔɔk^{3}; W hɔ^{4}; B hɔʔ^{5}; LNK (ka-) hɔɔk^{5}; LMY hɔɔk^{5}
CN - LP ɬook^{5}; LM lok^{5}; WN ðɔk^{5}
N - Y rok^{5}; Sk rɔɔk^{5}

0889 - a room, DS4, (cf. 0683)
SW - B luk^{5}; Sh luk^{4} (DS?)
CN - WN ðuk^{4} 'bedroom'
N - Y ruk^{1} 'bedroom'; WM ruk^{6}; P luk^{3}

0890 - spicy hot, DL4, (0639, 1065)
Not in SW languages
N - Y saat^{5}; Sk thaat^{5}

0891 - fishtrap, A4
SW - S say^{1}; W, B say^{4}; Sh shay^{4}; LNK say^{6}; LCH, LMY say^{4}
CN - LP ɬay^{4}; LM, WN say^{4}; LC ɬay^{4}
N - Y θay^{4}; Sk yay^{4}

0892 - splinter, C1
SW - S, B sian^{3}; Sh shen^{3}; LNK sian^{4}; LCH, LMY sen^{3}
CN - WN cen^{6} (C4)
N - Y sen^{6}; Sk kheel^{6} (OG), kheen^{6} (YG) (C4 in N languages)

0893 - to see (someone) off, B1
SW - S soŋ^{2}; W suŋ^{2}; B soŋ^{2}; Sh shoŋ^{2}; LNK soŋ^{3}; LCH, LMY suŋ^{2}
CN - LP ɬoŋ^{2}; LM soŋ^{2}; WN sɔŋ^{2}; LC ɬuŋ^{2}; PS, NM ɬoŋ^{2}
N - Sk cɔŋ^{6}

0894 - to put on, wear, C2, (cf. 1031)
Not in SW languages
N - Y tan^{3}; Sk tɛn^{3}; WM, P tan^{3}

0895 - to set up, C2
SW - S, W, B, Sh taŋ^{3}; LNK taŋ^{5}; LCH, LMY taŋ^{3}
CN - LP, LM, WN taŋ^{3}; LC taŋ^{3} 'to erect, build'; PS, NM taŋ^{3}
N - Y, Sk taŋ^{3}

0896 - shuttle of the loom, B2, (cf. 0197)
Not in SW languages
CN - LM pyaw^{5}; WN thaw^{2} (B1)
N - Y taw^{2}; WM raw^{5} (B?); P taw^{5}

0897 - turtle, B2
SW - S, W, B, Sh taw^{2}; LNK taw^{3}; LCH, LMY taw^{2}
CN - WN taw^{2}
N - Sk rɔɔ^{4} (A4, probably not cognate)

0898 - to hunt, B2?
Not in SW languages
CN - LP phyaw^{1} (A1); LM phyaw^{4} (A?); LC, PS phyaw^{2}
N - Y taw^{2}; P taw^{5}

0899 - to warn, A2
SW - S tɯan^{1}; LNK tɯan^{2}; LCH, LMY tɤn^{1}
CN - WN tɯn^{1}
N - Y tɯan^{2} (B2); WM tɯan^{1}; P tɯɯn^{1}

0900 - wild, forest, B1, (cf. 0258, 0448)
SW - S thɯan^{2}; W thɤn^{2}; B thɯan^{2}; Sh thɤn^{2}; LNK thɯan^{3}; LCH, LMY thɤn^{2}
CN - LP thɤɤn^{2}; LM thɯɯŋ^{2}; LC thɤɤn^{1} (A?)
N - Y tɯan^{5}; Sk thual^{5} (OG), thuan^{5} (YG); WM tɯan^{6}; P tɯɯn^{6}
(B4 in N languages)

0901 - to wake up (intransitive), B2, (cf. 0280)
SW - S tɯɯn^{2}; W, B, Sh tɯn^{2}; LNK tɯɯn^{3}; LCH, LMY tɯn^{2}
CN - LP tɤn^{5}; LM tɤn^{2}; WN tɯn^{2}; LC, PS tin^{2}; NM ten^{2}
N - Y rɯn^{2}

0902 - to castrate, A2
SW - S tɔɔn^{1}; W, B, Sh, LCH, LMY tɔn^{1}
CN - LP toon^{2}; LM toon^{1}; WN ton^{1}; LC, PS toon^{1}; NM toon^{2} (tone? toon^{1})
N - Y ton^{1}; Sk tɔɔn^{1}; WM tɤn^{1}

0903 - to argue, A1
SW - S thiaŋ^{5}; W theŋ^{1}; B thiaŋ^{1}; Sh theŋ^{1}; LNK thiaŋ^{1}; LCH, LMY theŋ^{1}
CN - LM khiiŋ^{1}; WN ceŋ^{1}
N - Y seŋ^{1}; Sk thiaŋ^{2}

0904 - to pull out, A1
SW - S thɔɔn^{5}; Sh thɔn^{1}; LNK thɔɔn^{1}; LMY thɔn^{1}
N - Sk tuun^{1} 'to take off, remove'

0905 - to flood, C1
SW - S thuam^{3}; W, Sh thom^{3}; LNK thuam^{4}; LCH, LMY thom^{3}
CN - LP thoom^{3} (thuum^{3}?); LM thuum^{3}; WN thum^{3}; LC, PS thuum^{3}
N - Y tum^{5} 'to flood' (B4), tum^{6} 'covered by water or earth' (C4) (which is cognate?); Sk thum^{6} (C4)

0906 - whole area of fields, B4
SW - S thuŋ^{3}; B toŋ^{5}; Sh toŋ^{3}; LNK thoŋ^{3}; LCH, LMY tuŋ^{5}
CN - LP thoŋ^{5}; LM toŋ^{5}; WN tɔŋ^{5}; NM toŋ^{5}
N - Y toŋ^{5}; Sk thɔŋ^{5}

0907 - rattan, A1
SW - S waay^{5}; W, B vaay^{1}; Sh, LNK waay ^{1}; LCH, LMY vaay^{1}
CN - LP, LM, WN, LC vaay^{1}
N - Y vaay^{1}; Sk vaay^{2}; WM waay^{1}

0908 - to fan, a fan, A4
SW - S wii^{1}; W, B vi^{4}; Sh wi^{4}; LNK wii^{6}; LCH, LMY vii^{4}
CN - LP vii^{4}; LM vey^{4}; WN, LC, PS vii^{4}; NM vey^{4}
N - Y vi^{2} 'to winnow' (B?); Sk phii^{4}; WM poy^{2}

0909 - to broil, C3
SW - S, W, B, Sh yaaŋ^{3}; LNK yaaŋ^{5}; LCH, LMY yaaŋ^{3}
CN - LM, WN yaaŋ^{3}
N - Y yiaŋ^{6}; Sk yuaŋ^{3} 'to smoke fish, meat, etc.'; WM ʔyɯaŋ^{3}

0910 - to smell bad, A1, (cf. 0867)
SW - S men^{5}; W min^{1}; Sh, LNK men^{1}; LCH, LMY min^{1}
CN - WN man^{1}

0911 - soft, C1, 2, 3 or B4?
SW - S nim^{3}

0912 - hundred, DL2, (cf. 0315)
SW - Sh, LCH, LMY paak^{2}
CN - LP paak^{5}; LM, WN, LC, PS, NM paak^{2}

0913 - figure, shape, B4
SW - S raaŋ^{3} 'frame, sketch'; Sh haaŋ^{3}; LCH, LMY haaŋ^{5}

0914 - mattress, B1
SW - S sɯa^{2} 'mat'; W sɤ^{2}; B sɯa^{2}; Sh shɤ^{2} 'to spread open, as a mat'; LNK sɯa^{3}; LCH, LMY sɤɤ^{2} 'to spread'
CN - WN sɯɯ^{2}
N - Sk sɯa^{6}

0915 - to bend or straighten, DS3
SW - S dat^{2}; Sh lat^{4}; LCH, LMY dat^{1}
CN - LM myat^{3}
N - Sk dɛt^{4}, blɛt^{4}

0916 - to pluck, DS2, (cf. 0440)
SW - S plit^{2}; W, B pit^{2}; Sh pit^{4}

0917 - kind of vegetable, DL2
SW - S, W, B, LCH, LMY kaat^{2}
CN - LP kaat^{5}; LM, WN kaat^{2}; LC laa^{4} kaat^{2} 'a kind of potato' (LC perhaps not the same vegetable); PS, NM kaat^{2}
N - Sk kɛk^{4} (DS2)

0918 - to be afraid, A2, (cf. 0728, 0840)
SW - S klua^{1}; Sh ko^{1}; LNK kua^{2}; LCH, LMY koo^{1}

0919 - half-grown, fairly large, B1
SW - S khɯaŋ^{2}; LCH, LMY xɤŋ^{2}
CN - LP khɤɤŋ^{2}; LM khɯɯŋ^{2}; WN khɯŋ^{2}

0920 - to kneel, DS4, (cf. 0970)
SW - S khuk^{4}; Sh khup^{5}; LCH, LMY xop^{5} (xaw^{2})
CN - LM kok^{4} 'to bend the knee'
N - Sk thuk^{6}

0921 - to surround, A4, (cf. 1102)
SW - S khum^{1}; Sh kum^{4}; LNK khum^{6}; LCH, LMY kum^{4}

0922 - vine, A1, (cf. 0538)
SW - S khaw^{5}; W khaw^{1}
CN - LP, LM, WN, PS khaw^{1}; NM haw^{1}

0923 - pond, A1
Not in SW languages
CN - LP, LM thom^{1}; LC thum^{1}; PS thom^{1}

0924 - dregs, B1, (cf. 0993)
SW - S saa^{2}; B saa^{2} 'yeast'; Sh, LCH, LMY saa^{2}
CN - LM saa^{2} 'wine dregs'; PS caa^{2} 'wine dregs'
N - Sk saa^{6}

0925 - millet, C1
SW - S, LCH, LMY faaŋ^{3}
CN - LP, LM, WN, NM phaaŋ^{3}
N - Sk viaŋ^{3}

0926 - tobacco, A3
Not in SW languages
CN - LP yiin^{2}; LM ʔiin^{4}; LC ʔiin^{2} (B?, Li says < Chinese); PS, NM yiin^{1}

0927 - to pickle, DL3, (cf. 0053)
SW - W ʔɤp^{2}; LNK ʔɯap^{2}
CN - LP ʔɤɤp^{5}; LM ʔɯɯp^{2}; LC, PS ʔɤɤp^{2}; NM ʔup^{2}
N - Sk ʔɯap^{6}

0928 - warm, B3
SW - S, W, B, Sh ʔun^{2}; LNK ʔun^{3}; LCH, LMY ʔun^{2}
CN - LP ʔon^{5}; LM ʔon^{2}; WN ʔun^{2}; LC ʔun^{2} 'to cook slowly for a long time'

0929 - to have sexual intercourse, C1
SW - W, B si^{3}; LNK sii^{4}; LCH, LMY sii^{3}

0930 - to hold in the mouth, A3
SW - S ʔom^{1}; W ʔum^{1}; B, Sh ʔom^{1}; LNK ʔom^{2}; LCH ʔum^{1}; LMY ʔum^{4}
CN - LP ʔom^{2}; LM ʔom^{4}; WN ʔum^{1}; PS ʔom^{1}; NM hom^{1}
N - Y ʔam^{2}, ʔum^{2} (B3); Sk ʔam^{1}

0931 - basin, B3
SW - S, W, B, Sh ʔaaŋ^{2}; LNK ʔaaŋ^{3}; LCH, LMY ʔaaŋ^{2}
CN - LP ʔaaŋ^{5}; LM, WN, LC, PS, NM ʔaaŋ^{2}
N - Y ʔaaŋ^{2}; Sk ʔaaŋ^{6}

0932 - to set up (a bed), A3, (cf. 0990)
Not in SW languages
CN - LP ʔaan^{2}; LM ʔaan^{4}; PS, NM ʔaan^{1}

0933 - to read, B3
SW - S, W, B ʔaan^{2}; Sh ʔaan^{2} - 'to read aloud, as a scholar, count'; LNK ʔaan^{3}; LCH, LMY ʔaan^{2} 'to read, to count'
CN - LP ʔaan^{5}; LM, WN ʔaan^{2}; LC ʔaan^{2} ('to count' in CN languages)
N - Sk ʔaan^{1} (A3?)

0934 - to lean back, A3, (cf. 0755)
Not in SW languages
CN - LP ʔaay^{2}; LM ʔaay^{4}; LC ʔii^{3} ʔaay^{1} 'arm-chair'; PS, NM ʔaay^{1}

0935 - father's younger brother, A3, (cf. 0752)
SW - S ʔaa^{1}; W, B ʔaaw^{1}; Sh ʔaaw^{1} 'father's younger brother or husband of father's younger sister', same as ʔaa^{1}; LNK ʔaaw^{2}; LCH ʔaaw^{1}; LMY ʔaaw^{4}
CN - LM, WN ʔaaw^{2}; LC ʔaaw^{2} 'father's younger brother or husband of father's younger sister'; PS ʔaaw^{2} (B3 in CN languages)
N - Y ʔaaw^{1}; Sk ʔaaw^{5} (B4); WM ʔaaw^{1}

0936 - classifier for things, A3
SW - S, W, B ʔan^{1}; Sh ʔan^{1} 'which, that which; a substantive particle'; LNK ʔan^{2}; LCH ʔan^{1}; LMY ʔan^{4}
CN - LP ʔan^{2}; LM ʔan^{4}; WN, LC, NM ʔan^{1}
N - Sk ʔal^{1} (OG), ʔan^{1} (YG)

0937 - mirror, B2
Not in SW languages
CN - LP kiiŋ^{5}; LM kiiŋ^{2}; WN ciŋ^{2}; PS, NM kiiŋ^{2}

0938 - gold, A2 (cf. 0117)
Not in SW languages
CN - LP kim^{2}; LM kim^{1}; WN cim^{1}; LC, PS kim^{1}; NM kyom^{1}
N - Y cim^{1}; WM kim^{1}

0939 - sword, B2, (cf. 0433)
Not in SW languages
CN - LP kiim^{5}; LM, LC, PS, NM kiim^{2}

0940 - a saw, to saw, B2, (cf. 0192)
SW - W kɯ^{5} (B4)
CN - LP kɤɤ^{5}; LM kɤɰ^{2}; WN chɯɯ^{2}; LC, PS kɯɯ^{2}; NM kaɰ^{2}
N - Y kɯ^{2}

0941 - work (noun), A2, (cf. 0722)
Not in SW languages
CN - LP koŋ^{2}; LM koŋ^{1}; WN kaŋ^{6} (C4); LC kuŋ^{1} (Li says < Chinese); PS, NM koŋ^{1}

0942 - buttocks, C2
SW - S kon^{3}; W kun^{3}; B, Sh kon^{3}; LNK kon^{5}; LCH, LMY kun^{3}
CN - LP kon^{3}; LM kom^{3}, kom^{2}; LC kun^{3}; PS, NM kon^{3}

0943 - seed, hard core, B2, (cf. 0213, 0457)
SW - S, W, B, Sh kɛn^{2}; LNK kɛɛn^{2} (A2); LCH kɛn^{2}; LMY kɛn^{1} (A2)
CN - LP keen^{5}; LM keen^{2}; WN cen^{2}; PS keen^{2} ('hard' in CN languages)
N - Sk keel^{6} (OG), keen^{6} (YG)

0944 - fishbone, C2
SW - S, W, B, Sh kaaŋ^{3}; LNK kaaŋ^{5}; LCH, LMY kaaŋ^{3}
CN - LP, LM, PS, NM kaaŋ^{3}
N - Sk kaaŋ^{3}

0945 - to take up in the two cupped hands, DL2
SW - S kɔɔp^{2}; B, Sh kɔp^{2}; LCH, LMY kɔɔp^{2}
CN - LP koop^{5}; LM koop^{2}; WN kɔp^{2}; LC, PS, NM koop^{2}

0946 - door latch, A2
SW - S klɔɔn^{1} 'door latch; rafter'; W kɔn^{1} 'roof beam'; B kɔn^{1}; Sh kɔn^{1} 'rafter'; LNK kɔɔn^{2}; LCH, LMY kɔn^{1}
CN - LP coon^{2}; LM, LC, PS, NM kyoon^{1} ('to close a door or window' in CN languages)

0947 - price, B2, (cf. 0500)
Not in SW languages
CN - LP kyaa^{5}; LM kyaa^{2}; WN caa^{2}; LC, PS kyaa^{2}

0948 - shelf above a fire, B?
SW - W caa^{3} (C?); Sh khaa^{2} (B?); LCH, LMY xaa^{2} (B?)
CN - LP kyaa^{5}; LM kyaa^{2}; WN chaa^{2}; PS kyaa^{2} (B2 in CN languages)
N - Sk thraa^{6} (C4)

0949 - melon, A2
SW - S kwaa^{1} 'cucumber'; LCH, LMY kwaa^{1} 'kind of gourd'
CN - LP kwaa^{2}; LM, LC, PS, NM kwaa^{1}

0950 -to roll up, C2
SW - W kon^{3}
CN - LP, LM kwiin^{3}; LC kwiin^{3} (Li says < Chinese); PS, NM kwiin^{3}

0951 - to chop, DL1, (cf. 0466)
SW - W khweʔ^{2}; B khiaʔ^{2}
CN - LP, LM, LC khiik^{2}

0952 - bridge, A4 (cf. 0544)
Not in SW languages
CN - LP khiiw^{4}; LM, LC, PS, NM kiiw^{4}
N - Y ciaw^{4}; Sk khaw^{4}; WM kiaw^{2}

0953 - penis, A4
SW - S khuay^{1}; W xway^{4}; B kuay^{4}; Sh kway^{4}, kay^{4}; LNK khoy^{6}; LCH, LMY kway^{4}
CN - LP, LM, WN, PS, NM vay^{4}

0954 - turbid, DS4, (cf. 0162)
Not in SW languages
CN - LP khot^{4}; LM kot^{4}; LC kut^{4} taat^{2}; PS, NM kot^{4}

0955 - to feed, A1, (cf. 0187)
SW - S khun^{5}; LNK khun^{1}
CN - LP, LM khon^{1}; LC khun^{1}; PS, NM khon^{1}

0956 - scissors, C2
SW - W, B kεw^{3}
CN - LP kheew^{4}; LM, LC, PS, NM keew^{4} (A4 in CN languages)
N - Sk kεεw^{3}
(Could all these be cognate with S khiaw^{1} 'sickle'?)

0957 - classifier for garments, A4
Not in SW languages
CN - LP khoη^{4}; LM luuη^{4}; WN, LC kuη^{4}; PS koη^{4}; NM toη^{4}

0958 - indigo, B1, (cf. 0534)
Not in SW languages
CN - LP khon^{5} (B?); LM khon^{2}; WN khun^{2}; PS, NM khon^{2}

0959 - to cut, B4, (cf. 0692)
Not in SW languages
CN - LP khee^{5}; LM kee^{5}, hee^{5}; WN hεε^{5}; LC, PS, NM kee^{5}

0960 - branch, B4, (cf. 0488)
SW - W xaa^{5}; B ηaa^{5}; Sh khaa^{3}; LNK ηaa^{3}; LCH, LMY xaa^{5} 'fork in a road'
CN - LP khaa^{5}; LM, WN ηaa^{5}; LC, PS kaa^{5}; NM ηaa^{5}
N - Sk ηaa^{5}

0961 - ape, B4
SW - S khaaη^{3}; Sh kaaη^{3}; LNK khaaη^{3}; LCH, LMY kaaη^{5}
CN - LP khaaη^{5}; LM, PS, NM kaaη^{5}
N - Sk khaaη^{5}, khaaη^{6} (C4)

0962 - threshold, C4
Not in SW languages
CN - LP khaam^{3}; LM, WN, LC, PS kaam^{6}

0963 - to squeeze, massage, C4
SW - S khan^{4}; W, B kan^{6}; Sh kan^{5} 'to wrestle, ravish'; LNK khan^{5}; LCH, LMY kan^{6}
CN - LP khan^{3}; LM kan^{6}; WN kan^{6} 'to wrestle'; NM kan^{6}
N - Sk khal^{6} (OG), khan^{6} (YG)

0964 - tight, DS4
SW - S khap^{4}; W kap^{4}; B, Sh kap^{5}; LNK khap^{3}; LCH, LMY kap^{5}
CN - LP kap^{2} (DS2?); LM kap^{3} (DS2?); WN kap^{4}; LC, PS, NM kap^{4} ('narrow' in CN languages)

0965 - shady, cloudy, A1
Not in SW languages
CN - LP, LM, LC, PS kham^{1}; NM ham^{1}

0966 - swollen, B4, (cf. 0769, 0785)
SW - W, B kaɰ^{5}; Sh kaɰ^{3}; LCH, LMY kay^{5}
CN - LP khaɰ^{5}; LM, WN, LC, PS, NM kaɰ^{5}

0967 - crooked, hunchback, A4, (cf. 0147)
SW - LCH, LMY kɔɔ^{4}; PS koo^{4}
CN - LP khoo^{4}; LM, LC koo^{4}

0968 - poor; difficult, C1, (cf. 0390)
SW - W khɔ^{3}; B khɔ^{2} (B?)
CN - LP khoo^{3}; LM hoo^{3}; LC, PS, NM khoo^{3}

0969 - a hook, A1
SW - S khɔɔ^{5}; W xɔ^{1}; B, Sh khɔ^{1}; LNK, LCH, LMY xɔɔ^{1}
CN - LP khoo^{4} (A4); LM, WN, PS khoo^{1}
N - Sk hɔɔ^{2}

0970 - to kneel down, B4, (cf. 0920)
Not in SW languages
CN - LP khwii^{5}; LM kwey^{5}; WN kii^{5}; LC kwii^{5}

0971 - cupboard, B4, (cf. 0705)
SW - W kuy^{2} (B2?)
CN - LP khwii^{5}; LM kwey^{5}; WN kii^{5}; LC, PS kwii^{5}; NM kwey^{5}

0972 - fist, A4
Not in SW languages
CN - LP khwiin^{4}; LM kwiin^{4}; WN kin^{4}; LC kam^{1} kwiin^{4} 'to make a fist'; PS, NM kwiin^{4}

0973 - trousers, B1
Not in SW languages
CN - LP, LM khwaa^{2}; WN khaa^{2}; LC, PS khwaa^{2}; NM vaa^{2}

0974 - cave (actually a recess beneath a projection in a cliff), A4, (cf. 0365)
Not in SW languages
CN - LP ŋɤɤm^{4}; LM ŋɯɯm^{4}; WN ŋum^{4}; LC ŋɤɤm^{4} (Li says < Chinese);
PS ŋɤɤm^{4}; NM ŋɯɯm^{4}

0975 - time, turn, DL4, (cf. 0597, 1058, 1155)
SW - S ŋuat^{3}; B ŋuat^{5}; LNK ŋuat^{5}
CN - LP vuut^{5}; LM ŋuut^{5}; LC ŋuut^{4} ('month' in CN languages)

0976 - to look, A4, (cf. 1094)
SW - Sh ŋɔy^{4} 'to look at slyly'
CN - LP, LM, LC, PS ŋooy^{4}

0977 - first (month), A2
SW - W ceŋ^{1}; B ciaŋ^{1}; Sh seŋ^{1}; LCH, LMY ceŋ^{1}
CN - LP ciŋ^{2}; LM ciiŋ^{1}; WN ciŋ^{1}; LC, PS, NM ciiŋ^{1}
N - Sk ciaŋ^{1}

0978 - blanket, A2, (cf. 1128)
SW - W cen^{1}
CN - LP ciin^{2}; LM, PS, NM ciin^{1}

0979 - to turn, B2
Not in SW languages
CN - LP ciin^{5}; LM, PS, NM ciin^{2}

0980 - wall, A4, (cf. 0058)
Not in SW languages
CN - LP ɬiŋ^{4}; LM, WN, LC, PS ciŋ^{4}; NM sɤŋ^{4}

0981 - to cook, C2
Not in SW languages
CN - LP cɤɤ^{3}; LM cɤɰ^{3}; LC, PS cɯɯ^{3}

0982 - to fry, A2
SW - W, B cɛn^{1}
CN - LP ceen^{2}; LM ceen^{1}; WN cen^{1}; PS, NM ceen^{1}

0983 - bottomless cage, C2
Not in SW languages
CN - LP, LM, LC, PS caam^{3}

0984 - raised net, A2, (the type of net called yɔɔ^{1} in S)
SW - Sh sam^{1}; LCH, LMY cam^{1}
CN - LP cam^{2}; LM, WN, LC, PS cam^{1}

0985 - thousand, A1
Not in SW languages
CN - LP, LM chiin^{1}; LC šiin^{1} (Li says < Chinese); PS siin^{1}; NM šiin^{1}

0986 - money, A4, (cf. 0250)
SW - W, B cɛn^{4}
CN - LP cheen^{4}; LM ceen^{4}; WN cen^{4}; LC ceen^{4} (Li says < Chinese);
PS ceen^{4}; NM seen^{4}

0987 - fork, A1
Not in SW languages
CN - LP, LM chaa^{1}; WN chaa^{6} (C4); LC šaa^{1}; PS, NM saa^{1}

0988 - wrong, incorrect, B1?, (cf. 0295)
SW - W caa^{5} 'false' (B4)
CN - LP, LM chaa^{2} (B1); WN šaa^{3} (C1?); LC šaa^{2} (B1?); PS, NM saa^{2} (B1)

0989 - it is, B4
SW - S chaɰ^{3}; W cɯ^{5}; Sh saɰ^{3} 'true, certain'; LCH, LMY cay^{5}
CN - LP chɤɤ^{5}; LM cɤɰ^{5}; WN caɰ^{5}; LC cɯɯ^{5} 'to be; to belong'; PS cɯɯ^{5};
NM caɰ^{5}

0990 - bed, A4, (cf. 0932)
SW - W cɔŋ^{4}; LCH, LMY cɔŋ^{4} 'bed of a monk'
CN - LP chooŋ^{4}; LM cooŋ^{4}; WN coŋ^{4}; LC cooŋ^{4} ('table' in CN languages)

0991 - to hide, C3, (cf. 0806, 1001)
Not in SW languages
CN - LP dii^{3}; LM nii^{3}; LC, PS dii^{3}

0992 - navel, C3 (cf. 0050)
Not in SW languages
CN - LP -dii^{3}; LM -ney^{3}; WN, PS -dii^{3}

0993 - wine dregs, B3, (cf. 0924)
Not in SW languages
CN - LP dɤɤ^{5}; LM nɯɯ^{2}; LC, PS dɯɯ^{2}; NM dɯɯ^{4}

0994 - to smell something, A3
SW - S dom^{1}; W dum^{1}; B dom^{1}; Sh nom^{1}; LNK dom^{2}; LCH dum^{1}; LMY dum^{4}
CN - LP dom^{2}; WN dom^{1}
N - Sk dam^{1}

0995 - numb, benumbed by cold, C3
SW - Sh laaη^{3}
CN- LP daaη^{3}; LM naaη^{3}; LC daaη^{3} ('cold' in CN languages)

0996 - idle, free, A3, (cf. 1105)
SW - S, W, B daay^{1}; Sh laay^{1} 'to be empty, barren, alone'; LCH daay^{1}; LMY daay^{4}
CN - LP daay^{2}; LM naay^{4}; WN daay^{1}; LC, PS, NM daay^{1}
N - Sk dɤɤy^{1}

0997 - to make a fire, A3, (cf. 0818)
SW - W daη^{1}
CN - LP daη^{2}; LM naη^{4}; WN, LC, PS, NM daη^{1}

0998 - to sting, C3
SW - B dan^{3}
CN - LP dan^{3}; LM nan^{3}; WN, LC dan^{3} ('to itch' in CN languages)

0999 - to swim under water, A3
SW - S, W, B dam^{1}; Sh lam^{1} 'to dive'; LCH dam^{1}; LMY dam^{4}
CN - LP dam^{2}; LM nam^{4}; WN, PS, NM dam^{1}

1000 - enough, A3, (cf. 0644)
SW - B nɔ^{1}
CN - LP doo^{2}; LM noo^{4}; LC, PS, NM doo^{1}

1001 - to hide, take shelter, C3, (0806, 0991)
Not in SW languages
CN - LP doo^{3}; LM noo^{3}; LC, PS doo^{3}

1002 - hill, C3, (cf. 0657, 0778)
Not in SW languages
CN - LP dooη^{3}; LM nooη^{3}; LC dooη^{3} 'wilderness; outskirts of a village'; PS, NM dooη^{3}

1003 - to hit, play, etc. (in phrases), DS2
SW - S, W, B tok^{2}; Sh tɯk^{4}; LNK, LCH, LMY tok^{1}
CN - LP tɤk^{2}; LM tɤk^{3}; WN tɤk^{6} (in many expressions, but thɔk^{6} paa^{1} 'to fish'); LC tik^{2} 'to do, to cause'
N - Sk tɯk^{4}

1004 - earth, dirt, A2, (cf. 0445)
SW - S tom^{1} 'mud'
CN - LP tom^{2}; LM tom^{1}; LC tum^{1}; PS, NM tom^{1}

1005 - to light (fire, lamp), C2, (cf. 0688)
Not in SW languages
CN - LP tiim^{3}, teem^{3}; LM tiim^{3}; WN tem^{3}; LC, PS, NM teem^{3}

1006 - hot; angry, C3, (cf. 0314)
Not in SW languages
CN - LP diiw^{3}; LM niiw^{3} ‘ to scorch’; LC, PS, NM diiw^{3}

1007 - plugged up, A2, (cf. 0014)
SW - S, W, B tan^{1}; Sh tan^{1} ‘to be solid, have no cavity’; LNK tan^{2}; LCH, LMY tan^{1}
CN - LP tan^{2}; LM tan^{1}
N - Sk tɛn^{1}

1008 - to hold, contain, A2
Not in SW languages
CN - LP too^{2}; LM too^{1}; WN too^{4} (A4); LC, PS, NM too^{1}

1009 - kind of wasp, B2
SW - S tɔɔ^{2}; W, B tɔ^{2}; Sh tɔ^{2} ‘a large hornet’; LNK tɔɔ^{3}; LCH, LMY tɔɔ^{2}
CN - LP too^{5}; LM, WN, PS, NM too^{2}
N - Sk tɔɔ^{6}

1010 - to gamble, C2
Not in SW languages
CN - LP, LM, LC, PS, NM too^{3}
N - Sk too^{3} ‘to challenge’

1011 - a piece, lump, B2
SW - B tɔn^{2}; LNK tɔɔn^{3}; LCH, LMY tɔn^{2}
CN - LP toon^{5} ‘a meal’; LM toon^{2} ‘a meal’; LC toon^{2} ‘meal, numeral classifier of meals’; PS toon^{2} ‘meal’

1012 - to listen, hear, B4, (cf. 0735, 0869)
Not in SW languages
CN - LP thiŋ^{5}; LM tiŋ^{5}; LC, PS tiŋ^{5}; NM tɤŋ^{5}

1013 - sugar, A1
Not in SW languages
CN - LP thɤɤŋ^{1}; LM thɯɯŋ^{1}; WN thɯŋ^{1}; LC thɤɤŋ^{1} (Li says < Chinese); PS thɤɤŋ^{1}; NM thɯɯŋ^{1}

1014 - to swallow, A1, (cf. 0816)
Not in SW languages
CN - LP, LM thɤn^{1}; WN thɯn^{6} (C4); PS thɤn^{1}; NM then^{1}

1015 - chopsticks, B1
SW - W, B, Sh thu^{2}; LCH, LMY thuu^{2}
CN - LP thuu^{2}; LM thow^{2}; WN, PS thuu^{2}; NM thaɰ^{2}
N - Sk thɯɯ^{5}, thuu^{5} (B4)

1016 - kind of basket, C1
SW - W thuη^{3}
CN - LP, LM thoη^{3} 'bucket'; PS, NM thoη^{3}

1017 - wet, A4
Not in SW languages
CN - LP thom^{4}; LM tom^{4}; LC tum^{4}

1018 - to carry on the back, C4, (cf. 1043)
Not in SW languages
CN - LP thee^{3}; LM, LC, PS tee^{6}

1019 - to smear, A4
SW - S thaa^{1}; W, B, Sh taa^{4}; LNK thaa^{6}; LCH, LMY taa^{4}
CN - LP thaa^{4}; LM, WN, LC, PS taa^{4}
N - Sk thaa^{4}

1020 - all, A4, (cf. 0225)
SW - S thaη^{4} (C4); W tɯη^{4}; Sh taη^{4}; LNK thaη^{6}; LCH, LMY tɯη^{4}, taη^{4} (frequently taaη^{4} in both places)
CN - LP thaη^{4}; LM taη^{4}; WN taη^{4}, tɯη^{4}; LC, PS, NM taη^{4}
N - Sk thɯη^{4}

1021 - place (in expressions for above, below, etc.), C1
Not in SW languages
CN - LP, LM than^{3}; LC than^{3} 'side, place'

1022 - to shave, B1
Not in SW languages
CN - LP, LM, LC, PS thay^{2}

1023 - bag, B4, (cf. 0717)
SW - W, B tay^{5}; LNK thay^{3}; LCH, LMY tay^{5}
CN - LP thay^{5}; LM, WN, LC, PS tay^{5}

1024 - rabbit, DL?
SW - W thɔʔ^{2}; B thɔʔ^{5}
CN - LP, LM, LC, PS, NM thoo^{2} (B1 in CN languages)

1025 - to gather, A4
Not in SW languages
CN - LP thoo^{4}; LM, WN too^{4}; LC too^{4} 'to provide, to store up'; PS, NM too^{4}

1026 - to do reciprocally, A4
Not in SW languages
CN - LP thoo^{4}; LM, LC, PS, NM too^{4}

1027 - brass, copper, A4
SW - S thɔɔŋ^{1}; W, B, Sh tɔŋ^{4}; LNK thɔɔŋ^{6} 'gold'; LCH, LMY tɔŋ^{4}
CN - LP thooŋ^{4}; LM tooŋ^{4}; WN toŋ^{4}; LC, PS, NM tooŋ^{4}
N - Sk thɔɔŋ^{4} (only in certain expressions < Lao or Siamese)

1028 - to flee, A1
SW - S nii^{5}; B, Sh ni^{1}; LNK, LCH, LMY nii^{1}
CN - LP nii^{1}; LM ney^{1}; WN nii^{1}, ɲii^{1}; LC, PS nii^{1}; NM ney^{1}

1029 - crop (of a chicken), A1
SW - S niaŋ^{5}; W neŋ^{1}; B niaŋ^{1}; Sh neŋ^{1}; LNK niaŋ^{1}; LMY neŋ^{1}
CN - LP, LM niiŋ^{1}

1030 - to be sticky, A1, (cf. 0603)
SW - Sh no^{1}
CN - LP, LM, WN nuu^{1}; LC khaw^{3} nuu^{1} 'glutinous rice'; PS nuu^{1}

1031 - to put on, wear, B4, (cf. 0894)
SW - S nuŋ^{3} (lower garment only); W, B nuŋ^{5}; Sh nuŋ^{3}, nɯŋ^{3}; LNK nuŋ^{3}; LCH, LMY nuŋ^{5}
CN - LP noŋ^{5}; LM loŋ^{5}; WN, LC nuŋ^{5}; PS noŋ^{5}

1032 - breast, A4
SW - S nom^{1}; W num^{4}; B, Sh nom^{4}; LNK nom^{6}; LCH, LMY num^{4}
CN - LP, LM, PS, NM nom^{4}
N - Sk nom^{4} (only in the meaning 'milk')

1033 - lady, A4
SW - S naaŋ^{1}; W, B, Sh naaŋ^{4}; LNK naaŋ^{6}; LCH, LMY naaŋ^{4}
CN - LP, LM naaŋ^{4}; WN naaŋ^{4} 'wife of older brother'; PS, NM naaŋ^{4}
N - Sk naaŋ^{4}

1034 - kind of deer, C4, (cf. 0109, apparently the same animal as 0782)
Not in SW languages
CN - LP naan^{3}; LM, WN, LC, PS, NM naan^{6}

1035 - dew, mist, A4
SW - Sh naay^{4}
CN - LP, LM, LC, PS, NM naay^{4}

1036 - top of the head, A4
Not in SW languages
N - Y naɰ^{4}; Sk nɤɤ^{4}

1037 - which, A?, (cf. 0438)
SW - S nay^{5}, day^{1}, ray^{1}; W, B daɰ^{1}; Sh laɰ^{1}, naɰ^{1}
C - LP naɰ^{4} (A4); LC naɰ^{1}; PS naɰ^{4} (A4); NM kaɰ^{4}
N - Y laɰ^{4} (A4); Sk nɤɤ^{4}, nɤɤ^{2} 'where' (A1)

1038 - the morning, A1, (cf. 0028)
SW - Sh laɰ^{1}, naɰ^{1}; LCH nay^{1}
CN - LP, LM, WN, LC, PS, NM naɰ^{1}

1039 - to rub, A1
Not in SW languages
CN - LP, LM noo^{1}; WN noo^{6} (C4); PS noo^{1}

1040 - flour, A3
SW - W bɤ^{1} 'yeast, leaven'; B bɯa^{1}; LCH bɤɤ^{1}
CN - LP bɤɤ^{2}; LM mɯɯ^{4}; LC, PS bɯɯ^{1}
N - Sk bɯa^{1}

1041 - to poison (fish), A3/B3?, (cf. 0411, 0598)
SW - S bɯa^{2} (B3); W bɤ^{2} (B3); B bɯa^{1} (A3); Sh mɤ^{2} (B3); LNK bɯa^{2} (A3); LCH bɤɤ^{1} (A3); LMY bɤɤ^{4} (A3)
CN - LP bɤɤ^{2} (A3); LM mɯɯ^{2} (B3); WN bɯɯ^{1} 'to poison' (A3), bɯɯ^{2} 'poisonous' (B3); LC, PS bɯɯ^{1} (A3)
N - Sk via^{1} 'to poison' (A3), via^{6} 'to be poisoned by' (B3)

1042 - an edible water plant, C3
SW - S, W buŋ^{3}; B boŋ^{3}; LCH, LMY buŋ^{3}
CN - LP boŋ^{3}; LM moŋ^{3}; WN bɯŋ^{3}; LC phyak^{2} buŋ^{3} buu^{2} ('sweet potato' in CN languages)

1043 - to carry on the back, DL3, (cf. 1018)
SW - S bɛɛk^{2}; W, B bɛʔ^{2}; Sh mɛk^{2}; LNK, LCH, LMY bɛɛk^{2}
CN - LP beek^{5}; LM meek^{2}; WN bɛk^{2}; LC, PS, NM beek^{2}

1044 - a package; to wrap up, A3
Not in SW languages
CN - LP been^{2}; LM meen^{4}; LC, PS, NM been^{1}

1045 - to spill, B3
SW - S, W baa^{2}; B baa^{2}, vaa^{2}; LNK naam^{5} baa^{3} 'flood'; LCH, LMY baa^{2}
CN - LP baa^{5}; LM maa^{2}; WN, LC, PS, NM baa^{2}

1046 - to squirm, struggle, C3
SW - S din^{3}; Sh lin^{3}; LNK din^{5}; LCH, LMY tin^{3}

1047 - crucible, C3
SW - S baw^{3}; W baw^{3} 'a cast, mold'; B baw^{3} taa^{1} 'eye socket'; Sh maw^{3}; LNK baw^{5}; LCH, LMY baw^{3}
CN - LP baw^{3} 'head'; LM maw^{3} 'jug'; WN baw^{3} 'gourd'; LC, PS baw^{3} 'head'
N - Sk baw^{3}

1048 - queue (referring to hair), A2
Not in SW languages
CN - LP piin^{2}; LM piin^{1}; LC piin^{1} (Li says < Chinese); PS, NM piin^{1}

1049 - half, B2
Not in SW languages
CN - LP puun^{5}; LM puun^{2}; LC puun^{2} (Li says < Chinese); PS, NM puun^{2}

1050 - a board, C2
SW - W, B, Sh pɛn^{3}; LNK pɛɛn^{5}; LCH, LMY pɛn^{3}
CN - LP, LM, LC, PS, NM peen^{3}
N - Sk peen^{3}

1051 - hemp, B2
SW - S, W, B, Sh paan^{2}; LNK paan^{3}; LMY paan^{2}
CN - LM, WN paan^{2} 'ramie'; LC paan^{2}

1052 - to divide, A2, (cf. 0761)
SW - S, W, B pan^{1}; Sh pan^{1} 'to give'; LNK pan^{2}; LCH, LMY pan^{1}
CN - LP pan^{2}; LM, WN, LC, PS, NM pan^{1}
N - Sk pan^{1}

1053 - to mold with the hands, C2
SW - S, W, B, Sh pan^{3}; LNK pan^{5}; LCH, LMY pan^{3}
CN - LP, LM, WN pan^{3}; LC pan^{3} 'to work in clay or clay-like substance'; NM pan^{3}
N - Sk val^{3} (OG), van^{3} (YG)

1054 - to feed (a child or invalid), C2
SW - S pɔɔn^{3}; W, B, Sh pɔn^{3}; LNK pɔɔn^{5}; LMY pɔn^{3}
CN - LP, LM poon^{3}; WN pon^{3}; LC, NM poon^{3}
N - Sk puun^{6} (B2)

1055 - white, DL1, (cf. 0509)
SW - S phɯak^{2}; LCH, LMY phɤɤk^{2}
CN - LP phɤɤk^{2}; LM phɯɯk^{2}; LC, PS phɤɤk^{2}; NM phɯɯk^{2}
N - Sk only in saaŋ^{6} phɯak^{6} 'white elephant'

1056 - goose, B4, (cf. 0068)
Not in SW languages
CN - LP phɤn^{5}; LM, LC, PS pɤn^{5}; NM pen^{5}

1057 - to whittle, A1
Not in SW languages
CN - LP, LM, PS, NM pheen^{1}

1058 - a time, A4, (cf. 0597, 0975, 1155)
Not in SW languages
CN - LP phay^{4}; LM, WN, LC, PS pay^{4}

1059 - bamboo, B1
SW - S phay^{2}; LNK phay^{3}; LCH, LMY phay^{2}
CN - LP phay^{2}; WN phay^{2} 'a kind of hardwood'; LC, PS phay^{2}
N - Sk phray^{6} 'a kind of wild bamboo'

1060 - a mound, A4
Not in SW languages
CN - LP phoo^{4}; LM poo^{4}; WN poo^{1} 'mountain' (A?); LC, PS poo^{4}

1061 - orphan, C4
SW - S (kam^{1}) phraa^{4}; LCH (kam^{2}) phaa^{6}; LMY (kam^{2}) faa^{6}
CN - LP phyaa^{3}; LM pyaa^{6}; WN paa^{6}; LC, PS, NM pyaa^{6}
N - Sk thraa^{6}

1062 - vinegar, B1
SW - B mi^{2}; Sh mi^{2} 'seasoning'; LCH, LMY nam^{6} mii^{2} 'pepper sauce' (mii^{2} 'to prepare food in the form of a salad')
CN - LP mii^{2}; LM mey^{2}; WN, LC, PS mii^{2}; NM mey^{2}

1063 - to return, A4
SW - S mɯa^{1} (obsolete); W mɤ^{4} 'to go upstream'; B mɯa^{4} 'to go upstream' (opposite of pay^{1} 'to go downstream'); Sh mɤ^{4}; LNK mɯa^{6}; LCH, LMY mɤɤ^{4} 'to go'
CN - LP mɤɤ^{4}; LM mɯɯ^{4}; LC, PS, NM mɯɯ^{4}
N - Sk mɯa^{4} (said to be < Lao)

1064 - frost, A1
SW - W mɤy^{1}; B mɯay^{1} 'dew'; Sh moy^{1}; LCH, LMY mɤy^{1} 'dew, mist'
CN - LP mɤɤy^{1}; LM muuy^{1}; WN mɯy^{1}; PS mɤɤy^{1}; NM muuy^{1}

1065 - spicy hot, B4, (cf. 0639, 0890)
Not in SW languages
CN - LP, LM, PS mɤn^{5}; NM men^{5}

1066 - round, A4, (cf. 0817)
SW - B, Sh mon^{4}; LCH, LMY mun^{4}
CN - LP, LM mɤn^{4}; WN man^{4}; LC, PS mɤn^{4}; NM men^{4}
N - Sk mɔn^{4}

1067 - plum, C4
SW - W man^{6}; LCH, LMY sum^{3} maak^{2} man^{6} 'a kind of fruit'
CN - LP man^{3}; LM, WN, PS, NM man^{6}

1068 - drunk, A4
SW - S maw^{1}; W, B maw^{4}; Sh maw^{4} 'giddy, dizzy'; LNK maw^{6}; LCH, LMY maw^{4}
CN - LP, LM, LC, PS, NM maw^{4}
N - Sk maw^{4}

1069 - ox, A4, (cf. 0256)
Not in SW languages
CN - LP, LM, WN moo^{4}; LC moo^{6} (C4); PS, NM moo^{4}
N - Sk bɔɔ^{4}

1070 - dawn, B1
Not in SW languages
CN - LM moon^{2}; LC moon^{2} 'twilight'; PS moon^{2}

1071 - to stretch out, DL3, (cf. 0742)
SW - S yiat^{2}; W yet^{2}; B yiat^{2}; Sh yet^{2}; LNK yiat^{2}; LCH, LMY yeet^{2}
CN - LP yiit^{5}; LM ʔiit^{2}; WN ʔit^{2}; LC, PS, NM yiit^{2}

1072 - to step on, DL3, (cf. 0392)
SW - S yiap^{2}; Sh yep^{2}; LNK yiap^{2}; LCH, LMY yeep^{2}
CN - LP yiip^{5}; LM ʔiip^{2}
N - Sk yiap^{6}

1073 - hawk, B1, (cf. 1100)
SW - S hiaw^{2}, yiaw^{2}; W hew^{2}, yew^{2}; B hiaw^{2}
CN - LP, LM, PS yiiw^{5} (B4)

1074 - a small shrimp, A4
SW - Sh ŋɛw^{4}
CN - LP, LM, LC, PS yiiw^{4}

1075 - Indian corn, B4
Not in SW languages
CN - LP yɤɤ^{5}; LM yɤɰ^{5}; LC khaw^{3} yɯɯ^{4} (A4); PS yɯɯ^{5}; NM ɲaɰ^{5}

1076 - oil, A4, (cf. 0584)
SW - W yaw^{4}; B yaw^{4} (said to be < Vietnamese); LCH, LMY maak^{2} yaw^{4} 'kind of fruit that yields oil' (cognate?)
CN - LP yuu^{4}; LM yow^{4}; WN yiw^{4}; LC, PS yuu^{4}; NM yow^{4}

1077 - to use, B4?, (cf. 0032)
SW - W yuŋ^{4} (A4)
CN - LP, LM yoŋ^{5}; WN yuŋ^{2} (B?); LC yuŋ^{5} (Li says < Chinese); PS, NM yoŋ^{5}

1078 - to cover, A4, (cf. 0282, 0794)
Not in SW languages
CN - LP, LM, WN yaa^{4}; LC yaa^{4} 'to cover up, to screen, to mend'

1079 - kind, B3
SW - S yaaŋ^{2}; LNK yaaŋ^{3}; LCH, LMY yaaŋ^{2}
CN - LP yɤɤŋ^{5}; LM yɯɯŋ^{5}; WN yiŋ^{5}; LC yɤɤŋ^{5} 'form, manner' (Li says < Chinese); PS yɤɤŋ^{5}; NM yɯɯŋ^{5} (B4 in CN languages)
N - Sk yaaŋ^{6}

1080 - slack, A4
SW - S yaan^{1}; W, B, Sh yaan^{4}; LNK ɲaan^{6}; LCH, LMY yaan^{4}
N - Sk yaal^{4} (OG), yaan^{4} (YG)

1081 - light, daybreak, B4, (cf. 0676)
SW - S ruŋ^{3}; W, B huŋ^{5}; Sh huŋ^{3} 'to shine'; LCH huŋ^{5} (also in the name Chieng Hung: ceŋ^{4} huŋ^{5}; literary ruŋ^{5}); LMY huŋ^{5}
CN - LP ɬoŋ^{5}; LM loŋ^{5}; WN ðuŋ^{5}; LC ɬuŋ^{5} 'to dawn; to be bright'; PS, NM ɬoŋ^{5}
N - Y roŋ^{5}; Sk rɔɔŋ^{5}

1082 - to fight, DS4
SW - S rop^{4}; Sh hop^{5} 'to find, meet with'; LNK hop^{3} 'to fight (only of cocks)'
CN - LP ɬop^{4}; LM lop^{4}; LC ɬup^{4} ('to meet' in CN languages)
N - Sk lop^{6}

1083 - gutter, trough, A4
SW - S raaŋ^{1}; W, B, Sh haaŋ^{4}; LNK haaŋ^{6}; LMY haaŋ^{4}
CN - LP ɬaaŋ^{4}; LM laaŋ^{4}; WN ðaaŋ^{4}; LC ɬaaŋ^{4}
N - Y ruaŋ^{4}; Sk haaŋ^{4}

1084 - to receive, DS4
SW - S rap^{4}; B, Sh hap^{5}; LNK hap^{3}
CN - LP ɬap^{4}; LM lap^{4}; WN ðap^{4}; LC, PS ɬap^{4}
N - Sk rap^{6}

1085 - to cry out, C4
SW - S rɔɔŋ^{4}; W, B hɔŋ^{6}; Sh hɔŋ^{5}; LNK hɔɔŋ^{5}, lɔɔŋ^{5}; LCH, LMY hɔŋ^{6}
CN - LP ɬooŋ^{3}; LM looŋ^{6}; WN ðoŋ^{6}; LC ɬooŋ^{6}

1086 - string, A4, (cf. 0323)
SW - W lin^{4}
CN - LP, LM lin^{4}; WN lan^{4}; LC, PS lin^{4}; NM len^{4}

1087 - lotus, A4
Not in SW languages
CN - LP, LM liin^{4}; WN lin^{5} (B4); LC liin^{4} (Li says < Chinese); PS liin^{4}

1088 - sickle, A4
Not in SW languages
CN - LP liim^{4}; LM niim^{4}; LC, PS, NM liim^{4}
N - Sk liam^{4}

1089 - to sharpen, A1, (cf. 0463, 0556, 0560, 1107)
Not in SW languages
CN - LP liiw^{1} 'to peel'; LM liiw^{1}; LC, PS liiw^{1} 'to peel'

1090 - to play, B4, (cf. 0184)
Not in SW languages
CN - LP, LM liiw^{5}; WN liw^{5}; LC, PS, NM liiw^{5}

1091 - wife of man's younger brother, A4, (cf. 0289)
SW - W lo^{4}; B lua^{4} 'wife of father's younger brother'; Sh lo^{4} 'one's elder brother's wife'
CN - LP, LM, WN, LC, PS luu^{4} ('daughter-in-law' in CN languages)
N - Sk luaw^{4} 'wife of father's younger brother'

1092 - blunt-pointed, B1
Not in SW languages
CN - LP, LM, LC, PS luu^{2}

1093 - all (day, etc.), B4
Not in SW languages
CN - LP, LM lɤn^{5}; PS lin^{5}; NM len^{5}

1094 - to look, A4, (cf. 0976)
SW - S lɛɛ^{1}; W, B lɛ^{4}; LNK lɛɛ^{6}; LCH, LMY lɛɛ^{4} 'to look sideways'
CN - LP, LM lee^{4}

1095 - lightning, DL4
SW - S lɛɛp^{3}; B mɛp^{5} 'to stick out (the tongue)'; Sh maap^{3} 'to blaze, flame; to glitter, glance as a ray of light'; LNK lɛɛp^{5} 'to stick out'; LCH, LMY mɛɛp^{5}
CN - LP, LM meep^{5}; WN maap^{5}; LC meep^{4} 'to glitter', faa^{6} meep^{4} 'lightning'; PS, NM meep^{5}

1096 - to run, B4
SW - S lɛn^{3}; W, B lɛn^{5}; Sh lɛn^{3}; LNK lɛɛn^{3}; LCH, LMY lɛn^{5}
CN - LP, LM leen^{5}; WN len^{5}; LC, PS leen^{5}

1097 - (rice) cooked in a bamboo tube, A1
SW - S (khaaw^{3}) laam^{5}; B laam^{1}; Sh laam^{1} 'to hold in the fire'; LNK (khaw^{4}) laam^{1}; LCH, LMY (xaw^{3}) laam^{1}
CN - LP, LM, WN laam^{1}; LC khaw^{3} laam^{1}; PS laam^{1}

1098 - soybeans, C1
Not in SW languages
CN - LP haŋ^{3}; LM laŋ^{3}; PS haŋ^{3}

1099 - to water (plants), A4, (cf. 0887)
Not in SW languages
CN - LP, LM, LC, PS, NM lam^{4}

1100 - hawk, B4, (cf. 1073)
Not in SW languages
CN - LP lam^{5} 'eagle'; LM, WN lam^{5}; LC lam^{5} 'a kind of eagle or hawk'; PS lam^{5}
N - Sk lam^{5}

1101 - road, B4, (cf. 0364, 0474)
Not in SW languages
CN - LP, LM, WN, LC, PS, NM loo^{5}

1102 - to surround (as with a fence), C4, (cf. 0921)
SW - S lɔɔm^{4}; W, B lɔm^{6}; Sh lɔm^{5}; LNK lɔɔm^{5}; LCH, LMY lɔm^{6}
CN - LP loom^{3}; LM loom^{6}; WN hom^{6}, hum^{6}; LC, PS loom^{6}

1103 - thunder, A4, (cf. 0878)
Not in SW languages
CN - LM, LC looy^{4}; PS poo^{5} looy^{4}

1104 - tile, C4
Not in SW languages
CN - LP vaa^3; LM vaa^6; LC, PS vaa^6; NM ηwaa^6

1105 - free, idle, B1, (cf. 0996)
SW - S waaη^3 (B4); W vaaη^2; Sh waaη^2 'to assist gratuitously'; LNK waaη^3
CN - LP, LM, LC, PS, NM vaaη^2

1106 - heart, A1, (cf. 0022)
Not in SW languages
CN - LP ɬim^1; LM sim^1; LC, PS ɬim^1; NM ɬom^1

1107 - to sharpen to a point, C1, (cf. 0436, 0556, 0560, 1089)
SW - S siam^3; Sh shem^3; LNK siam^4; LCH, LMY sem^3
CN - LP ɬiim^3; LM siim^3; LC ɬiim^3 'sharp'

1108 - pillar, A1, (cf. 0675)
Not in SW languages
CN - LP ɬiiw^1; LM seew^1; LC ɬaw^1, ɬiiw^1; PS ɬiiw^1

1109 - to swim, A1
Not in SW languages
CN - LP ɬiiw^1; LM seew^1; LC, PS ɬiiw^1

1110 - to embroider, B1
SW - W, B sɛw^2; Sh shɛw^2 'to sew for decoration'; LNK sɛɛw^3 'to baste'; LCH, LMY sɛw^2
CN - LP ɬiiw^2; LM seew^2; WN sɛw^3 (C?); PS ɬiiw^2; NM ɬiiw^3 (tone?)

1111 - day before yesterday, A4
SW - S sɯɯn^1; W, B sɯn^4; Sh shɯn^4 (in 'day before yesterday', 'month before last', 'year before last'); LNK, LCH, LMY sɯn^4
CN - LP ɬɤɤn^4; LM sɤn^4; WN sin^4; LC van^4 ɬin^4; PS ɬin^4; NM ɬen^4

1112 - a part, B1
SW - S, B suan^2; LNK suan^3; LCH, LMY son^2
N - Sk sual^6 (OG), suan^6 (YG)

1113 - classifier for long, thin objects, C1
SW - S sen^3; Sh shen^3 'string, rope'; LNK sen^4; LCH, LMY sin^3
CN - WN san^3
N - Sk sɛl^3 (OG), sɛn^3 (YG)

1114 - a lock, C1
Not in SW languages
CN - LP ɬaa^3; LM saa^3; WN saa^2 (B?); LC, PS ɬaa^3

1115 - cockroach, DL1
SW - S, B, LNK, LCH, LMY saap^{2}
CN - LP ɬaap^{2}; LM, WN saap^{2}; LC, PS ɬaap^{2}; NM ɬaak^{2}
N - Sk saap^{6}

1116 - to wash, A4, (cf. 0325, 0552)
SW - S saaw^{1}; Sh taaw^{4} ‘to wash for gold’; LNK thaaw^{6} ‘to seek in water with a stick, hook, spoon, etc.’; LCH, LMY taaw^{4} ‘to feel about in water; to wash (rice) in water’
CN - LP ɬaaw^{4}; LM saaw^{4}; WN taaw^{4} ‘to wash for gold’; LC, PS, NM ɬaaw^{4}

1117 - one or so, any, DS1
SW - S, W, B sak^{2}; Sh shak^{4} ‘particle denoting separation’; LCH, LMY sak^{1}
CN - LP ɬak^{2}; LM sak^{3}; WN sak^{6}; LC, PS ɬak^{2}
N - Sk sak^{4}

1118 - pig-feed, C1, (cf. 0661)
Not in SW languages
CN - LM sam^{3}; LC ɬam^{3}

1119 - small, B1, (cf. 0246)
Not in SW languages
CN - LP ɬay^{2}; LM say^{2}; LC, PS, NM ɬay^{2}

1120 - to poke, C2, (cf. 0034)
SW - S cii^{3}; W ci^{3}; Sh si^{3} ‘to sting as an insect’; LNK cii^{5} ‘to hold up, rob’; LMY cii^{3} ‘to sting’

1121 - to teach, A1
SW - S sɔɔn^{5}; W sɔn^{1} ‘to imitate’; B sɔn^{1}; Sh shɔn^{1} ‘to study, learn, acquire knowledge’; LCH, LMY sɔn^{1}
CN - LP ɬoon^{1}; LM soon^{1}; WN son^{1}, sɔn^{1}; LC, PS ɬoon^{1}
S - Sk sɔɔl^{2} (OG), sɔɔn^{2} (YG)

1122 - to pound (rice) again, C4
SW - S sɔɔm^{4}; W, B sɔm^{6}; Sh shɔm^{5}; LCH, LMY sɔm^{6}
CN - LP ɬoom^{3}; LM soom^{6}; LC khaw^{3} ɬoom^{6} ‘husked rice’; PS ɬoom^{6}

1123 - necklace, C1
SW - S sɔy^{3}; W sɔy^{3} ‘earring’; B sɔy^{3} ‘necklace; chain’; Sh shɔy^{3} ‘a tuft, a tassel’; LCH, LMY sɔy^{3}
CN - LP ɬooy^{3} ‘earring’; LM sooy^{3} ‘earring’; WN sɔy^{3} ‘necklace, bracelet’; LC, PS ɬooy^{3} ‘earring’
N - Sk sɔɔy^{3}

1124 - a harrow, A1
SW - Sh phɤ^{1}; LCH phɤɤ^{1}; LMY fɤɤ^{1}
CN - LP phɤɤ^{1}; LM, WN, LC, PS, NM phɯɯ^{1}
N - Sk phia^{2}

1125 - to braid, A1
SW - W fɤ^{1}; B fɯa^{1}; Sh phɤ^{1}; LNK fɯa^{1}; LCH, LMY fɤɤ^{1}
CN - LP phɤɤ^{1}; LM, WN phɯɯ^{1}; LC phɯɯ^{1} 'to dress (hair)'; PS, NM phɯɯ^{1}
N - Sk pia^{1}

1126 - mat, DL4, (cf. 0763)
SW - S fuuk^{3} 'mattress'; W fuʔ^{4}; B fuʔ^{5}; LNK fuuk^{5} 'mattress'
CN - LP fok^{5}; LM fook^{5}; WN fuk^{5}; LC fuk^{4}; PS fok^{4} (DS4); NM fuuk^{5}

1127 - water tortoise, A1
SW - W faa^{1}; LNK (paa^{2}) faa^{1}; LCH, LMY faa^{1}
CN - LP, LM, WN, PS phaa^{1}
N - Sk via^{3} (probably not cognate)

1128 - blanket, A4, (cf. 0978)
SW - B faa^{4}
CN - LP, LM, WN, LC, PS, NM faa^{4} 'quilt'

1129 - to bury, A1
SW - S faŋ^{5}; W, B faŋ^{1}; Sh phaŋ^{1}; LNK, LCH, LMY faŋ^{1}
CN - LP, LM, WN, LC phaŋ^{1}

1130 - to make (rope), C1
SW - S, W, B fan^{3}; Sh phan^{3} 'to twist tight and hard'; LNK fan^{4}; LCH, LMY fan^{3}
CN - LP, LM phan^{3}; LC phan^{3} 'to twist'; NM phan^{3}

1131 - market, B4
Not in SW languages
CN - LP, LM faɰ^{5}; LC faɰ^{4} (A4); PS, NM faɰ^{5}

1132 - mole, A1
SW - S fay^{5}; LCH, LMY fay^{2} 'freckles' (B1, cognate?)
CN - LP, LM, PS may^{1}

1133 - vagina, A1
SW - S hii^{5}; W, B, Sh hi^{1}; LNK, LCH hii^{1}
CN - LP, LM hii^{1}; WN šii^{1}; PS hii^{1}; NM hey^{1}

1134 - to do, to make, DS4?, (cf. 0823)
SW - S yet^4 'to have intercourse'; W yet^4; B yet^5; Sh het^4 (DS1); LNK het^3; LCH, LMY het^5
CN - LP het^2 (hit^2?); LM hat^3; LC hit^2; PS het^2; NM het^4 (DS1 in CN languages)
N - Sk hit^6

1135 - cage, B1
Not in SW languages
CN - LP hoŋ^2; LM loŋ^2; LC huŋ^2; PS hoŋ^2; NM khyoŋ^2

1136 - pot, frying pan, DL1, (cf. 0227)
SW - B hɛʔ^2 'pot'
CN - LP, LM heek^2 'frying pan'; LC heek^2 'pot, caldron, kettle'; PS, NM heek^2 'round-bottomed frying pan'
N - Sk hɛɛk^6

1137 - edge, side, A4, (cf. 0309)
Not in SW languages
CN - LP, LM heen^4

1138 - to guard, A1
SW - S hɛɛn^5
CN - LP, LM, LC, PS, NM heen^1

1139 - cholera, B?
SW - S haa^2 (B1); W haa^4 (A4); Sh haa^3 (B4); LNK haa^3; LCH, LMY haa^5 (B4)
CN - LP ɬaa^5; LM laa^5; WN ðaa^5 (B4 in CN languages)
N - Sk haa^6 (C4)

1140 - to set (a trap), C1, (cf. 0774)
SW - W haaŋ^3; B haaŋ^3 'platform for hunting'; Sh haaŋ^3 'to construct, arrange, array, prepare, hunter's platform in a tree'; LNK haaŋ^4 'a trap, hunter's platform'; LCH, LMY haaŋ^3 'platform; to prepare, set up'
CN - LP haaŋ^3; LM, WN thaaŋ^3; LC, PS haaŋ^3

1141 - shoe, A4
SW - W, B haay^4
CN - LP, LM, WN haay^4; LC, PS kaay^4; NM haay^4

1142 - lime, A1, (same as 0085?)
Not in SW languages
CN - LP, LM hooy^1; WN hɔy^1; LC hooy^1 (Li says < Chinese); PS, NM hooy^1

1143 - to hang down, C1
SW - S, W, B, Sh hɔy^3; LNK hɔɔy^4; LCH, LMY hɔy^3
CN - LP, LM hooy^3; WN hɔy^3; PS hooy^3

1144 - slave, I, C1, (cf. 0494, 0533)
SW - S khaa^{3} (khaa^{2} 'mountain people'); W chaa^{3} 'mountain people'; B saa^{3} 'mountain people'; Sh khaa^{3}; LNK khaa^{4} 'servant; I' (latter said to be from Bangkok); LCH, LMY xaa^{3}
CN - WN chaa^{3} 'mountain people'

1145 - paternal grandfather, B2
SW - S puu^{2}; W, B, Sh pu^{2}; LNK puu^{3}; LCH, LMY puu^{2}

1146 - tree; beginning, C2
SW - S ton^{3}; W tun^{3}; B, Sh ton^{3}; LNK ton^{5}; LCH, LMY tun^{3}

1147 - cool, A3
SW - S, B yen^{1}; Sh yen^{1} 'to be quiet, still'; LNK yen^{2}; LCH yin^{1}; LMY yin^{4}
CN - LM nin^{4} 'gooseflesh'
N - Sk yen^{1} (only in certain expressions < Lao)

1148 - to hire, C2
SW - S, W, B caaη^{3}; Sh saaη^{3}; LNK caaη^{5}; LCH, LMY caaη^{3}
N - Sk caaη^{3}

1149 - anvil, B4
SW - S thaη^{3}; B taη^{5}; Sh taη^{3}; LNK thaη^{3}; LCH, LMY taη^{5}
CN - LM, WN taη^{5}
N - Sk thaη^{6} (C4)

1150 - calf of the leg, B4, (cf. 0131, 0501)
SW - S nɔη^{3}; W, B, nɔη^{5} 'underside of the knee'; Sh nɔη^{3} 'the inside of the bend of the knee'; LNK nɔɔη^{3}; LCH, LMY nɔη^{5}
CN - LM, NM nooη^{5}

1151 - to toast, C2
SW - S, W, B, Sh piη^{3}; LNK piη^{5}; LCH, LMY piη^{3}
CN - LM piη^{3} 'to bake in ashes'

1152 - level; only, A4
SW - S phiaη^{1}; B piaη^{4}; Sh peη^{4}; LNK phiaη^{6}; LCH, LMY peη^{4}
CN - LP phiiη^{1}; LM piη^{4}; WN phiη^{1}, peη^{5}
N - Sk phiaη^{4}

1153 - to mend, A1
SW - W, B fuη^{1}; Sh phuη^{1}; LNK fuuη^{1}; LCH, LMY fuη^{1}
CN - LP, LM phoη^{1}; WN phuη^{1}, phoη^{1}; NM phooη^{1}

1154 - blind, having poor eyesight, A4, (cf. 0416)
SW - S faaη^{1}; W, B faaη^{4}; LNK faaη^{6}; LCH, LMY faaη^{4}

1155 - long (of time), A1, (cf. 0597, 0975, 1058)
SW - S hɯŋ^{5} (literary); W hɯŋ^{1}; B hɤŋ^{1}; Sh hɯŋ^{1}; LNK hɤɤŋ^{1}; LCH, LMY hɯŋ^{1}
CN - LP, LC hɤŋ^{1}; PS hɯŋ^{1}; NM haŋ^{1}

1156 - to sift, A1
SW - S khɯŋ^{5}; W chɯŋ^{1}; B sɤŋ^{1}; Sh khɯŋ^{1}; LNK khɤŋ^{1} 'a sieve'; LMY xɯŋ^{1}
CN - LM lɤŋ^{1}; WN chaŋ^{1}; LC khyɤŋ^{1}; PS khiŋ^{1}
N - Sk raŋ^{2}

1157 - petal; section of fruit, DL2
SW - S kliip^{2}; W, B kip^{2}; LNK kiip^{2}; LCH liip^{2} 'a clove of garlic' (cognate?)
CN - LP kiip^{5}; WN cip^{6}; LC kip^{2}
N - Sk tliip^{6} (OG), triip^{6} (YG)

1158 - mouth, DS1, (cf. 0623)
SW - W, B sop^{2}; Sh shop^{4}; LNK sop^{1} 'lips'; LCH, LMY sop^{1}

1159 - strange, DL2
SW - S plɛɛk^{2}; W, B pɛʔ^{2} 'alike, similar' (cognate?); Sh pɛk^{2} 'different'; LNK pɛɛk^{2}
CN - LM peek^{2} 'to exchange by mistake'; WN pɛk^{2} 'to leave, separate from'

REFERENCES

Abramson, Arthur S. 1962. *The Vowels and Tones of Standard Thai: Acoustical Measurements and Experiments*. Publication 20. Bloomington: Indiana University Research Center in Anthropology, Folklore, and Linguistics.

Aymonier, Étienne. 1895. *Voyage dans le Laos*. Paris: Annals du Musée Guimet, Bibliothèques d'Études vols. 5, 6. Reference to "savages" called Sâk, vol. 5, pp. 112–13.

Baccam, Don, Falaung Baccam, Hung Baccam, and Dorothy Fippinger. 1989. *Tai Dam-English English Tai-Dam Vocabulary*. Eastlake, CO: Summer Institute of Linguistics.

Benedict, Paul K. 1997. Linguistic Prediction: The Case of Saek. In *Comparative Kadai: The Tai Branch*, edited by Jerold A. Edmondson and David B. Solnit, 161–87. Arlington, TX: Summer Institute of Linguistics and The University of Texas at Arlington.

Bickner, Robert J., John Hartmann, Thomas John Hudak, and Patcharin Peyasantiwong, eds 1989. *Selected Papers on Comparative Tai Studies: William J. Gedney*. Michigan Papers on South and Southeast Asia, no. 29. Ann Arbor, MI: Center for South and Southeast Asian Studies, University of Michigan.

Blanchard, Wendell. 1957. *Thailand, Its People, Its Society, Its Culture*. New Haven: HRAF Country Survey Series.

Bonifacy, Auguste Louis. 1907. Étude sur les Tày de la Rivière Claire au Tonkin et dans la Chine Méridionale (Yünnan et Kouangsi). *Toung Pao*, series 2, 8:77–98.

———. 1919. *Cours d'ethnographie indochinoise*. Hanoi-Haiphong: Imprimerie d'Extrême-Orient. Sek listed on p. 81.

Creder, Wilhelm. 1935. *Siam, das Land der Tai*. Stuttgart: J. Engelhorns nachf.

Cushing, Josiah Nelson. [1881]1914. *A Shan and English Dictionary*. 2nd ed. Rangoon: American Baptist Mission Press. (Reprint: Farnborough, England: Gregg International, 1971.)

Davis, Sara L.M. 2005. *Song and Silence: Ethnic Revival on China's Southwest Borders*. New York: Columbia University Press.

Điêu, Chinh Nhim, and Jean Donaldson. 1970. *Păp san khhăm pak Tãy-Keo-Eng: Ngử-vưng Thai (Trang)-Viêt-Anh: (White) Tai-Vietnamese-English Vocabulary*. Saigon: Department of Education.

Diguet, Edouard. 1895. *Étude de la langue taï, précedée d'une notice sur les races des hautes régions du Tonkin: comprenant grammaire, méthode d'écriture taï et vocabulaires*. Hanoi: F.H. Schneider.

Donaldson, Jean. 1963. *White Tai Phonology*. M.A. thesis, Hartford Seminary Foundation, Hartford, CT.

Donaldson, Jean, and Jerold A. Edmondson. 1997. A Preliminary Examination of Tay Tac. In *Comparative Kadai: The Tai Branch*, edited by Jerold A. Edmondson and David B. Solnit, 235–66. Arlington, TX: Summer Institute of Linguistics and The University of Texas at Arlington.

Durand, Maurice. 1952. Notes sur les pays tai de Phong-thô. *Bulletin de la Société des Études Indochinoises*. N.s. 27:193–231.

Edmondson, Jerold A. 2000a. Personal Communication, 6 May.

———. 2000b. The Language Corridor: New Evidence from Vietnam. In *Proceedings: The International Conference on Tai Studies, July 29–31, 1988*, edited by Somsonge Burusphat, 129–50. Bangkok: Institute of Language and Culture for Rural Development, Mahidol University.

Edmondson, Jerold A., and Kenneth J. Gregerson. 2001. Four Languages of the Vietnam-China Borderlands. In *Papers from the Sixth Annual Meeting of the Southeast Asian Linguistics Society: 1996*, edited by Karen L. Adams and Thomas John Hudak, 101–33. Tempe, AZ: Program for Southeast Asian Studies, Arizona State University.

Edmondson, Jerold A., and David B. Solnit. 1997a. Comparative Shan. In *Comparative Kadai: The Tai Branch*, edited by Jerold A. Edmondson and David B. Solnit, 337–59. Arlington, TX: Summer Institute of Linguistics and The University of Texas at Arlington.

———, eds 1997b. *Comparative Kadai: The Tai Branch*. Arlington, TX: Summer Institute of Linguistics and The University of Texas at Arlington.

Egerod, Søren. 1957. Essentials of Shan Phonology and Script. *Academia Sinica Bulletin of the Institute of Ethnology* 29:121–29.

———. 1960. The Romanization of Shan. *Burma Research Society Fiftieth Anniversary Publication* I:47–49.

———. 1961. Three Shan Texts. *Acta Orientalia* 26(3/4):149–88.

Esquirol, Joseph, and Gust Williatte. 1908. *Dictionnaire Dioi-Français*. Hong Kong: Imprimerie de la Société des Missions-Étangères.

Fippinger, Jay. 1975. Black Tai Sentence Types. In *Studies in Tai Linguistics in Honor of William J. Gedney*, edited by Jimmy G. Harris and James R. Chamberlain, 130–69. Bangkok: Cemtral Institute of English.

Fippinger, Jay, and Dorothy Fippinger. 1970. Black Tai Phonemes, with Reference to White Tai. *Anthropological Linguistics* 12(3):83–97.

Fraisse, André. 1950. Les tribus Sek et Kha de la province de Cammon (Laos). *Bulletin de la Société des Études Indochinoises* 25(3):333–48. Saek vocabulary on pp. 338–40.

Gedney, William J. 1947. *Indic Loanwords in Spoken Thai*. Ph.D. dissertation, Yale University.

———. 1961. Special Vocabularies in Thai. In *Georgetown University Round Table on Language and Linguistics*, edited by Michael Zarechnak, 109–14. Washington, D.C.: Georgetown University Press.

———. 1964. A Comparative Sketch of White, Black, and Red Tai. *The Social Science Review*, Special Number, 1–47. Bangkok.

———. 1965. Yay, A Northern Tai Language in North Vietnam. *Lingua* 14: 180–93.

———. 1970. The Saek Language of Nakhon Phanom. *Journal of the Siam Society* 57(1):67–87.

———. 1972. A Checklist for Determining Tones in Tai Dialects. In *Studies in Linguistics in Honor of George L. Trager*, edited by M. Estellie Smith, 423–37. The Hague: Mouton.

———. 1989. Siamese Verse Forms in Historical Perspective. In *Selected Papers on Comparative Tai Studies: William J. Gedney*, edited by Robert J. Bickner, John Hartmann, Thomas John Hudak, and Patcharin Peyasantiwong, 489–544. Ann Arbor, MI: Center for South and Southeast Asian Studies, University of Michigan.

———. 1993a. Saek Final -l: Archaism or Innovation? In *William J. Gedney's The Saek Language: Glossary, Texts, and Translations*, edited by Thomas John Hudak, 917–74. Ann Arbor, MI: Center for South and Southeast Asian Studies, University of Michigan.

———. 1993b. The Twelve Year Names in Saek. In *William J. Gedney's The Saek Language: Glossary, Texts, and Translations*, edited by Thomas John Hudak, 975–89. Ann Arbor, MI: Center for South and Southeast Asian Studies, University of Michigan.

———. 1995a. Linguistic Diversity Among Tai Dialects in Southern Kwangsi. In *William J. Gedney's Central Tai Dialects: Glossaries, Texts, and Translations*, edited by Thomas John Hudak, 803–22. Ann Arbor, MI: Center for South and Southeast Asian Studies, University of Michigan.

———. 1995b. A Comparative Central Tai Wordlist. In *William J. Gedney's Central Tai Dialects: Glossaries, Texts, and Translations*, edited by Thomas John Hudak, 883–962. Ann Arbor, MI: Center for South and Southeast Asian Studies, University of Michigan.

———. 1995c. An Areal Vowel Change in Tai Dialects in Kwangsi and Kweichow. In *William J. Gedney's Central Tai Dialects: Glossaries, Texts, and Translations*, edited by Thomas John Hudak, 823–58. Ann Arbor, MI: Center for South and Southeast Asian Studies, University of Michigan.

———. 1995d. Notes on the Tai Dialect of Ning Ming: Part One. In *William J. Gedney's Central Tai Dialects: Glossaries, Texts, and Translations*, edited by Thomas John Hudak, 859–82. Ann Arbor, MI: Center for South and Southeast Asian Studies, University of Michigan.

———. 1997. Saek, A Displaced Northern Tai Language. In *William J. Gedney's Tai Dialect Studies: Glossaries, Texts, and Translations*, edited by Thomas John Hudak, 1281–1302. Ann Arbor, MI: Center for South and Southeast Asian Studies, University of Michigan.

Haas, Mary R. 1942a. Types of Reduplication in Thai. *Studies in Linguistics* 1(1):1–6.

———. 1942b. The Use of Numeral Classifiers in Thai. *Language* XVIII:201–05.

———. 1946. Techniques of Intensifying in Thai. *Word* II:125–30.

———. 1956. *The Thai System of Writing*. Washington D.C.: American Council of Learned Societies.

———. 1964. *Thai-English Student's Dictionary*. Stanford: Stanford University Press.

Hartmann, John F. 1981. Computations on a Tai Dam Origin Myth. *Anthropological Linguistics* 23(5):183–202.

———. 1984. *Linguistic and Memory Structures in Tai-Lue Oral Narratives*. Pacific Linguistics Series B-No. 20. Canberra: The Australian National University.

———. 1985. Dating White Thai and Black Thai Scripts. A paper presented at the 18th International Conference on Sino-Tibetan Languages and Linguistics, Ramkhamhaeng University, Bangkok, August 27–29. Published in Thai: 1987. Kaan-kaamnot ?aayu? tua-?aksoun tay khaaw lae? tay dam. *Ruam Bot Khwaam Prawatisaat* [Royal Thai Historical Society Review] 5:121–39.

———. 1986. Varieties of Tai Dam Scripts. *Crossroads* 3(1):97–103.

———. 1992. Tai Dam Poetics and Proto-tone Categories. In *Papers on Tai Language, Literature, and Linguistics*, edited by Carol J. Compton and John F. Hartmann, 262–77. DeKalb, IL: Center for Southeast Asian Studies, Northern Illinois University.

———. 1994. Pronominal Strategies in Tai Dam Poetic Discourse. In *Papers from the Second Annual Meeting of the Southeast Asian Linguistics Society: 1992*, edited by Karen L. Adams and Thomas John Hudak, 187–99. Tempe, AZ: Program for Southeast Asian Studies, Arizona State University.

Haudricourt, André-Georges. 1956. De la restitution des initiales dans les langues monosyllabiques: le problème du thai commun. *Bulletin de la Société de Linguistique de Paris* 52(1):307–22.

———. 1958. Les Sek de la province du Cammon (Laos), migration thai ou déportation chinoise? *Journal Asiatique* 246:107–08.

———. 1960. Notes sur les dialectes de la région de Moncay (Vietnam du Nord). *Bulletin de l'École Française d'Extrême Orient* 50:161–77.

———. 1963a. Remarques sur les initiales complexes de la langue Sek. *Bulletin de la Société Linguistique de Paris* 58:156–63.

———. 1963b. La langue Sek. *Proceedings of the International Congress of Orientalists* 25 (Moscow) 4:414–15. Abstract.

———. 1972. *Problèmes de phonologie diachronique*. Paris: Société pour l'étude des langues africaines.

———. 1976. La tonologie du Sek. *Bulletin de la Société Linguistique de Paris* 71(1):299–304.

Henderson, Eugenie J.A. 1949. Prosodies in Siamese: A Study in Synthesis. *Asia Major* New Series 1(Part III):189–215.

Hudak, Thomas John. 2004. William J. Gedney's Elicitation Questionnaire. *Journal of the American Oriental Society* 124(3):549–59.

Hudak, Thomas John, ed. 1991a. *William J. Gedney's The Yay Language: Glossary, Texts, and Translations*. Michigan Papers on South and Southeast Asia, no. 38. Ann Arbor, MI: Center for South and Southeast Asian Studies, University of Michigan.

———, ed. 1991b. *William J. Gedney's The Tai Dialect of Lungming: Glossary, Texts, and Translations*. Michigan Papers on South and Southeast Asia, no. 39. Ann Arbor, MI: Center for South and Southeast Asian Studies, University of Michigan.

———, ed. 1993. *William J. Gedney's The Saek Language: Glossary, Texts, and Translations*. Michigan Papers on South and Southeast Asia, no. 41. Ann Arbor, MI: Center for South and Southeast Asian Studies, University of Michigan.

———, ed. 1994. *William J. Gedney's Southwestern Tai Dialects: Glossaries, Texts, and Translations*. Michigan Papers on South and Southeast Asia, no. 42. Ann Arbor, MI: Center for South and Southeast Asian Studies, University of Michigan.

———, ed. 1995. *William J. Gedney's Central Tai Dialects: Glossaries, Texts, and Translations*. Michigan Papers on South and Southeast Asia, no. 43. Ann Arbor, MI: Center for South and Southeast Asian Studies, University of Michigan.

———, ed. 1996. *William J. Gedney's The Lue Language: Glossary, Texts, and Translations*. Michigan Papers on South and Southeast Asia, no. 44. Ann Arbor, MI: Center for South and Southeast Asian Studies, University of Michigan.

———, ed. 1997. *William J. Gedney's Tai Dialect Studies: Glossaries, Texts, and Translations*. Michigan Papers on South and Southeast Asia, no. 45. Ann Arbor, MI: Center for South and Southeast Asian Studies, University of Michigan.

———, ed. 2000. *Cushing's Shan-English Dictionary: A Phonetic Version*. Tempe, AZ: Program for Southeast Asian Studies, Arizona State University.

———, ed. 2001. *Minot's White Tai Dictionary: A Phonetic Version*. Tempe, AZ: Program for Southeast Asian Studies, Arizona State University.

Khanitthanan, Wilaiwan. 1975. Saek Revisted. In *A Tai Festschrift for William J. Gedney on the Occasion of his Fifth Cycle of Life Birthday Anniversary, April 14, 1975*, edited by Thomas W. Gething, 128–39. Honolulu: University of Hawai‘i Southeast Asian Studies Program.

———. 1976. *Phaasaa Saek* [The Saek Language]. Bangkok: Thammasat University Press. In Thai.

Lebar, Frank M., Gerald C. Hickey, and John K. Musgrave. 1964. *Ethnic Groups of Mainland Southeast Asia*. New Haven: HRAF Press.

Li, Fang-Kuei. 1940. The Tai Dialect of Lungchow. Institute of History and Philology Monographs, Series A, No. 16. Academia Sinica. Shanghai: The Commercial Press, Ltd. In Chinese.

———. 1944. The Influence of the Primitive Tai Glottal Stop and Pre-glottalized Consonants on the Tone System of Po-ai. *Bulletin of Chinese Studies* 4:59–68.

———. 1956. *The Tai Dialect of Wu-ming*. Institute of History and Philology Monographs, Series A, No. 19. Academia Sinica. Taipei, Taiwan. In Chinese.

———. 1957a. The Jui Dialect of Po-ai: Phonology. *Bulletin of the Institute of History and Philology* 28:551–66.

———. 1957b. The Jui Dialect of Po-ai and the Northern Tai. *Bulletin of the Institute of History and Philology* 29:315–22.

———. 1959. Classification by Vocabulary: Tai Dialects. *Anthropological Linguistics* 1(2):15–21.

———. 1960. A Tentative Classification of Tai Dialects. In *Culture in History: Essays in Honor of Paul Radin*, edited by Stanley Diamond, 951–59. New York: Columbia University Press.

———. 1964. The Phonemic System of the Tai-Lü Language. *Bulletin of the Institute of History and Philology* 35:7–14.

———. 1977. *A Handbook of Comparative Tai*. Honolulu: The University Press of Hawai'i.

Luo, Yongxian. 1996. *The Subgroup Structure of the Tai Languages: A Historical-Comparative Study*. Ph.D. dissertation, The Australian National University.

Macey, Paul. 1905. Étude ethnographique sur diverses tribus, aborigènes ou autochtones habitant les provinces des Hua-phano, Ha-tang-hoc et du Cammon, au Laos. *Actes 14e Congrès International des Orientalistes, Alger 1905.* 1re Partie, 5e Sect.:3–63. Description of "Sèks" on pp. 36–43; vocabulary on pp. 52–57.

Mark, Lindy Li, and Fang-kuei Li. 1966. Speech Tone and Melody in Wu-Ming Folk Songs. In *Essays Offered to G.H. Luce by his Colleagues and Friends in Honour of his Seventy-fifth Birthday*, vol. 1, edited by Ba Shin, Jean Boisselier, and A.B. Griswold, 167–86. Ascona, Switzerland: Artibus Asiae.

Maspero, Henri. 1912. Étude sur la phonétique historique de la langue annamite. Les initiales. *Bulletin de l'École Française d'Extrême-Orient* 12(1): 1–127. Saek tones on pp. 3–5.

McFarland, George Bradley. 1944. *Thai-English Dictionary*. Stanford: Stanford University Press.

Minot, Georges. 1940. Dictionnaire tay blanc-français avec transcription latine. *Bulletin de l'École Française d'Extrême Orient* 40(1):1–237.

———. 1949a. *Vocabulaire Français-Thay Blanc et Éléments de Grammaire*, vol. I. Hanoi: L'École Française d'Extrême-Orient.

———. 1949b. *Vocabulaire Français-Thay Blanc et Éléments de Grammaire*, vol. II. Hanoi: L'École Française d'Extrême-Orient.

Mix, Mrs. H.W., ed. 1920. *An English and Shan Dictionary*. Rangoon: American Baptist Mission Press.

Moeng, Sao Tern. 1995. *Shan-English Dictionary*. Kensington, MD: Dunwoody Press.

Moerman, Michael. 1965. Ethnic Identification in a Complex Civilization: Who are the Lue? *American Anthropologist* 67:1215–30.

———. 1988. *Talking Culture: Ethnography and Conversational Analysis*. Philadelphia: University of Pennsylvania Press.

Morev, L.N. 1988. *Yozik sek* [The Saek Language]. Moscow: Nauka. In Russian.

Noss, Richard B. 1964. *Thai Reference Grammar*. Washington D.C.: Foreign Service Institute.

Rivière, Armand. 1902. Vocabulaire Hang-thcek, khas Xos, Harème. In *Mission Pavie, Géographie et Voyages IV*, 285–90. Paris: E. Leroux.

Sarawit, Mary. 1973. *The Proto-Tai Vowel System*. Ph.D. dissertation, University of Michigan.

Siedenfaden, Erik. 1930. Ethnology. In *Siam, Nature and Industry*, 82–106. Bangkok: Ministry of Commerce and Communications.

Snyder, Wil C., and Lu Tianqiao. 1997. Wuming Zhuang Tone Sandhi: A Phonological, Syntactic, and Lexical Investigation. In *Comparative Kadai: The Tai Branch*, edited by Jerold A. Edmondson and David B. Solnit, 107–37. Arlington, TX: Summer Institute of Linguistics and The University of Texas at Arlington.

Thongkum, Theraphan L. 1976. The Saek Language of Ban Ba Wa: Some Phonetic Notes. In *Genetic Relationship, Diffusion, and Typological Similarities of East and Southeast Asian Languages*, edited by Mantaro J. Hashimoto, 398–409. Tokyo: Japan Society for the Promotion of Science.

Tingsabadh, M.R.K. 1976. A Phonetic Description of Tai Nong. In *A Festschrift for Richard B. Noss*, edited by A. Wansotorn and J.D. Palmer, 159–75. Bangkok: Central Institute of English Language.

Young, Linda Wai Ling. 1985. *Shan Chrestomathy: An Introduction to Tai Mau Language and Literature*. Lanham, MD: University Press of America.

INDEX

[Note: Locator numbers refer to the gloss, not the page]

OCEANIC LINGUISTICS SPECIAL PUBLICATIONS

Oceanic Linguistics Special Publications are occasional publications issued under the sponsorship of the Department of Linguistics of the University of Hawai'i. The series consists of independently subsidized studies bearing on the languages of the Oceanic area. The "Oceanic area" is defined for this purpose as the combined Austronesian, Papuan, and Australian language areas. The Special Publications are published and distributed for the Department by the University of Hawai'i Press.

Manuscripts may be submitted to:

Oceanic Linguistics Special Publications
Department of Linguistics
1890 East-West Road
Moore Hall 569
University of Hawai'i
Honolulu, Hawai'i 96822